The USA 1910–1929 & Germany 1919–1947

John Wright, Steve Waugh
Editor: R. Paul Evans

Orders: please contact Bookpoint Ltd, 130 Milton Park, Abingdon, Oxon OX14 4SB. Telephone: (44) 01235 827720. Fax: (44) 01235 400454. Lines are open 9.00–5.00, Monday to Saturday, with a 24-hour message answering service. Visit our website at www.hoddereducation.co.uk

First published in 2010 by
Hodder Education,
An Hachette UK Company
338 Euston Road
London NW1 3BH

Impression number 10 9 8 7
Year 2014

Cover photos © Stapleton Collection/Corbis, © Bettmann/Corbis
Illustrations by Barking Dog and Richard Duszczak
Typeset in Minion Pro 11pt by Fakenham Prepress Solutions, Fakenham, Norfolk
Printed in Italy

A catalogue record for this title is available from the British Library

ISBN: 978 1444 112207

CONTENTS

The Publishers would like to thank the following for permission to reproduce copyright material:

Photo credits

p.7 Courtesy of Library of Congress, Prints and Photographs Division, Alfred Bendiner Memorial Collection, LC-DIG-ppmsca-05646; **p.10** Cartoon on the popular reduction of immigrants to the United States, 1914 (litho), American School, (20th century)/Private Collection/Peter Newark American Pictures/The Bridgeman Art Library; **p.11** © Library and Archives, Historical Society of Western Pennsylvania; **p.12** © Labadie Collection, University of Michigan; **pp.13, 14** and **16** © Bettmann/Corbis; **p.19** © The Granger Collection, NYC/TopFoto; **p.20** *t* © The Granger Collection, NYC/TopFoto, *b* © Bettmann/Corbis; **p.23** © Library of Congress, Prints and Photographs Division; **p.26** © Bettmann/Corbis; **p.27** © Elliott Erwitt/Magnum Photos; **p.30** *t* © The Granger Collection/TopFoto, *b* © Ohio State University; **p.31** © Minnesota Historical Society/Corbis; **p.32** © Library of Congress, Prints and Photographs Division, LC-USZ62-100533; **p.34** *l* Cartoon showing Uncle Sam exhausted by the flow of bootleg produced by the devil, during the Prohibition era (1920–33) (colour litho), German School, (20th century)/Private Collection/Peter Newark American Pictures/The Bridgeman Art Library, *r* © IMAGNO/Austrian Archives/Getty Images; **p.36** © Corbis; **p.37** *l* The Gusenberg Brothers, St Valentine Day's Massacre, front page of *The Chicago Daily News*, 14 February 1929 (newsprint) St Valentine's Day Massacre, front page of the 'Chicago Daily News', 14 February 1929 (newsprint) by American School, (20th century) © Private Collection/Peter Newark American Pictures/The Bridgeman Art Library, *r* © The Granger Collection/TopFoto; **p.39** © MPI/Getty Images; **p.40** *t* 'The National Gesture' by Clive Weed, from Judge, 12 June 1926 © American Social History Project/City University of New York, *b* © Library of Congress, Prints & Photographs Division, NYWT&S Collection, LC-USZ62-123252; **p.44** 'Welcome All' cartoon, 1880 (colour litho), Keppler, Joseph (1838–94)/Private Collection/Peter Newark American Pictures/The Bridgeman Art Library; **p.45** © Ullsteinbild/Topfoto; **p.46** © Mary Evans Picture Library; **p.51** © Bettmann/Corbis; **p.52** © The Granger Collection/TopFoto; **p.53** © Corbis; **p.55** © Swim Ink 2, LLC/Corbis; **p.56** © Ullsteinbild/TopFoto; **p.57** © Bettmann/Corbis; **p.58** © Library of Congress, Prints and Photographs Division; **p.59** © Mary Evans/Classic Stock/H. Armstrong Roberts; **p.60** © Bettmann/Corbis; **p.61** © Bettmann/Corbis; **p.63** © Brown Brothers; **p.65** © Ullsteinbild/Topfoto; **p.67** © The Granger Collection, NYC/TopFoto; **p.70** © Bettmann/Corbis; **p.72** © Charles Deering McCormick Library of Special Collections, Northwestern University Library; **p.77** © Hulton-Deutsch Collection/Corbis; **p.81** © Frank Driggs Collection/Getty Images; **p.83** © Bettmann/Corbis; **p.84** © Bettmann/Corbis; **p.86** © Bettmann/Corbis; **p.87** © Granger Collection, New York/Topfoto; **p.90** © Bettmann/Corbis; **p.94** © John Iacono/Sports Illustrated/Getty Images; **p.95** © Bettmann/Corbis; **p.97** © The Granger Collection, NYC/TopFoto; **pp.98** and **99** © Bettmann/Corbis; **p.100** *l & r* © Bettmann/Corbis, *b* © Ullsteinbild/TopFoto; **p.101** © Mark Rucker/Transcendental Graphics, Getty Images; **p.102** *l* © Bettmann/Corbis, *r* © Ohio State University; **p.103** © Everett Collection Historical/Alamy; **p.115** © akg-images; **p.116** © Hulton-Deutsch Collection/Corbis; **p.118** *l* © Popperfoto/Getty Images, *r* Courtesy of the United States Holocaust Memorial Museum Photo Archives; **p.121** © Walter Ballhause/akg-images; **p.122** © akg-images; **p.123** *l* © Randall Bytwerk, German Propaganda Archive, *r* © Ullstein Bild/akg-images; **p.125** *l* © Randall Bytwerk, German Propaganda Archive, *tr* © akg-images, *br* © SZ-Photo/Scherl; **p.126** *r* Bildarchiv preussischer Kulturbesitz © The Heartfield Community of Heirs/VG Bild-Kunst, Bonn and DACS, London 2010; **p.127** © SZ-Photo/Scherl; **p.128** © Mary Evans/Weimar Archive; **p.129** *t* © Bildarchiv preussischer Kulturbesitz, *r* Portrait of Adolf Hitler (1889–1945), 1933 (oil on canvas), Jacobs, B. von (fl.1933)/Private Collection/The Bridgeman Art Library; **p.131** © Punch Limited/Topham/TopFoto; **pp.134** and **135** © Bettmann/Corbis; **p.137** © R. Paul Evans; **p.138** © Bettmann/Corbis; **p.139** 'They salute with both hands now' by David Low, 1934 © Evening Standard/Solo Syndication (photo: British Cartoon Archive, University of Kent); **p.140** © Hulton Archive/Getty Images; **p.141** © 2000 Topham Picturepoint/TopFoto; **p.143** © Bundesarchiv, Plak 003-002-046, Grafiker: Ahrlé, René; **p.144** © Institut für Stadtgeschichte Frankfurt am Main; **p.146** © R. Paul Evans; **p.147** © SZ-Photo/Scherl; **p.148** © akg-images; **p.149** © The Wiener Library; **p.152** *l* © akg-images, *r* © Bundesarchiv, Plak 003-011-012, Grafiker: Daehler, Jupp; **pp.153** and **154** © akg-images; **p.157** Police in Nazi Germany arrest communists on Hitler's orders, 1933 (b/w photo), German Photographer (20th Century)/Private Collection/Peter Newark Military Pictures/The Bridgeman Art Library; **p.158** © 2000 Topham Picturepoint/TopFoto; **p.159** © Bildarchiv preussischer Kulturbesitz; **p.161** © SZ-Photo/Scherl; **p.162** *l* © 2006 TopFoto, *r* © Ullstein Bild/akg-images; **p.163** *c* © akg-images, *b* © Hulton-Deutsch Collection/Corbis; **p.164** © Mary Evans/Weimar Archive; **p.165** © Everett Collection Historical/Alamy; **p.168** © akg-images; **p.169** © Mary Evans/Weimar Archive; **p.170** © 1999 Topham Picturepoint/TopFoto; **p.174** © akg-images; **p.177** © Bildarchiv preussischer Kulturbesitz; **p.178** © Robert Hunt Library; **p.179** © Mary Evans Picture Library 2010; **p.180** *l* © Randall Bytwerk, German Propaganda Archive, *r* © Mary Evans Picture Library 2008; **p.183** © APIC/Getty Images; **p.184** 'Volkssturm, For Liberty and Life', German recruitment poster, 1944 (colour litho) by Jolnir, M. (fl.1932–45) © Private Collection/Archives Charmet/The Bridgeman Art Library; **p.186** © akg-images; **p.187** © Painting by Wadyslaw Siwek, Courtesy Muzeum Auschwitz-Birkenau; **p.188** German World War II recruitment poster for women Auxiliaries (Blitzmadchen) for the Luftwaffe (colour litho), German School, (20th century)/© Private Collection/Peter Newark Military Pictures/The Bridgeman Art Library; **p.189** © SZ Photo/Scherl; **p.191** © akg-images/Wittenstein; **p.194** © akg-images/ullstein bild; **p.198** © Bettmann/Corbis; **p.200** © Heinrich Hoffman/Bildarchiv Preußischer Kulturbesitz; **p.201** © Yevgeny Khaldei/Corbis; **p.203** © The Art Archive/Eileen Tweedy; **p.204** © Bettmann/Corbis; **p.206** *t* © St Louis Post-Dispatch, used with permission, State Historical Society of Missouri, Columbia, *b* © Corbis; **p.207** 'Well, that's the end of the Nazis' by David Low, 1946 © Evening Standard/Solo Syndication (Photo: British Cartoon Archive, University of Kent); **p.208** © Bettmann/Corbis.

Acknowledgements

pp.4–5 WJEC sample examination paper, reproduced by permission of WJEC; **p.14** Woody Guthrie, 'Two good men' (1946); **p.17** Abel Meeropol. 'Strange Fruit' (Music & Words by Lewis Allan) © 1939 – Edward B Marks Music Company – copyright renewed; extended term of copyright derived from Lewis Allan assigned and effective July 21, 1995 to Music Sales Corporation – all rights for the world outside of USA controlled by Edward B Marks Music Company – All Rights reserved – Lyric reproduced by kind permission of Carlin Music Corp., London NW1 8BD; **p.47** M. Chandler and J. Wright, Table showing selected share prices 1927–29 from *Modern World History for Edexcel* (Heinemann Educational, 2001); **p.58** John Vick, Table of selected US farm prices, 1919–25 from *Modern America* (Collins Educational, 1991); **p.62** Dave McCarn, 'Cotton Mill Colic' from *The Folksongs of North America*, edited by Alan Lomax (Doubleday, 1960); **pp.101–3 & 210** WJEC sample examination questions, reproduced by permission of WJEC.

Every effort has been made to trace all copyright holders, but if any have been inadvertently overlooked the Publishers will be pleased to make the necessary arrangements at the first opportunity.

INTRODUCTION

About the Route A course

During this course you must study four units:

- A study in depth focusing on source evaluation (Unit 1).
- A study in depth focusing on key historical concepts (Unit 2).
- An outline study focusing on change over time (Unit 3).
- An investigation into an issue of historical debate or controversy (Unit 4).

These are assessed through three examination papers and one controlled assessment:

- For Unit 1 you have one hour and fifteen minutes to answer the set questions. You must answer all the questions on the paper.
- For Unit 2 you have one hour and fifteen minutes to answer the set questions. You must answer all the questions on the paper.
- For Unit 3 you have one hour and fifteen minutes to answer questions on the outline study you have studied.
- In the internal assessment (Unit 4) you have to complete two tasks under controlled conditions in the classroom.

About the book

This book covers two depth studies and is divided into two parts (one part per depth study). Each part is then divided into three sections, each with three chapters.

Part 1: The USA, a nation of contrasts, 1910–29

- **Section A** examines the main political and social challenges facing the USA, including the attempts to restrict immigration, fear of political extremism, racial and religious intolerance, as well as organised crime and corruption.
- **Section B** concentrates on the rise and fall of the American economy, including the reasons for the economic boom, how this prosperity affected American society and why the prosperity came to a sudden end in 1929.
- **Section C** explains changes in American culture and society, including the popularity of entertainment such as the cinema, changes in the lifestyle and status of women, the increasing popularity of sport and fads, crazes and passion for the unusual.

Part 2: Germany in transition, 1919–47

- **Section A** examines the rise of the Nazi Party and its consolidation of power, including the political and economic problems of the Weimar Republic, the impact of the Treaty of Versailles, the early development of the Nazi Party, the impact and effect of the Wall Street Crash, political scheming 1932–33, the reasons for Nazi electoral success, Hitler as Chancellor and the move to dictatorship.
- **Section B** concentrates on the changing life for the German people in Nazi Germany, including how the Nazis tackled economic problems, the treatment of women and young people, how the Nazis extended political control and used propaganda and censorship, Nazi racial policy and the treatment of religion.
- **Section C** explains war and its impact on life in Germany, including how life changed in Germany during the Second World War, the treatment of Jews, opposition from civilians and the military, the defeat and punishment of Germany.

Each chapter:

- contains activities – some develop the historical skills you will need, others are exam-style questions that give you the opportunity to practise exam skills, exam-style questions are highlighted in blue.
- gives step-by-step guidance, model answers and advice on how to answer particular question types in Units 1 and 2.

About Unit 1

The examination of Unit 1 is a test of:

- knowledge and understanding of the key developments in each of the three topic areas for each depth study
- the ability to answer a range of skills questions and source questions.

The exam paper will include a mix of written and illustrative sources:

- Written sources could include extracts from diaries, speeches, letters, poems, songs, biographies, autobiographies, memoirs, newspapers, modern history textbooks, the views of historians, or information from the internet.

- Illustrations could include photographs, posters, cartoons or paintings.

You have to answer the following types of questions, which ask you to demonstrate different source and writing skills:

- Comprehension of information from different sources.
- Comprehension of a source linked to the recall of your own knowledge – asking you to explain what is in the source and place it within its historical context.
- Utility – asking you to analyse and evaluate how useful a source is.
- Describe – asking you to give a detailed description, usually of the key events in a period.
- Context – asking you to explain why a primary source has been created at a particular time.
- Interpretation – asking you to explain differing historical interpretations about the same event.
- Essay writing – asking you to assess the importance of causes, changes or consequences, and to make a judgement on a historical issue.

Example questions

Below and on page 5 is a set of specimen questions for Unit 1 (without the sources). You will be given step-by-step guidance throughout each part of the book on how to best approach and answer these questions.

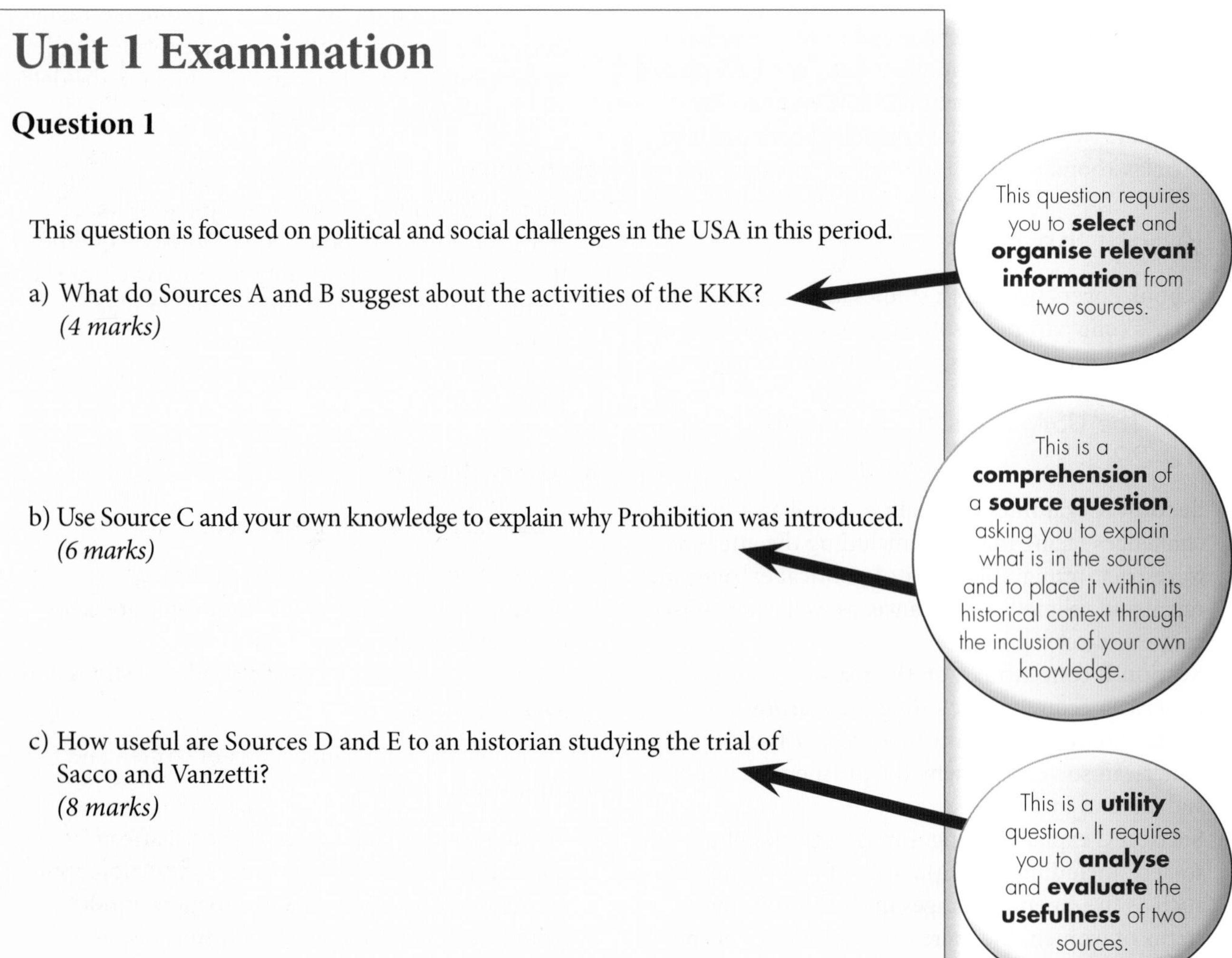

Unit 1 Examination

Question 1

This question is focused on political and social challenges in the USA in this period.

a) What do Sources A and B suggest about the activities of the KKK?
(4 marks)

b) Use Source C and your own knowledge to explain why Prohibition was introduced.
(6 marks)

c) How useful are Sources D and E to an historian studying the trial of Sacco and Vanzetti?
(8 marks)

Question 2

This question is focused on the consolidation of Hitler's power, 1933–34.

a) Describe the events of the Reichstag Fire.
(4 marks)

This is a **describe** question which tests your **knowledge** and **understanding** of an historical event.

b) Why was Source F produced in 1934?
(6 marks)
(Use the source and your own knowledge to explain your answer.)

This is a question about **historical context**. It requires you to **explain the purpose** of the **creation** of a primary source at a specific time.

c) Historians have made different interpretations about why the Night of the Long Knives took place.
One interpretation is that Röhm was planning to overthrow Hitler and make himself leader of Germany. How far do you agree with this interpretation?
(10 marks)
(In your answer you should use the evidence above and your own knowledge of how and why there are different interpretations of the Night of the Long Knives.)

This question is about **differing historical interpretations**. It requires you to **analyse** differing interpretations about the same event.

Question 3

This question is about changing life for people in Germany between 1933 and 1939.

Did the Nazis improve life for all people in Germany between 1933 and 1939?
(12 marks & 3 marks for SPaG)
(In your answer you should discuss the impact of Nazi rule upon the lives of German people, including those who did not see an improvement in their lifestyles.)

This is an **essay** question. You are required to use your own knowledge to debate an issue, examining both sides of an argument. You should also provide a judgement upon the set question. Your answer will also be awarded marks for good spelling, punctuation and grammar (SPaG).

Section A
The main political and social challenges facing America

Source A From an interview with Al Capone, in the 1920s

If people didn't want beer and wouldn't drink it a fellow would be crazy going round trying to sell it. I've seen gambling houses too in my travels and I never saw anyone point a gun at a man and make him go in. I never heard of anyone being forced to go to a place and have some fun.

I help the public. You can't cure thirst by law. They call me a bootlegger. Yes. It's bootleg while it's on the trucks, but when your host hands it to you on a silver plate it's hospitality.

This section examines the main political and social challenges facing America in the period 1910–29 which were two decades of great change for the country and its people. Initially, the USA was seen as a place where the underprivileged of the world could make their fortune and live in freedom. However, after the First World War foreigners were resented and feared and this section looks at the attempts to restrict immigration and considers the problems of religion and race at this time.

It also considers **Prohibition** (see Source A), which had the unintended consequence of ushering in the age of the gangster at a time when the USA was experiencing some of its most difficult challenges.

Each chapter explains a key issue and examines important lines of enquiry as outlined below:

Chapter 1: Why did immigration become such a major issue in American society?

- Why did people emigrate to the USA?
- Why was there opposition to immigration?
- Why was there a fear of political extremism in the USA?
- Why was the Sacco and Vanzetti case important?

Chapter 2: Was America a country of religious and racial intolerance during this period?

- What was religious Fundamentalism?
- What was the experience of black Americans and racial minorities in the 1920s?
- What was the Ku Klux Klan?
- Why was no action taken against the Ku Klux Klan?
- How were Native Americans treated?

Chapter 3: Was the 1920s a decade of organised crime and corruption?

- Why was Prohibition introduced?
- What effects did Prohibition have on US society?
- Why did Prohibition come to an end?
- What was the era of the gangster?
- What was the extent of government corruption and scandal?

1 Why did immigration become such a major issue in American society?

Source A A postcard produced in the USA by the Hebrew Publishing Company, c.1910

TASK

Study Source A. What does it tell you about the attitude of many Americans towards immigration in 1910?

During the late nineteenth and early twentieth centuries about 40 million people emigrated to the USA. The majority of these came from Southern and Eastern Europe and became known as the 'new immigrants'. This distinguished them from the 'old immigrants' who had arrived from western and northern Europe in the earlier part of the nineteenth century. However, by the early 1920s, there was not only open hostility towards immigrants but also a growing **xenophobia** (fear of foreigners) in the USA.

This chapter answers the following questions:

- Why did people emigrate to the USA?
- Why was there opposition to immigration?
- Why was there a fear of political extremism in the USA?
- Why was the Sacco and Vanzetti case important?

Examination guidance

Throughout this chapter you will be given the opportunity to practise different exam-style questions and detailed guidance on how to answer questions from Unit 1 of the examination paper.

Why did people emigrate to the USA?

Source A From the autobiography of Louis Adamic who emigrated to the USA from Slovenia in 1913. His book *From Laughing in the Jungle* was published in 1932

My notion of the United States is that it was a grand, amazing, somewhat fantastic place – the Golden Country – huge beyond conception, very exciting. In America one could make pots of money in a short time, acquire immense holdings, wear a white collar and have polish on one's boots – and eat white bread, soup and meat on weekdays as well as on Sundays, even if you were only an ordinary workman. In America even the common people were 'citizens' and not 'subjects' as in many European countries.

People made the journey to the USA for many different reasons. These can be grouped into the 'push' and 'pull' factors. The push factors explain why immigrants wanted to leave their homeland and the pull factors relate to the attractions of a new life in the USA. Land was available for farming, though by 1900 good cheap agricultural land was becoming scarce. The USA was booming industrially, there were many employment opportunities and those with any business acumen could start new ventures quite easily. The USA was the land of opportunity for all. It was seen as the land of the free and a country which guaranteed basic human rights. For example, Jews from Eastern Europe were seeking religious freedom and an escape from the **pogroms** of Russia, where many thousands had been massacred.

Source B From an interview with a Polish farm labourer in 1912, explaining why he wanted to go to the USA

I have a very great wish to go to America. I want to leave my native country because we are six children and we have very little land. My parents are still young, so it is difficult for us to live. Here in Poland, one must work plenty and wages are very small, just enough to live, so I would like to go and perhaps I would earn more there.

In short, the homelands of the immigrants offered none of these attractions. Moreover, the US government followed an **'Open Door' policy** which meant that entry to the country was quite straightforward.

Source C Official government statistics showing the number of immigrants arriving in the USA, 1871–1920

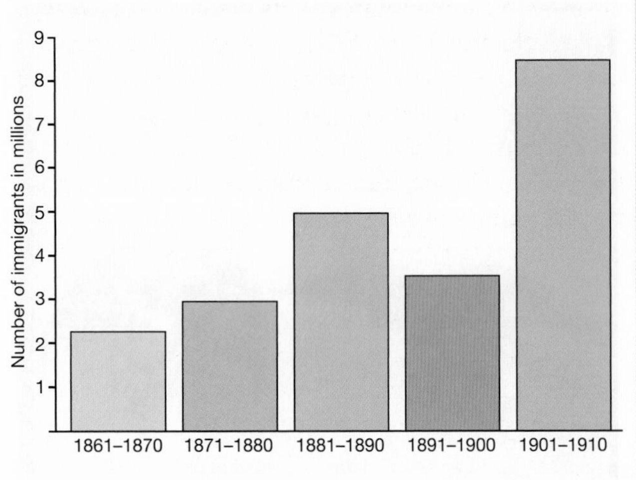

TASKS

1 Use Source B and your own knowledge to explain why people wanted to emigrate to the USA.
(For guidance on how to answer this type of question, see pages 40–41.)

2 How useful are Sources A and C to an historian studying immigration into the USA?
(For guidance on how to answer this type of question, see pages 49–50.)

3 Working in pairs, devise a suitable poster or advertisement to attract people to the USA in the early twentieth century.

Why was there opposition to immigration?

By 1910 there were many in the USA who began to oppose the mass immigration. The immigrants moved to cities where they tended to live with people from their own country of origin and hence **ghettos** developed. Intolerance began to grow and there was a feeling that the 'new' immigrants would take jobs and work for very low wages. It was also thought that the immigrants were responsible for increases in crime, drunkenness and prostitution.

There was opposition to further immigration when the USA became involved in the First World War and hostility to German immigrants increased alarmingly. Indeed, the teaching of German was banned in schools in several states. Furthermore, involvement in the First World War caused many Americans to fear future entanglements in European affairs. They wanted the USA to isolate itself from events in Europe and restricting immigration was a way of doing this.

In the larger cities, the more established immigrant groups such as Irish and German Americans tended to look down on the more recent immigrants from Eastern Europe and Italy. For many Americans in the 1920s, the ideal citizen was a '**WASP**' – white, Anglo-Saxon and Protestant. Asian immigrants were not white whilst many recent European immigrants were Catholics, Greek Orthodox or Jewish. Above all, many Americans feared that immigrants would bring with them dangerous political beliefs, especially **communism**.

Government action to restrict immigration

Immigration was restricted by a series of measures, as detailed in the table below. In addition to the restrictions on the numbers of immigrants, measures were introduced to Americanise them. The Federal Bureau of Naturalisation organised naturalisation proceedings and patriotic 'Americanisation Day' rallies. The Americanisation Day was designed for citizens to re-affirm their loyalty to the USA and the heritage of freedom. People were invited to put on appropriate ceremonies in schools and similar places. Courses on politics and democracy were organised by the Federal Bureau of Education to prepare immigrants for the citizenship examination.

TASKS

1 Describe the key features of restrictions placed on immigration into the USA in the 1920s. (For guidance on how to answer this type of question, see page 73)

2 What was meant by 'Americanisation'?

Date	Measure	Key features
1917	Literacy Test	All foreigners wishing to enter the USA had to take a literacy test. They had to prove that they could read a short passage in English. Many people from poorer countries, especially in Eastern Europe, could not afford to take English lessons and failed the test. In addition, the act banned all immigration from Asia, and charged an immigration fee of $8.
1921	Emergency Quota Act	This act introduced a quota system. New immigrants were allowed in as a proportion of the number of people of the same nationality who had been living in the USA in 1910. The figure was set at three per cent. In other words, the Act reduced the numbers of immigrants from Eastern Europe.
1924	National Origins Act	The quota was reduced to two per cent of the 1890 census. In other words, since there had been a lot more people arriving from Northern Europe by 1890, more of these groups were allowed to enter. (See Source C on page 10.)
1929	Immigration Act	This restricted immigration to 150,000 per year. There were to be no Asians at all. Northern and Western Europeans were allocated 85 per cent of places. By 1930 immigration from Japan, China and Eastern Europe had virtually ceased.

Measures to reduce immigration 1917–29.

Source A From a speech by a senator from Alabama in 1921 who was in favour of the laws to restrict immigration

The steamship companies haul them over to America, and as soon as they step off the decks of their ships the problem of the steamship companies is settled, but our problem has begun – Bolshevism, red anarchy, black-handers, kidnappers, challenging the authority and integrity of the flag. Thousands come here who never take the oath to our Constitution and to become citizens of the USA. They pay allegiance to our country while they live upon the substance of their own. They fill places that belong to the loyal wage-earning citizens of America. They are of no service whatever to our people. They are a menace and a danger to us every day.

Source B President Calvin Coolidge, a republican, speaking to **Congress** in 1923

We must remember that every object of our institutions of society and government will fail unless America is kept American. New arrivals should be limited to our capacity to absorb them into the ranks of good citizenship. America must be kept American. I am convinced that our present economic and social conditions warrant a limitation of those to be admitted. Those who do not want to be partakers of the American spirit ought not to settle in America.

Source C Annual immigration quotas (in thousands) for some countries under the 1924 National Origins Act

Country	Quota
Germany	51,227
Great Britain and Northern Ireland	34,007
Sweden	9,561
Norway	6,453
Italy	3,845
Czechoslovakia	3,073
Russia	2,248
Romania	603

Source D A US cartoon of 1921 commenting on the immigrant quotas

TASKS

3 Explain why there was a growth in opposition to immigration into the USA.

4 How useful are Sources A and B to an historian studying the reasons for restricting entry to immigrants? (For guidance on how to answer this type of question, see pages 49–50.)

5 What do Sources C and D suggest about the attempts to restrict immigration in the early 1920s? (For guidance on how to answer this type of question, see pages 27–28.)

6 How successful had the US government been in its attempts to restrict immigration by 1929?

Why was there a fear of political extremism in the USA?

The 'Red Scare'

The '**Red Scare**' was an almost hysterical reaction from many US citizens to developments in Europe in the years 1917–19, especially the fear of communism. In Russia in 1917 the **Bolshevik Revolution** led to the establishment of a **communist** government. In Germany, a group of communists attempted to seize power in January 1919.

The majority of Americans believed that the government should not interfere in the lives of ordinary citizens and that the individual was responsible for his/her own fate. This theory was '**rugged individualism**'. The idea that a government might take control of land, property and industry was abhorrent to them. Any threat to the US system – **capitalism** – had to be countered.

Source A From *The Case Against the Reds*, an essay by Attorney General Mitchell Palmer, 1920

It is my belief that while they have stirred discontent in our midst, while they have caused irritating strikes, and while they have infected our social ideas with the disease of their own minds and their unclean morals we can get rid of them and not until we have done so shall we have removed the menace of Bolshevism for good.

Many Americans were convinced that revolutionary ideas were being brought to the USA by immigrants, especially from Eastern Europe. This led to a growth in xenophobia – an irrational fear of foreigners. Moreover, Americans tended to see any new political ideas, especially **radicalism** and **anarchism**, as branches of communism. All people who believed in these ideas were classified as 'Reds' (communists). When a communist party was formed in the USA in 1919, many Americans began to fear that there would be a revolution in their own country.

American fears were then heightened by a series of events that occurred in the years immediately after the First World War.

Strikes

There were 3600 strikes in 1919. They were protests against poor working conditions and low pay. Even the police went on strike in Boston. To many members of the American public, the strikes seemed to herald the beginnings of a communist revolution.

A **general strike** in Seattle was led by an organisation known as the Industrial Workers of the World (IWW), a name that many found strongly suggestive of communist ideals. The strike failed and one consequence was the loss of orders for the dockyards, which resulted in an increase in unemployment.

During the steelworkers' dispute, the steel company owners published circulars which attacked foreign-born strikers. The press generally portrayed the strikes as anti-American actions which threatened the US government.

Source B An advertisement in a US newspaper encouraging steelworkers to return to work, 1919. It was written in eight languages, which linked union leadership with foreigners and the un-American teachings of radical strike agitators

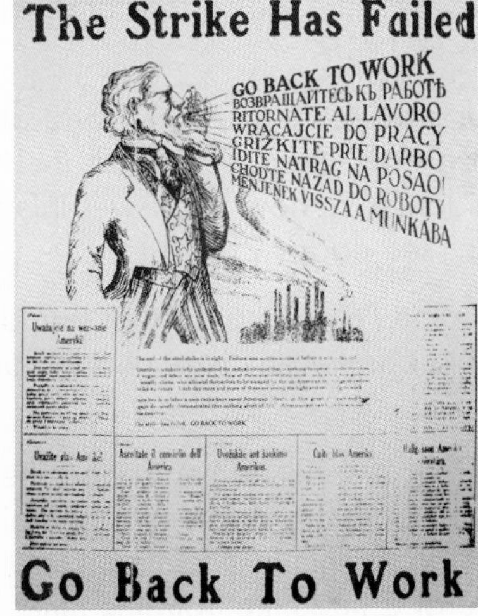

TASK

1 Why was this advertisement (Source B) published in 1919? (For guidance on how to answer this type of question, see page 84.)

Bomb outrages and the actions of anarchists

In the same year (1919), there was a series of bombings by extreme anarchist groups. In one famous attack, the home of Mitchell Palmer, the Attorney-General (Head of the US Department of Justice), was bombed. In April 1919, a bomb planted in a church in Milwaukee killed ten people. In May, letter bombs were posted to 36 well-known Americans.

Source C An anarchist pamphlet called the *Plain Truth*, found near the house of Mitchell Palmer in 1919

There will have to be bloodshed. We will not dodge. There will have to be a murder. We will kill. There will have to be destruction. We will destroy. We are ready to do anything to suppress the capitalist system.

TASKS

2 What is meant by the following terms: rugged individualism, communism, anarchism, radical?

3 Explain why there was a fear of revolution in the USA in 1919.

4 What do Sources C and D suggest about the fear of revolution in the USA in 1919? (For guidance on how to answer this type of question, see pages 27–28.)

5 Describe the Palmer Raids. (For guidance on how to answer this type of question, see page 73.)

6 Put together a series of newspaper headlines for 1919 about the strikes and bombings, to whip up anti-communist feeling. Here is one example of a headline from the time:

REDS PLANNED BOMBING MURDERS

The Palmer Raids

The press whipped up public feeling and insisted that this was further evidence of a widespread communist takeover plot. The police attacked socialist parades on May Day 1920 and raided the offices of socialist organisations. Many innocent people were arrested because of their supposed dangerous political beliefs. Amongst those arrested were trade unionists, black people, Jews and Catholics. These arrests were known as the 'Palmer Raids' as they were organised by Mitchell Palmer. These raids were illegal but there were few who protested against them. In all, more than 6000 suspected communists were arrested in 36 cities across the USA. Several hundred Russian immigrants were sent back in a ship nicknamed the 'Soviet Ark'.

Source D The aftermath of one of the Palmer Raids on the offices of the Industrial Workers of the World (IWW), 15 November 1919

Why was the Sacco and Vanzetti case important?

On 5 May 1920, two Italian labourers, Nicola Sacco and Bartolomeo Vanzetti, were arrested and charged with the murder of Fred Parmenter. Parmenter was the paymaster of a factory in South Braintree, Massachusetts. Parmenter and a security guard had been shot by two armed robbers on 15 April 1920. Both men died, but not before Parmenter had described his attackers as slim foreigners with olive skins.

The Sacco and Vanzetti trial began in May 1921 and lasted 45 days. Owing to the heavy publicity given to the case, it took several days to find a jury of 12 men who were acceptable to both the prosecution and defence. In all, 875 candidates were called to the court. On 14 July 1921, the jury delivered a guilty verdict. There were demonstrations all over the USA in support of the two condemned men.

Sacco and Vanzetti took their case to appeal in several higher courts but all attempts failed. The last appeal was in 1927. The two men were executed by electric chair on 24 August 1927.

The evidence against Sacco and Vanzetti

- They were anarchists who hated American capitalism and the US system of government.
- Vanzetti had been convicted of armed robbery in 1919.
- 61 eyewitnesses identified the two men as the killers.
- Sacco and Vanzetti were carrying guns on the day they were arrested.
- The two men told lies in their statements to the police.
- Forensic evidence matched the pistol that killed the guard with the one carried by Sacco.
- Vanzetti refused to take the stand at the trial.

Bartolomeo Vanzetti (left) and Nicola Sacco (right).

The evidence in their defence

- Vanzetti refused to take the stand because he feared that his political activities would become a major focus and that he would be found guilty of these rather than the robbery.
- 107 people confirmed the two men's alibi (their claim that they were somewhere else when the robbery was committed). However, many of these witnesses were recently arrived Italian immigrants whose English was poor.
- Some believe that the forensic evidence about Sacco's gun was rigged.
- Evidence from the 61 prosecution witnesses often disagreed in important details. Some witnesses had changed their stories by the time the trial started.
- The two men said they lied to the police because they feared that they would be discriminated against because of their support for anarchism.
- Several other men confessed to the crime.
- The judge, Webster Thayer, seemed determined to find the two men guilty.

Importance of the trial

- The trial was reported all over the world and showed the intolerance of US society. As Italian immigrants, the two men were victims of racial discrimination and were denied rights that they were entitled to.
- It exposed the unfairness of the American legal system. The two men were convicted on flimsy evidence – although subsequent evidence suggests that Sacco may have been guilty.
- In the 1970s the **Governor** of Massachusetts granted Sacco and Vanzetti a formal pardon and agreed that a mistrial had taken place (see Source D).

Source A A comment made about Judge Thayer who presided over the original Sacco and Vanzetti case. It was made in 1930 by Felix Frankfurter, a lawyer who campaigned for a retrial, and who wrote a book which criticised the original trial

I have known Judge Thayer all my life. I say that he is a narrow-minded man; he is an unintelligent man; he is full of prejudice; he is carried away by fear of Reds, a fear which has captured about ninety per cent of the American people.

TASKS

1. What do Sources A and B suggest about the Sacco and Vanzetti case? (For guidance on how to answer this type of question, see pages 27–28).
2. Describe the events surrounding the trial of Sacco and Vanzetti. (For guidance on how to answer this type of question, see page 73).

Source B Demonstrators in Boston in 1925 in support of Sacco and Vanzetti

Source C Freda Kirchwey was in Germany during the last few weeks before Nicola Sacco and Bartolomeo Vanzetti were executed. She wrote about her reaction to the execution in *The Nation*, 28 August 1927. *The Nation* was a radical US magazine

We've hardly talked about it – but every time we got within range of a newspaper we've rushed to it hoping, without any real hope, that some miracle of mercy would have descended on the Governor or someone else. It was hard to sleep through some of those nights. And everywhere we went – from Paris and Berlin to Heiligenblut in the Austrian Tyrol – people talked to us about it with horror and a complete inability to understand. It whipped up further opposition to immigrants, intensified the 'Red Scare' and seemed to strengthen the case for restrictions on immigration.

Source D Proclamation from the Governor of Massachusetts, August 1977

Therefore I, Michael S. Dukakis, hereby proclaim Tuesday, August 23, 1977, Nicola Sacco and Bartolomeo Vanzetti Memorial Day and declare, further, that any stigma and disgrace should be forever removed from the names of the two men.

Source E From the song 'Two Good Men' by Woody Guthrie, written in 1946

Vanzetti docked in nineteen eight;
Slept along the dirty street,
Told the workers 'Organize',
And on the 'lectric chair he dies.

All you people ought to be like me,
And work like Sacco and Vanzetti,
And everyday find ways to fight
On the union side for the workers' rights.

TASKS

3 Study Source C. What information does it contain to support the view that Sacco and Vanzetti were used as scapegoats?

4 Examine the evidence for and against the two men on pages 13–15. Copy and complete the table below.

	Guilty	Not guilty
Most convincing evidence		
Least convincing evidence		

Now make your own decision: guilty or not guilty? Write two paragraphs explaining your decision.

5 Study Source E. What message is the writer trying to put across about Sacco and Vanzetti?

6 Was the fear of communism the most important reason for the restrictions on immigration in the USA in the 1920s?

In your answer you should discuss the various factors which led to the restriction of immigration, including the fear of communism.

(For guidance on how to answer this type of question, see pages 91–92.)

Examination guidance

This section is intended to provide you with some guidance on how to evaluate the usefulness and reliability of an historical source. These evaluation skills can be applied to many of the source-based questions throughout this book.

Considering the usefulness of a source

When evaluating the usefulness of a source to the historian you need to ask a series of probing questions about the source:

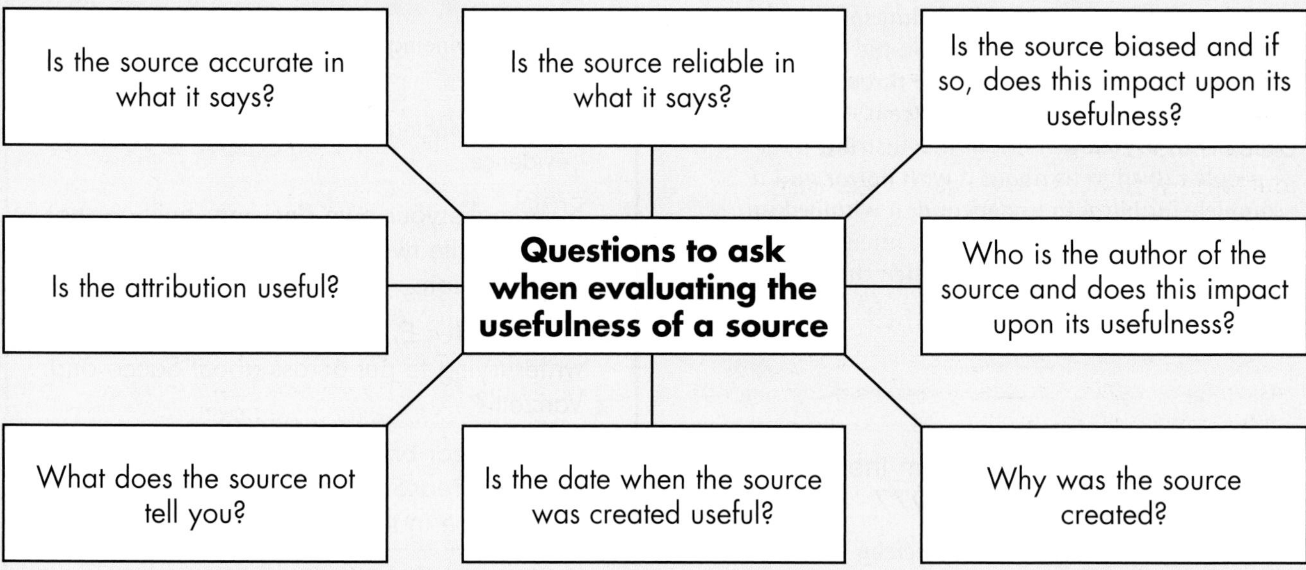

Considering the reliability of a source

When evaluating the reliability of a source as a piece of evidence to the historian you need to ask a series of questions about the source:

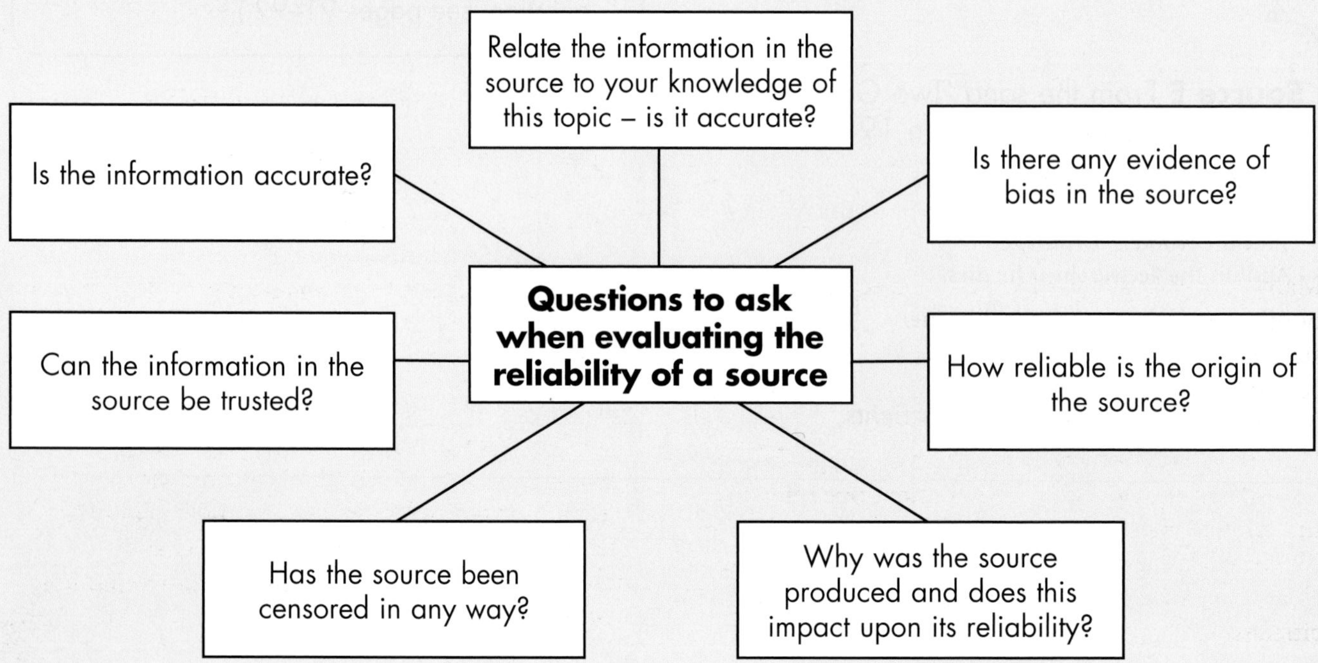

Was America a country of religious and racial intolerance during this period?

Source A A report from the *Washington Eagle,* 1921. It describes the death of a black American who had been accused of murdering a white woman in Georgia

The negro was taken to a grove where members of the Ku Klux Klan had placed a fine pine knot around a stump. The negro was chained to the stump and asked if he had anything to say. Castrated and in indescribable pain, the negro asked for a cigarette and blew the smoke in the face of his tormentors. The fire was lit and a hundred men and women danced, old and young, joined hands and danced around while the negro burned.

Source B The poem 'Strange Fruit' by Abel Meeropol, written in 1936 in response to lynchings of black Americans in the 1920s

Southern trees bear strange fruit
Blood on the leaves
Blood at the root
Black bodies swinging in the southern breeze
Strange fruit hanging from the poplar trees
Pastoral scene of the gallant south
The bulging eyes and the twisted mouth
The scent of magnolia sweet and fresh
Then the sudden smell of burning flesh
Here is a fruit for the crows to pluck
for the rain to gather
for the wind to suck
for the sun to rot
for the tree to drop
Here is a strange and bitter crop

TASKS

1 What do Sources A and B suggest about the treatment of black Americans during the 1920s? (For guidance on how to answer this type of question, see pages 27–28.)

Many Americans benefited from the economic boom of the 1920s and experienced an improved standard of living, including a wider range of leisure activities and entertainment. However, many people living in the USA suffered from racism and bigotry. During the 1920s there was a great deal of hatred towards black Americans and tremendous religious intolerance which was reflected in the growth of the Ku Klux Klan. Furthermore, the notorious Monkey Trial also showed the gulf in beliefs between many US citizens.

This chapter answers the following questions:

- What was religious Fundamentalism?
- What was the experience of black Americans and racial minorities in the 1920s?
- What was the Ku Klux Klan?
- Why was no action taken against the Ku Klux Klan?
- How were Native Americans treated?

Examination guidance

Throughout this chapter you will be given the opportunity to practise different exam-style questions and detailed guidance on how to answer question 1(a). This requires you to select and organise relevant information from two sources. It is worth 4 marks.

What was religious Fundamentalism?

In the 1920s most rural Americans were very religious people. The south-east of the USA (including states such as Alabama, Arkansas, Kentucky and Tennessee) had been given the name of the '**Bible Belt**' and the people viewed themselves as righteous, God-fearing Christians. Many in these areas were known as **Fundamentalists** following the formation of the World's Christian Fundamentals Association. They were Protestants who believed that everything in the Bible was to be taken literally and must not be questioned.

During the 1920s, many people in the Bible Belt sought to hold back the changes that were taking place in the USA. They disliked the provocative clothes and dancing, the gambling and what they saw as the general decline in moral standards. One of the most famous Fundamentalist preachers was Aimee Semple McPherson. She went round the USA in the early 1920s raising money for her Four Square Gospel Church. She raised more than $1.5 million in 1921 for the building of her Angelus Temple.

The gap in belief between the rural and urban Americans was most clearly seen with the argument over the theory of evolution. Most people living in the towns and cities of the USA accepted Charles Darwin's theory of evolution, which stated that over a period of millions of years human beings had evolved from ape-like creatures. However, these views were not accepted by many people in rural areas, especially in the Bible-Belt states.

Source A A sermon delivered by Billy Sunday, a well-known Fundamentalist preacher in 1925

If anyone wants to teach that God-forsaken hell-born, bastard theory of evolution, then let him ... but do not expect the Christian people of this country to pay for the teaching of a rotten, stinking professor who gets up there and teaches our children to forsake God and makes our schools a clearing-house for their God-forsaken dirty politics.

The Monkey Trial

In 1924 the state of Tennessee passed the Butler Act, which made it illegal for any public school 'to teach any theory which denied the story of the Divine Creation of man as taught in the Bible and to teach that man has descended from a lower order or animals'. Five other states passed similar laws.

A biology teacher called John Scopes decided to challenge this ban. He deliberately taught evolution in his class in Tennessee in order to be arrested and put on trial.

Both sides hired the best lawyers for a trial, which took place in July 1925. Its proceedings captured the imagination of the public. Scopes was supported by the American Civil Liberties Union and defended by Clarence Darrow, a famous criminal lawyer, and the prosecutor was William Jennings Bryan, a Fundamentalist. Scopes was convicted of breaking the law and was fined $100. However, the trial was a disaster for the public image of the Fundamentalists. The trial became a debate between science and religion. Bryan was shown to be confused and ignorant whilst the media mocked the beliefs of those who opposed the theory of evolution. Many saw the Fundamentalist viewpoint as an attempt to stifle freedom of thought.

Source B A report on the trial in the *Baltimore Evening Sun*, July 1925

For nearly two hours Mr Darrow goaded his opponent. He asked Mr Bryan if he really believed that the serpent had always crawled on its belly because it tempted Eve, and if he believed Eve was made from Adam's rib. Bryan's face flushed under Mr Darrow's searching words and when one stumped him he took refuge in his faith and either refused to answer directly or said in effect: 'The Bible states it; it must be true'.

Source C A cartoon which appeared in a national newspaper in July 1925

CLASSROOM IN PROPOSED BRYAN UNIVERSITY OF TENNESSEE

TASKS

1 Explain why John Scopes was put on trial in 1925.

2 Use Source A and your own knowledge to explain why there was opposition from some Americans to the teaching of the theory of evolution. (For guidance on how to answer this type of question, see pages 40–41.)

3 How far does Source B support the view that the Monkey Trial was really a debate between science and religion?

4 Why was the cartoon (Source C) published in July 1925? (For guidance on how to answer this type of question, see page 84.)

What was the experience of black Americans and racial minorities in the 1920s?

The Jim Crow Laws

Black people had been brought to America as slaves in the seventeenth and eighteenth centuries. By the time slavery was ended in the 1860s, there were more black Americans than whites living in the southern states. White-controlled state governments, fearing the power of black Americans, introduced laws to control their freedom. These were known as the **Jim Crow Laws**, after a nineteenth-century comedian's act which ridiculed black people. They segregated blacks in schools, parks, hospitals, swimming pools, libraries and other public places. New Jim Crow laws were passed in some states so that there were segregated taxis, race tracks and boxing matches.

Blacks found it hard to get fair treatment. They could not vote and were denied access to good jobs and a reasonable education. They were intimidated by whites who tried to control them through fear and terror. In the First World War, 360,000 black Americans served in the armed forces. They returned home to find that racism was part of everyday life. Between 1915 and 1922 more than 430 black Americans were lynched.

Source B Lige Daniels, a black American, lynched on 3 August 1920 at Center, Texas

Source A A segregated drinking fountain

The Great Migration

Faced by racism and living in often chronic poverty, thousands of black Americans moved to the cities of the north in the years after 1910, hoping to find a better life. In the years 1916–20, almost 1 million black Americans left the south for jobs in the north. This became known as '**the Great Migration**'.

Source C From an article published in a newspaper for black Americans, 1921

Look around at your cabin, look at the dirt floor and the windows without glass. Then ask your folks already up North about the bathrooms with hot and cold water. What chance has the average black man to get these back home? And if he does get them, how can he be sure that some night some poor white man won't get his gang together and come round and drive him out?

However, conditions were not much better in the north. Black Americans were given low-paid jobs and were the first to be laid off in bad times. They generally lived in squalid tenement ghettos and faced even more racial intolerance. In New York and Chicago they often lived in poorer housing than whites and yet paid higher rents. They had poorer education and health services than whites. There was some progress: for example, the Ford Motor Company employed only 50 black Americans in 1916 but by 1926 it employed 10,000. Nevertheless, the majority of black Americans did not benefit from the economic **boom** of the 1920s. They were still seen as second-class citizens and, especially in the southern states, suffered from segregation, discrimination and often terrible intimidation.

Northern white Americans frequently objected to the arrival of southern black Americans and feared the competition for jobs and housing. Racial tension grew and in 1919 there were race riots in more than 20 US cities, which resulted in 62 deaths and hundreds of injuries. The worst riots were in Chicago and Washington DC where the army had to be used to restore order. In Chicago, 38 people died, including 15 white and 23 black Americans, and 537 people were injured.

Improvements

However, there were some improvements for black Americans, especially in the northern states.

- In Chicago and New York there was a growing black middle class. In Chicago in 1930 blacks boycotted department stores until they agreed to employ black assistants.
- Jazz brought fame to several black singers and musicians such as Louis Armstrong.
- The black neighbourhood of Harlem in New York became the centre of the Harlem Renaissance for black singers, musicians, artists, writers and poets.
- Black theatre attracted big audiences whilst black performing artists, including singers, comedians and dancers, were popular in clubs and musical shows.
- Life expectancy for blacks increased from 45 in 1900 to 48 in 1930.

On page 22 are examples of some influential black Americans of the 1920s.

TASKS

1. What do Sources A and B suggest about the treatment of some black Americans during the 1920s? (For guidance on how to answer this type of question, see pages 27–28.)
2. Explain why segregation was introduced into the southern states.
3. Use Source C and your own knowledge to explain why black Americans migrated to the north. (For guidance on how to answer this type of question, see pages 40–41.)
4. Describe the race riots of 1920. (For guidance on how to answer this type of question, see page 73.)
5. Study Source D. What does it tell you about black American migration in the 1920s?

Source D Urban black population, 1920–30

City	1920	1930	Percentage increase
New York	152,467	327,706	114.9
Chicago	109,458	233,903	113.7
Philadelphia	134,229	219,599	63.6
Detroit	40,838	120,066	194.0
Los Angeles	15,579	38,894	149.7

Biography Paul Robeson 1898–1976

Paul Robeson was a trained lawyer who was unable to find work because he was black. Instead, he turned to acting and became well known due to his part in the hit musical *Showboat.* With songs such as his trademark 'Ol' Man River', he became one of the most popular concert singers of his time. His *Othello* was the longest-running Shakespeare play in Broadway history. More than any other performer of his time, he believed that the famous have a responsibility to fight for justice and peace.

Biography Countee Cullen 1903–46

Countee Cullen had an unusual education which went against the prejudices of the time. He attended DeWitt Clinton High School, mainly consisting of all white, male students, and became Vice-President of his class during his senior year. He attended New York University and graduated in 1925. He became a renowned poet whose works were published in various literary magazines. His poems attacked racism and black poverty.

Biography Marcus Garvey 1887–1940

Marcus Garvey thought that black people should not try to be part of white society. He insisted that they should celebrate their blackness and their African past. In 1914 he set up the **Universal Negro Improvement Association** (**UNIA**). By 1920 the UNIA had 2000 members. At its peak, UNIA had about 250,000 members.

Garvey wanted to establish close contacts with Africa and asked black Americans to use their skills, education and knowledge to make Africa strong and powerful in the world. He encouraged black Americans to return to Africa (his slogan was 'Back to Africa') to 'establish a country and a government on their own'. However, in 1925 Garvey was put in prison for 'postal fraud' and, on his release, he was deported to Jamaica. The UNIA fell apart.

Nevertheless, he passed on the idea taken up by the **Black Power Movement** of the 1960s that 'black is beautiful'.

Biography W E B Du Bois 1868–1963

William Du Bois set up the **National Association for the Advancement of Colored People** (**NAACP**) in 1909. He wanted America to accept all people, with equal opportunities for all. By 1919 NAACP had 90,000 members in 300 branches. Du Bois used the NAACP to challenge **white supremacy**, especially the segregation laws. He made black Americans much more aware of their civil rights, especially the right to vote.

The NAACP also campaigned against the practice of lynching in the south. It investigated and publicised the number of lynchings. Although the NAACP failed to get a law passed banning lynchings, the publicity gained led to a great reduction in the number being carried out.

TASKS

6 Describe the work of the NAACP and UNIA in the 1920s. (For guidance on how to answer this type of question, see page 73.)

7 Use the information from pages 20–22 to compile a mind map showing how black Americans were treated as second-class citizens in the USA during the 1920s.

8 Did all black Americans experience a life of poverty and discrimination during the 1920s?

> In your answer you should discuss the bad treatment received by black Americans and also the improvements experienced by others.

(For guidance on how to answer this type of question, see pages 91–92.)

9 Working in groups, draw up a petition to present to the President of the USA explaining why life for black Americans should be improved.

What was the Ku Klux Klan (KKK)?

Origins

The Ku Klux Klan (KKK) was set up in the 1860s by soldiers who had fought in the American Civil War. Its aim was to terrorise black people newly freed from slavery. However, it died out in the years after 1870 when a federal Grand Jury determined that the Klan was a 'terrorist organisation'. It was revived after the release of a film, *The Birth of a Nation,* in 1915 which was set in the south after the Civil War and showed the Klan saving white families from gangs of blacks intent on raping and looting. The film attracted huge audiences and seemed to reinforce the idea of white supremacy.

After the First World War, labour tensions rose as veterans tried to enter the workforce. In reaction to new groups of immigrants and migrants (see pages 7–10), the membership increased.

Source A Hiram Wesley Evans, the leader of the KKK, speaking in 1924

> It is the way of the world that each race must fight for its life, must conquer or accept slavery or die. The Klan wants every state to make sex between a white and black person a crime. Protestants must be supreme. Rome shall not rule America. The Roman Catholic Church is un-American and usually anti-American.

Beliefs

The Klan members were WASPs. They identified themselves as white, Anglo-Saxon, Protestants, and they saw themselves as being superior to other races. They were also anti-communist, anti-black, anti-Jew, anti-Catholic and against all foreigners.

Source B Members of the Ku Klux Klan marching through Washington DC, 18 August 1925

Organisation

Klansmen dressed in white sheets and wore white hoods. This outfit was designed to conceal the identity of Klan members, who often attacked their victims at night. The white colour symbolised white supremacy. Members carried American flags and lit burning crosses at their night-time meetings. Their leader, a dentist called Hiram Wesley Evans, was known as the Imperial Wizard. Officers of the Klan were known as Klaliffs, Kluds or Klabees.

Membership

In 1920 the Klan had 100,000 members. By 1925, it claimed to have more than 5 million. It attracted members all over the USA, but especially in the south. Most members were white, Protestant and racist. The state governors of Oregon and Oklahoma were members of the Klan. The growth of the Klan after 1920 arose in response to:

- Industrialisation, which brought more and more workers to cities. The Klan grew rapidly in cities such as Memphis and Atlanta, which expanded quickly after 1910.
- Many of these workers were immigrants from Eastern and Southern Europe, or black Americans migrating from the southern states to the urban centres of the north.
- Southern whites resented the arming of black soldiers during the First World War.

Activities

Members of the Klan carried out lynchings of black people and they beat up and mutilated anyone they considered to be their enemy. They stripped some of their victims and put tar and feathers on their bodies. For example:

- In 1921 Chris Lochan, a restaurant owner, was run out of town because he was accused of being a foreigner. His parents were Greek.
- George Arnwood was a mentally retarded black man who, in October 1933, was accused of assaulting an 82-year-old white woman. Members of the Klan dragged him from jail and beat him to death. His body was strung up on a tree and then dragged through the town before being set on fire. The police watched and did nothing.

Source C A description of Klan activities in Alabama in 1929

A lad whipped with branches until his back was ribboned flesh ... a white girl, divorcee, beaten into unconsciousness in her home; a naturalised foreigner flogged until his back was a pulp because he married an American woman; a negro lashed until he sold his land to a white man for a fraction of its value.

Source D A report of KKK activities by the New York magazine *World* in 1921

5 kidnappings
43 orders to negroes to leave town
27 tar and featherings
41 floggings
1 branding with acid
1 mutilation
4 murders

Decline

The Klan declined after 1925 when one of its leaders, Grand Wizard David Stephenson, was convicted of the rape and mutilation of a woman on a Chicago train. The scandal destroyed Stephenson's reputation and when the Governor of Indiana refused to pardon him, he produced evidence of illegal Klan activities. This discredited the Klan and led to a sharp decline in its membership.

TASKS

1. What do Sources A and B suggest about the beliefs of the Ku Klux Klan? (For guidance on how to answer this type of question, see pages 27–28.)
2. Describe the activities of the Ku Klux Klan. (For guidance on how to answer this type of question, see page 73.)
3. Using Sources B (page 23), C and D, design a poster for those people who opposed the activities of the KKK. The poster should aim to shock people.

Why was no action taken against the Ku Klux Klan?

Some states believed that the **federal government** had no right to interfere in what was happening with the Klan. In addition, many politicians in the south knew that if they spoke out against the Klan, they would lose votes and might not be elected to Congress. When campaigning for re-election in 1924, one Congressman said 'I was told to join the Klan or else.'

Source A A cartoon published in the *Heroes of the Fiery Cross,* a magazine of the Pillar of Fire Church during the presidential campaign of 1928. The Democrat candidate, Alfred Smith, was Roman Catholic. The Pillar of Fire Church was closely linked to the Ku Klux Klan in the 1920s

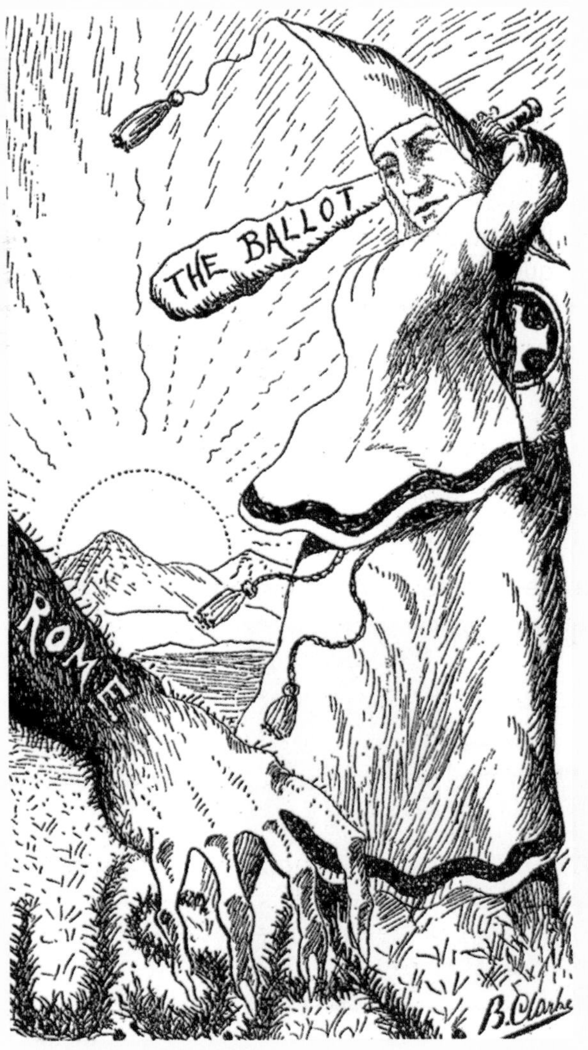

Source B From *Konklave in Kokomo*, a book about the Ku Klux Klan by the historian Robert Coughlan (1949). Coughlan grew up in Kokomo during the 1920s

Literally half the town (Kokomo) belonged to the Klan when I was a boy. At its peak, which was from 1923 through 1925, the Nathan Hale Den had about five thousand members, out of an able-bodied adult population of ten thousand. With this strength the Klan was able to dominate local politics. It packed the police and fire departments with its own people, with the result that on parade nights the traffic patrolmen disappeared and traffic control was taken over by sheeted figures whose size and shape resembled those of the vanished patrolmen.

Source C A historian writing about the Ku Klux Klan in 1992

The Ku Klux Klan believed White, Protestant America had to be saved from black people, immigrants, Jews and Catholics. They used extreme violence against people from all these groups, especially black people. Klan members swore an oath of loyalty to the USA and promised to defend the USA against 'any cause, government, people, sect or ruler that is foreign to the country'.

TASKS

1. Why was Source A published in 1928? (For guidance on how to answer this type of question, see page 84.)
2. How useful are Sources B and C to an historian studying why the Ku Klux Klan was able to operate freely in the 1920s? (For guidance on how to answer this type of question, see pages 49–50.)

How were Native Americans treated?

At the beginning of the twentieth century, Native Americans had been placed on reservations. In 1924 the Indian Citizenship Act was passed. This at last granted full US citizenship to America's native peoples (they were called 'Indians' in the Act).

Native Americans were really only seen when they were demonstrating Indian crafts, speaking Indian languages, or performing in stereotypical Indian costume. In the states of Vermont and New Hampshire, the Eugenics Project had a programme which managed Native Americans and other 'undesirables' by means of social planning, education, and reproductive control. Some white reformers argued that Native Americans could only survive by rejecting their own culture and merging fully into white society. As a result, special boarding schools were established for this purpose and thousands of Native American children were taken from their families and cultures. This tended to destroy the identity of tribes and the children were encouraged not to speak their own language and convert to Christianity. It was another attempt to Americanise those people who were not the original migrants in the USA (see pages 9–10).

In 1928 the Meriam Report was prepared for the US government. The report stated that the boarding schools were underfunded and understaffed and run too harshly. The attempt to bring assimilation by means of education had failed. The Report recommended that the curriculum, which taught only European–American cultural values, should be dropped. The report went on to say that the Native Americans should be provided with the skills and education for life in their own traditional rural communities as well as American urban society.

TASKS

1. Describe the treatment of Native Americans by the US government during the 1920s. (For guidance on how to answer this type of question, see page 73.)
2. Explain why the US government wanted to 'Americanise' the Native Americans.
3. Were the Jim Crow laws the worst examples of intolerance in the USA between 1910 and 1929?

   In your answer you should discuss the impact of various types of racial and religious intolerance within American society during the period 1910–1929, including the Jim Crow laws.

   (For guidance on how to answer this type of question, see pages 91–92.)

Source A An Indian logger and his family outside their home in Washington State, 1916

Examination guidance

This section provides guidance on how to answer a source comprehension question. This requires you to select and organise relevant information from two sources. It is worth 4 marks.

What do Sources A and B suggest about the treatment of black Americans in the southern states?

(4 marks)

Source A A segregated drinking fountain. These were common across the southern states of America.

Source B From a school textbook

*Some southern states tried to keep control over black people by passing laws which separated them from white people. This involved making sure that black people went to separate schools and were kept in poorly paid, unskilled jobs with few **trade union** rights.*

Tips on how to answer

This is an inference question involving the comprehension of information extracted from two sources.

- In the case of a **visual source** you will need to **look into the picture** and **extract relevant details**
- You will need to **pick out at least two relevant points** which are well developed and supported
- You should **make use of the written statement attached to the source** which is intended to provide you with additional information
- In the case of a **written source** you will need to **read the extract carefully, underlining** or **highlighting** key points
- You should then **try to rephrase and explain these points** in your own words, making sure you discuss **at least two key points**
- Aim to bring in your own **background knowledge** to expand upon these points
- To obtain maximum marks you need to ensure that you have **referred to both sources in equal measure**
- An **imbalanced answer** which concentrates too much on one source will not score you top marks

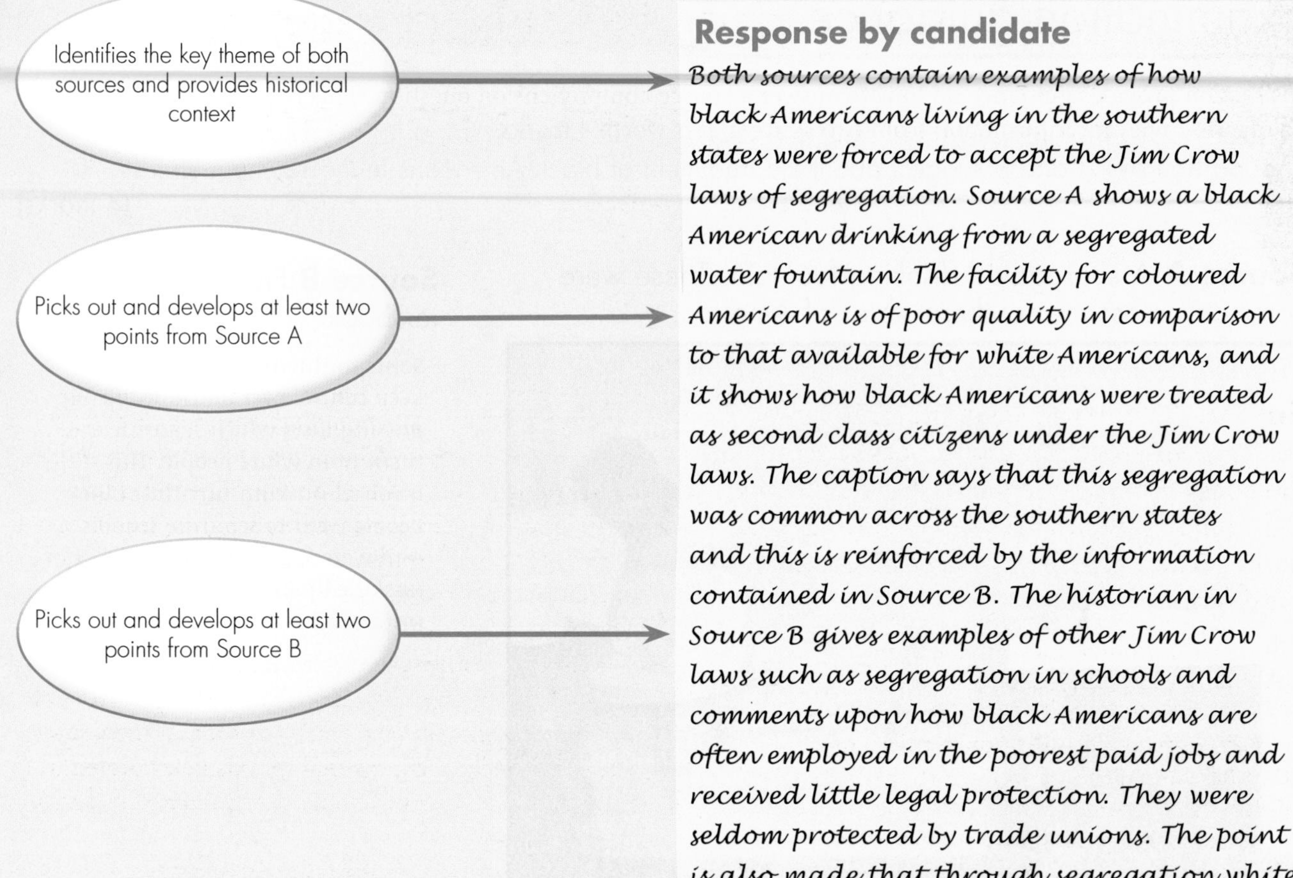

Response by candidate

Both sources contain examples of how black Americans living in the southern states were forced to accept the Jim Crow laws of segregation. Source A shows a black American drinking from a segregated water fountain. The facility for coloured Americans is of poor quality in comparison to that available for white Americans, and it shows how black Americans were treated as second class citizens under the Jim Crow laws. The caption says that this segregation was common across the southern states and this is reinforced by the information contained in Source B. The historian in Source B gives examples of other Jim Crow laws such as segregation in schools and comments upon how black Americans are often employed in the poorest paid jobs and received little legal protection. They were seldom protected by trade unions. The point is also made that through segregation white Americans aimed to control the lives of black Americans.

Comment on candidate performance

The candidate has made a number of valid observations based upon both sources and has displayed an understanding of how black Americans were treated in the southern states during the 1920s. Historical context is provided through specific reference to key terms such as the Jim Crow laws of segregation. At least two relevant points are extracted from each source and discussed in some detail. Both sources are afforded equal weighting and this, together with an informed discussion, makes the answer worthy of maximum (4) marks.

Was the 1920s a decade of organised crime and corruption?

Source A From the memoirs of Alice Longworth, 1933. She was very active in the social and political life of Washington DC in the 1920s. Here she describes life at the White House when Harding was president

Though violation of the 18th Amendment (Prohibition) was a matter of course in Washington DC, it was rather shocking to see the way President Harding disregarded the Constitution and laws that he was sworn to uphold. Though nothing to drink was served downstairs, there were always, at least before the unofficial dinners, cocktails in the upstairs hall outside the President's room and guests were shown up there instead of waiting below … One evening, the study was heavy with tobacco smoke, there were trays with bottles containing every imaginable brand of whisky, people had their feet on the desk, there was a spittoon … Harding was not a bad man. He was just a slob.

TASK

Study Source A. What does it tell you about the age of prohibition?

The 1920s was an unsettling decade for the USA and its citizens. It was a time of great prosperity for many and poverty for others. There was racial tension and bigotry which often led to violence. However, the decade is most often remembered for gangsters such as Al Capone and the period of Prohibition. Gangsters brought much corruption and violence to the cities of the USA and in some cases whole cities were controlled by them. Nor did people see cases of corruption only in the cities; they also saw it in the federal government under the presidency of Warren Harding in the years 1919–23. The feeling grew that morals deteriorated in the USA and that many people were prepared to break the law.

This chapter answers the following questions:

- Why was Prohibition introduced?
- What effects did Prohibition have on US society?
- Why did Prohibition come to an end?
- What was the era of the gangster?
- What was the extent of government corruption and scandal?

Examination guidance

Throughout this chapter you will be given the opportunity to practise different exam-style questions and detailed guidance on how to answer question 1(b). This requires you to use the source material and your own knowledge to explain a development. It is worth 6 marks.

Why was Prohibition introduced?

Source A A poster issued by the Anti-Saloon League in 1917 to highlight the evils of alcohol

Daddy's in There---

And Our Shoes and Stockings and Clothes and Food Are in There, Too, and They'll Never Come Out. —*Chicago American.*

During the nineteenth century, there had been many groups in the USA who had supported the idea of prohibiting the sale of alcohol. The Women's Christian Temperance Union (1873) and **Anti-Saloon League** (1895) were very powerful organisations and they made the idea of Prohibition one of the top political issues.

Momentum for Prohibition had been building up and this is shown by the fact that, in the years 1906–19, 26 states in the USA passed laws to limit the sale of alcohol. Female reformers had argued for some time that there were clear links between the consumption of alcohol and wife beating and child abuse. Henry Ford and other **industrialists** were concerned that drinking reduced efficiency and output at work. Many religious groups saw alcohol as the root of sin and evil and were keen to support Prohibition. It was felt that Prohibition would support and strengthen the traditional values of the American people, who were God-fearing, hard-working, family-orientated and thrifty. Moreover, it would encourage immigrants to follow these values.

America's participation in the First World War created many problems around the issue of Prohibition. Many brewers were of German origin and when the USA declared war on Germany, the **Temperance Movement** and the Anti-Saloon League saw prohibiting the sale of alcohol as patriotic. Their followers viewed the sale and consumption of alcohol as a betrayal of the USA. As anti-German feeling grew in the USA, beer was given the nickname 'the ***Kaiser***'s brew' (the *Kaiser* was the German emperor).

Source B Part of a song written in 1903, called 'When the Prohibs Win the Day'

There'll be plenty of food for eating, There'll be plenty of clothes for wear, There'll be gladness in ev'ry meeting, There'll be praise to outmeasure prayer, There'll be toys each day for baby, And then Papa at home will stay, And a heaven on earth will the bright home be, When the Prohibs win the day.

Source C A cartoon published in a US newspaper during the First World War

Source D From an Anti-Saloon League pamphlet, 1918

The American's patriotic duty is to abolish the un-American, pro-German, crime-producing, food-wasting, youth-corrupting, home-wrecking, treasonable liquor traffic.

In September 1918 President Woodrow Wilson banned beer production until the war ended. There was little opposition to this move – there were not even any organised bodies to counter the arguments of the Prohibition lobby. The Prohibition Amendment, which stopped the 'manufacture, sale or transportation of intoxicating liquors' was ratified in Congress in January 1919 and was scheduled to come into effect one year later. The amendment did not outlaw buying or drinking alcohol, nor did it define the term 'intoxicating liquors'. In 1920, Congress passed the Volstead Act which defined 'intoxicating liquors' as anything containing more than 0.5 per cent alcohol. The Internal Revenue Service (IRS) became responsible for enforcing Prohibition.

Source E Women demonstrating in favour of Prohibition in Madison, Minnesota, 1917

TASKS

1. What do Sources A and B suggest about American attitudes to alcohol? (For guidance on how to answer this type of question, see pages 27–28.)
2. Use Source C and your own knowledge to explain why there was support for prohibition. (For guidance on how to answer this type of question, see pages 40–41.)
3. Describe the different types of groups within American Society who campaigned for the introduction of prohibition. (For guidance on how to answer this type of question, see page 73.)
4. What can you learn from Sources D and E about the supporters of Prohibition?
5. Copy and complete the mind map to show why Prohibition was introduced.

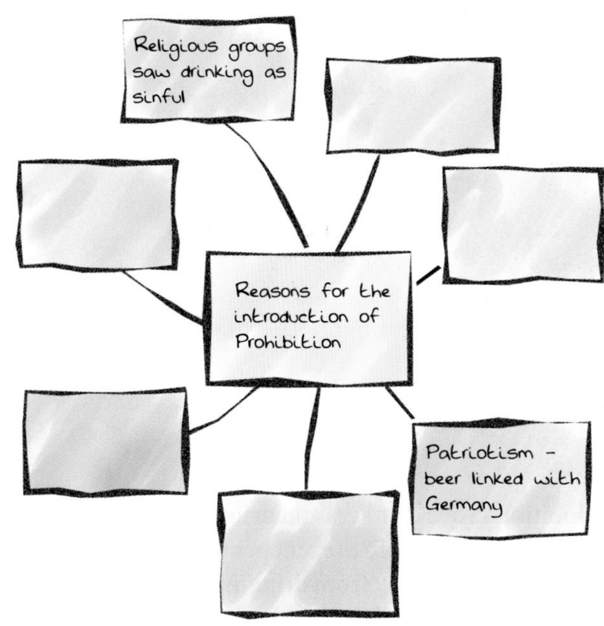

What effects did Prohibition have on US society?

Source A This 1920s cartoon shows Uncle Sam and a man labelled 'State' arguing, each demanding of the other, 'You do it!' In the background a smiling '**Bootlegger**' stands next to boxes labelled 'Gin', 'Beer', 'Choice Liquor' and 'Handmade Liquor'

Prohibition drove drinkers and drinking underground. It became impossible to prevent people from drinking alcohol – and crucially from drinking beverages with an alcoholic content of greater than 0.5 per cent. Huge numbers of people were prepared to break the law not only to produce alcohol but to go to private bars to consume it. For many ordinary people, consuming alcohol or visiting a '**speakeasy**' did not feel like breaking the law. Prohibition created a situation where consumers wanted a product which could not be provided by legitimate means. To satisfy this demand, organised crime stepped in. Thus began the age of the gangster.

Prohibition terms

speakeasy	illegal drinking saloon
bootlegger	one who produced or sold alcohol illegally
bathtub gin	home-brewed gin
still	a device for distilling alcohol
moonshine	illegally distilled or smuggled alcohol
rum runner	someone who illegally transports liquor across a border

Smuggling

It was never difficult to get hold of alcohol. There were many people who produced it illegally and many who smuggled it from Europe, Mexico, Canada and the Caribbean. The USA had more than 30,000 kilometres of coastline and land borders to guard, and so it was difficult to prevent smuggling. It was even possible to find doctors who would prescribe 'medicinal whiskey'.

Speakeasies

Within a short time after the introduction of Prohibition, there were more speakeasies than there had been legal saloons in the old days. In New York alone there were more than 30,000 speakeasies by 1930. An owner of a speakeasy had many overheads. As well as purchasing the illegal alcohol, he would have to pay off the federal agents, senior police officers, city officials (and also the police on the beat when deliveries were made). This situation was replicated across the USA.

Health

Prohibition had mixed consequences for the health of Americans. Deaths from alcoholism had fallen by 80 per cent by 1921, but by 1926 about 50,000 people had died from poisoned alcohol. Male deaths from cirrhosis of the liver fell from 29.5 per 100,000 in 1911 to 10.7 per 100,000 in 1929, yet doctors reported an increase in cases of blindness and paralysis – again as a result of drinking poisoned alcohol.

Many pointed out that Prohibition reduced the number of people killed on the roads and the incidence of drink-related accidents at work did diminish. Moreover, per capita consumption of alcohol fell during Prohibition.

The brewing industry

Prohibition had a lasting effect on the nation's brewing industry. St Louis had 22 breweries before Prohibition. Only nine re-opened after Prohibition ended in 1933. The Anheuser-Busch company survived only because it diversified into soft drinks, developed a bottling industry and even manufactured car and lorry parts. In 1915 there were 1345 breweries in the USA. In 1934 there were only 756.

Source B A speech given by Pauline Sabin in 1929 in which she calls for the repeal of Prohibition. Sabin founded the Women's Organisation for National Prohibition Reform in Chicago in 1929

In pre-Prohibition days, mothers had little fear in regard to the saloon as far as their children were concerned. A saloon-keeper's license was revoked if he was caught selling liquor to minors. Today in any speakeasy in the United States you can find boys and girls in their teens drinking liquor and this situation has become so acute that the mothers of the country feel something must be done to protect their children.

TASKS

1. Study Source A. What does it tell you about prohibition?
2. How successful was the US government in preventing the smuggling of alcohol into the country?
3. Use Source B and your own knowledge to explain why some Americans wanted to end prohibition. (For guidance on how to answer this type of question, see pages 40–41).
4. Design a poster showing how Prohibition helped to create unemployment in the USA.

Why did Prohibition come to an end?

The enforcement of Prohibition

Enforcing Prohibition proved impossible. The Internal Revenue Service (IRS) never had more than 2500 agents and some of them became paid hands of the gang leaders. The most famous of the IRS agents was Eliot Ness, the man who eventually arrested Al Capone (see page 35). Most Americans were prepared to break the Prohibition law, and so a new criminal age began. Making and selling alcohol brought profits. Police and city officials were aware of the spread of speakeasies and bootleggers, but the lawbreakers realised that bribery would buy silence. One New York politician said it would take 250,000 federal agents to enforce Prohibition and that hundreds more would be needed to check the police. What followed in the 1920s was a growth of public corruption on a scale never before seen in the USA.

Source A A cartoon, published in the late 1920s, showing Uncle Sam exhausted by the devil's flow of bootleg liquor

The end of Prohibition

By the early 1930s, there was clear and growing opposition to Prohibition. However, since the Volstead Act (see page 31), attention had focused on the moral dimension of the drinking culture. Just as women had attacked the sale of alcohol before Prohibition, they now formed groups to highlight the new alcohol-related problems Prohibition had created.

Many felt that if Prohibition were removed, the legal brewing industry would create jobs. People would pay more in taxes and duties, thus helping to combat the **Depression** in the USA. Franklin Roosevelt called for the end of Prohibition in his presidential campaign. On becoming president, he carried out his promise in December 1933.

Source B People in New York celebrating the end of Prohibition, December 1933

TASKS

1. Why was Source A produced in the 1920s? (For guidance on how to answer this type of question, see page 84.)
2. Explain why it was difficult to enforce prohibition.
3. Study Source B. What does it show you about the ending of prohibition?

What was the era of the gangster?

There were criminal gangs in the USA before Prohibition, but the 1920s saw a rapid growth in their power. Prohibition gave criminals the opportunities to broaden their involvement in such activities as bootlegging. The gangs bought out hundreds of breweries and transported illegal beer in armoured lorries. Gang leaders saw themselves as businessmen and when faced with competition they took over their rivals. However, the takeovers were often carried out violently and usually ended with the murder of the opposition. Gangs frequently used the Thompson sub-machine gun, which was nicknamed the 'Chicago Piano' and the 'Chicago Typewriter'.

Gangs were involved in what were known as **rackets** – for example, protection, prostitution, 'numbers' (illegal lottery).

Al Capone

Biography Al Capone 1899–1947	
1899	Born in New York
1917	Joins the Five Points Gang led by Johnny Torrio
1921	Moves to Chicago to work with Torrio
1922	Partner in Torrio's saloons, gambling houses, and brothels
1925	Takes over operations when Torrio leaves Chicago
1929	Is responsible for the St Valentine's Day Massacre
1931	Is indicted for **income tax** evasion and found guilty as charged
1939	Wins release from prison
1947	Dies in Palm Island, Florida

Al Capone epitomises the gangster of the Prohibition era. The son of Italian immigrants, he left school at an early age and became involved in small-time criminal activities. Capone was given the nickname 'Scarface' following a fight when he was a bouncer at a New York club. His links to the crook Johnny Torrio led him to Chicago where he eventually rose through the ranks to take over Torrio's operations. Capone cemented his position as one of the leading gangsters in Chicago by bribing local officials. Before long, he had half of the city's employees on his payroll.

Source A A reporter, E Mandeville, talking about corruption in Detroit in 1925 in the *Outlook Magazine*

Ten years ago a dishonest policeman was a rarity ... Now the honest ones are pointed out as rarities ... Their relationship with the bootleggers is perfectly friendly. They have to pinch two out of five once in a while, but they choose the ones who are least willing to pay the bribes.

Capone controlled the mayor 'Big Bill' Thompson and senior police officers, and fixed local elections. In Chicago, he controlled speakeasies, bookmakers' joints, gambling houses, brothels, horse and race tracks, nightclubs, distilleries and breweries. He drove around in a bullet-proof Cadillac, which always contained his bodyguards who were armed with machine guns. In order to ensure that he controlled Chicago, Capone had more than 200 of his rivals killed in the years 1925–29. There were no convictions for any of these murders.

Source B A description of an election in Cicero, a suburb of Chicago, from a local newspaper, 1924

Cars filled with gunmen paraded the streets slugging and kidnapping election workers. Polling places were raided by armed thugs and ballots taken at the point of a gun from the hands of voters waiting to drop them in the box. Voters and workers were kidnapped, taken to Chicago and held prisoners until the polls closed.

TASKS

1 Describe Al Capone's rise to become Chicago's chief gangster. (For guidance on how to answer this type of question, see page 73.)

2 What do Sources A and B suggest about the power exercised by some gangsters? (For guidance on how to answer this type of question, see pages 27–28.)

Source C 'Big Al's soup kitchen', Chicago 1930. The soup kitchen was set up for unemployed workers by Al Capone

Despite his criminal activities, Capone was seen by many Americans as a glamorous person. He moved in the highest social circles and 'put Chicago on the map'. He was the first to open soup kitchens after the 1929 **Wall Street Crash** and he ordered stores to give clothes and food to the needy at his own expense.

TASK

3 a) Study Source C. Write a newspaper headline for the source.

b) Suggest reasons why Capone opened soup kitchens for the unemployed.

The St Valentine's Day Massacre

In his quest for the control of all gangs, Capone was involved in the infamous St Valentine's Day Massacre. Bugs Moran, the leader of a rival Chicago gang, narrowly escaped death but seven of his men were machine-gunned in a garage by Capone's men who entered the building dressed as police officers. Capone himself was in Florida with the perfect alibi. It was this incident which made many Americans realise that the gangsters, and Capone in particular, were not the glamorous characters they had imagined.

Source D The front page of *The Chicago Daily News* newspaper carrying the news of the St Valentine's Day massacre

THREE CENTS THE CHICAGO DAILY NEWS BLUE STREAK

THURSDAY, FEBRUARY 14, 1929.—FORTY-EIGHT PAGES. FINAL EDITION

MASSACRE 7 OF MORAN GANG

HAFFA CHANGES HIS MIND; WILL FIGHT PRISON

MAY STAY IN COUNCIL

TWO OF VICTIMS AND SCENE OF LATEST GANGSTER OUTBREAK

KILLING SCENE TOO GRUESOME FOR ONLOOKERS

View of Carnage Proves a Strain on Their Nerves.

IS LIKE A SHAMBLES

VICTIMS ARE LINED AGAINST WALL; ONE VOLLEY KILLS ALL

Assassins Pose as Policemen; Flee in "Squad Car" After Fusillade; Capone Revenge for Murder of Lombardo, Officers Believe.

STAYS GIVEN 2 OF 3 KILLERS DUE TO DIE TONIGHT

1929 FLAPPERS JUST EAT UP VALENTINES

DECIDE TO CUT COOK ADRIFT IN TAX TANGLE

War to Finish Russell's Plan

Source E Poster advertising the 1932 gangster film *Scarface*

Arrest

In 1931 Capone was prosecuted for income tax evasion for the years 1925–29. It was claimed that he owed more than $200,000 in taxes from gambling profits. He was subsequently found guilty and his role as gang leader was over. The demise of Capone seemed to herald the end of the age of the gangster. With the Depression setting in, the American people had plenty of other issues to contend with.

TASKS

4 Use Source D and your own knowledge to explain why gangsters were responsible for an increase in violent crime during the 1920s. (For guidance on how to answer this type of question, see pages 40–41.)

5 Describe the events which led to the arrest and prosecution of Al Capone. (For guidance on how to answer this type of question, see page 73.)

6 Study Source E. Working in pairs, design your own poster for a film glamorising the gangster age.

What was the extent of government corruption and scandal?

President Harding and the 'Ohio Gang'

Just as there was corruption in towns and cities in the USA during Prohibition, there were examples of corruption in the government in Washington DC.

In 1919 the new president, Warren Harding, promised the USA that there would be a return to '**normalcy**' after the distress caused by the First World War. Harding surrounded himself in his cabinet with friends and colleagues from Ohio who were given the nickname the 'Ohio Gang', see the biographies below. However, some of Harding's friends used their position to line their pockets with money. The Head of the Veterans' Bureau was fined and sent to jail for selling off veterans' hospital supplies for personal profit. Another colleague resigned in disgrace and two more committed suicide rather than face a public disgrace over the scandal.

Biography Harry Daugherty 1860–1941

1881	Qualified as lawyer
1890–94	Republican member of Ohio legislature
1920	Leader of Republican Party in Ohio
1921–24	Attorney-General
1924	Resigned as Attorney-General

Biography President Warren Harding 1865–1923

1900–04	Republican member of Ohio legislature
1904–06	Lieutenant-Governor of Ohio
1915–21	Senator for Ohio
1921–23	President

Biography Albert Fall 1861–1944

1891	Qualified as a lawyer
1893	Appointed judge in New Mexico
1912	Republican Senator for New Mexico
1921	Appointed Secretary of the Interior by Harding
1923	Resigned
1929	Imprisoned for one year over the Teapot Dome Scandal

The Teapot Dome Scandal

Harding and his government were disgraced even more with the so-called Teapot Dome Scandal. Albert Fall, Harding's Secretary of the Interior, leased government oil fields to wealthy friends in exchange for hundreds of thousands of dollars in bribes. The oil fields were to be specifically used for the US navy following a decision in Congress in 1920 to ensure that there would always be sufficient reserves in times of a national emergency. Harry Sinclair (Head of Mammoth Oil Company) obtained leases to drill for oil at Teapot Dome, Wyoming, and Edward Doheny (owner of the Pan-American Petroleum and Transport Company) acquired leases for reserves at Elk Hills, California. Fall received about $400,000 in cash and gifts from Doheny and Sinclair. The deals were secret but when Fall began spending large amounts of money, suspicions grew about how he had come by it. By the time he had finished leasing the navy's reserves, Fall had given Sinclair and Doheny oil reserves which were estimated to be worth $100 million. He himself had collected from them $409,000 in cash and bonds.

Some details of the deals were published in newspapers in April 1922 and President Harding defended the actions of Fall saying that he had, in fact, approved them. At first, Fall's leasing of the oil deposits seemed unimportant. When asked about the secrecy of the arrangements, Fall replied that national security required it. Doheny similarly claimed patriotism and security to justify his actions. However, there was an

TASKS

1 Describe the corruption in the government under President Harding. (For guidance on how to answer this type of question, see page 73.)

2 Use Source A and your own knowledge to explain why there was a scandal over events at Teapot Dome. (For guidance on how to answer this type of question, see pages 40–41.)

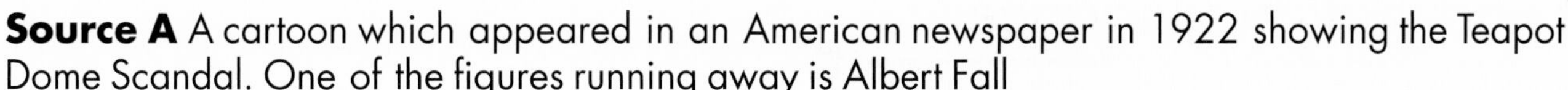

Source A A cartoon which appeared in an American newspaper in 1922 showing the Teapot Dome Scandal. One of the figures running away is Albert Fall

outcry from many leading US oil companies because they had not been able to bid openly for the leases. The Senate began to demand an investigation and Harding became so distressed by the events that he fell ill and contracted pneumonia. At the height of the crisis, President Harding said: 'I have no trouble with my enemies. I can take care of them. It is my friends that are giving me trouble.' Harding died in August 1923 and was succeeded by Calvin Coolidge, who was gradually able to restore faith in the government.

Senator Thomas Walsh, a Democrat from Montana, led the Senate's investigation. He was criticised by many newspapers and Republicans for his sensationalism during the investigation. He was also harassed by the FBI who tapped his phones, opened his mail and made anonymous threats to his life. The Senate inquiry dragged on for several years and finally, in 1927, the **Supreme Court** ruled that the oil leases had been corruptly obtained and invalidated the leases. The navy regained control of the Teapot Dome and Elk Hills reserves. Albert Fall was found guilty of bribery in 1929, fined $100,000 and sentenced to one year in prison. He became the first ever US government official to be imprisoned. Harry Sinclair, who refused to co-operate with the government investigators, was charged with contempt and received a short sentence for tampering with the jury. Edward Doheny was acquitted in 1930 of the attempt to bribe Fall.

During the inquiry Harry Daugherty, the Attorney-General, was himself accused of obstructing investigations and was forced to resign in 1924.

TASKS

3 Can you suggest reasons why Senator Walsh was harassed during the Teapot Dome investigation?

4 Write a newspaper headline for the Teapot Dome Scandal.

5 Was organised crime the biggest problem facing American society during the 1920s?

> In your answer you should discuss the impact of the various problems which faced America during the 1920s, including problems faced by organised crime.

(For guidance on how to answer this type of question, see pages 91–92.)

Examination guidance

This section provides guidance on how to answer a question which requires you to use source material and your own knowledge to explain a development. It is worth 6 marks.

Use Source A and your own knowledge to explain why Prohibition was difficult to enforce. (6 marks)

Source A From a school textbook

The Volstead Act proved difficult to police. Corruption increased as gangsters bribed police officers, judges and politicians to ignore their illegal activities. High-ranking police accepted bribes from criminals such as Al Capone and John Torrio. It soon became evident that the legal system was unable to cope.

There are two responses to this question. One is below and one is on page 41.

Tips on how to answer

- Read through the source, **underlining or highlighting** the key points.
- In your answer you should **try to rephrase and explain these points** in your own words.
- Aim to bring in your own **background knowledge** to expand upon these points.
- Think about any **other relevant factors** which are not included in the source and bring them into your answer.
- To obtain maximum marks **you need to do two things** – refer to information from the source and add to this with information from your own knowledge of this topic area.
- You should try to **explain and develop** at least **three points**.

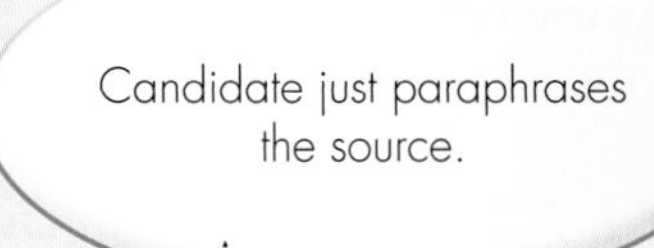

Response by candidate one

Prohibition was difficult to enforce because police officers and judges were bribed to ignore what went on. Criminals like Al Capone and John Torrio put pressure on the police, judges and politicians to allow them to carry on with their business of supplying illegal alcohol. Corruption was common and this made the Volstead Act very difficult to enforce.

Comment on candidate performance

This answer lacks development. The candidate has paraphrased sections of the source and has demonstrated little attempt to explain these points or to illustrate them with additional knowledge. Little effort has been made to place the source into its historical context. This is a generalised answer which would score less than half marks.

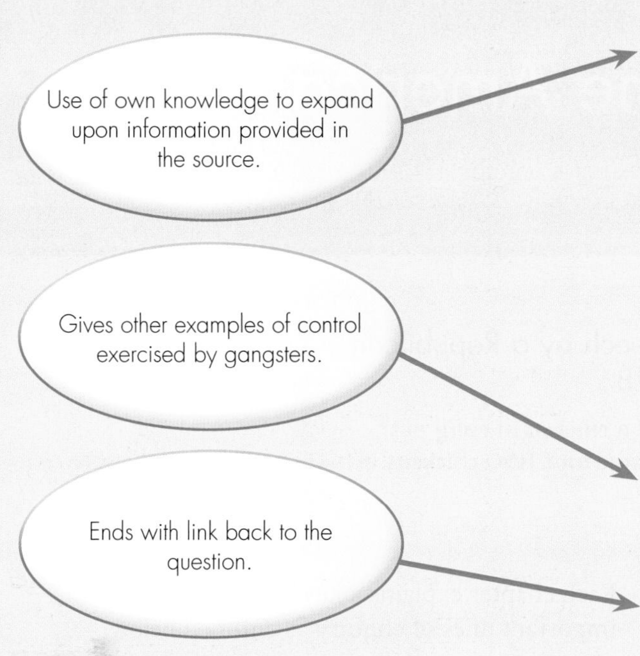

Response by candidate two

Gangsters like Al Capone ignored the Volstead Act and developed their own vast empires of organised crime, supplying illegal alcohol through their speakeasies and rum running businesses. These gangsters became rich and powerful and they used their wealth to bribe officials at all levels. Police officers, judges, lawyers and even politicians were bought off. Capone's gang controlled large areas of Chicago and even bribed the city's Mayor, Big Bill Thompson. Rival gangs often engaged in street violence to control their patch, and the police were unable to do much to stop them. As there was such a demand for illegal alcohol many Americans did not consider the breaking of the prohibition law to be a real crime and this made it difficult for the authorities to enforce prohibition.

Comment on candidate performance

This is a well-developed answer. The candidate demonstrates a sound understanding of this topic and has worked the source material well. There is a good blend of own knowledge to explain and expand upon the information given in the source. There has been a clear attempt to provide at least three reasons why prohibition was difficult to enforce. The answer displays a clear use of content material with accurate and detailed background knowledge and is therefore worthy of a mark within the highest level of response (6 marks).

Now you have a go

Use Source B and your own knowledge to explain why there was a scandal over oil reserves at Teapot Dome. (6 marks)

Source B From a school textbook

The scandal in the Harding administration centred on some naval oil reserves, including one at Teapot Dome, near Casper, Wyoming. Congress was concerned that the US military had enough oil in case of emergencies, so it had set aside certain oil-rich areas for government use. The Secretary of the Interior, Albert Fall, leased out land in the Teapot Dome oil fields to individuals and private companies who got rich on oil meant for public use.

Section B
The rise and fall of the American economy

Source A From a speech by a Republican Party politician in 1928

A car in every garage and a chicken in every pot? No, TWO cars in every garage and TWO chickens in every pot.

This section examines the fortunes of the US economy in the years 1910–29, including the causes for the economic boom, long- and short-term reasons for the end of prosperity, and the immediate effects of the **Wall Street Crash**.

This was a time of boom and bust for the USA. It was a time when, at the beginning, it was thought that the country would prosper and could create wealth for all its citizens (see Source A). However, at the end of the period, the Wall Street Crash ushered in a period of depression in which more than 16 million people were unemployed and the country faced economic ruin.

Each chapter explains a key issue and examines important lines of enquiry as outlined below:

Chapter 4: What were the causes of the economic boom?

- How did America's assets and development contribute to the economic boom?
- How did the attitude and policies of the Republican presidents contribute to the economic boom?

Chapter 5: How did this prosperity affect American society?

- What were the features of the new consumer society?
- What was the influence of the car industry?
- Which other industries experienced a boom?
- Which groups and sectors did not prosper?

Chapter 6: Why did this prosperity come to a sudden end in 1929?

- What were the long-term reasons for the end of prosperity?
- What were the short-term reasons for the end of prosperity?
- What were the events of the Wall Street Crash?
- What were the immediate effects of the Wall Street Crash?

What were the causes of the economic boom?

Source A A graph comparing US industrial production to the rest of the world

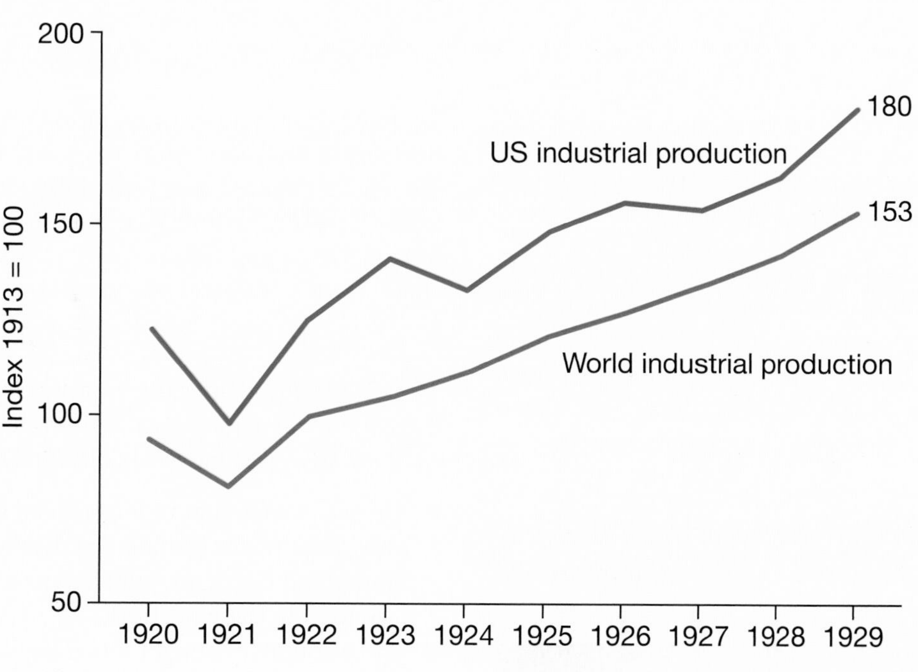

TASK

Study Source A. What does it tell you about the US economy in the 1920s?

This chapter answers the following questions:

- How did America's assets and development contribute to the economic boom?
- How did the attitude and policies of the Republican presidents contribute to the economic boom?

The USA greatly benefited economically from the First World War and, in the 1920s, experienced an economic **boom** which was encouraged by the policies of successive **Republican** presidents as well as the advanced techniques of production used by the car industry. There was a rapid growth in newer industries together with a dramatic rise in the values of **stocks and shares** on the US **stock market**.

Examination guidance

Throughout this chapter you will be given the opportunity to practise different exam-style questions and detailed guidance on how to answer question 1(c). This requires you to analyse and evaluate the utility of two sources. It is worth 8 marks.

How did America's assets and development contribute to the economic boom?

A boom occurs when the economy of a country is rapidly developing. Factories make and sell a lot of goods which, in turn, make money that is put back into factories, to make and sell goods and make even more money. In other words, an economy experiences the multiplier effect, whereby the growth of one industry benefits and stimulates the growth of another. For example, in the USA in this period:

- The growth of the car industry benefited the rubber and glass industries.
- The development of electricity stimulated the growth of new industries which made electrical products such as vacuum cleaners and fridges.

The US boom was due to a number of long-term factors such as the availability of natural resources, a cheap labour force and the impact of the First World War. More immediate factors included technological change, **consumerism**, the availability of **credit** and confidence and the policies of the Republican governments.

Source A This cartoon from 1880 shows a figure representing the USA and immigrants arriving in the USA

Natural resources

The USA had a plentiful supply of raw materials which included oil, coal, wood and iron. These resources had provided the foundation for US economic growth in the years before the First World War and stimulated further growth in the 1920s.

Cheap labour force

There was continuous immigration from Europe to the USA in the years before the First World War. This provided a plentiful supply of cheap, unskilled labour from Germany, Scandinavia, Italy, Poland, Russia, Ireland, China and Japan.

The impact of the First World War

The USA did not enter the First World War until 1917. Its economy benefited greatly from the war. Indeed, by 1918 the USA was the world's leading economy.

- The war was fought in Europe and badly affected the economies of leading countries such as Britain, France and Germany, who had to divert their resources to the war effort.
- These countries bought much-needed supplies from the USA. Money poured into the USA for food, raw materials and **munitions**. This led to the growth of US industry and agriculture.
- Many countries ended up borrowing huge sums of money from the USA. American bankers and businessmen increasingly invested in Europe and made money once the economies of these countries recovered in the 1920s.
- In addition, during the war, European countries were unable to maintain their pre-war export levels. USA manufacturers and farmers took over European overseas markets and further expanded. For example, the USA took over from Germany as the leading producer in the world for fertilisers and chemicals.
- The war stimulated technological advances, especially **mechanisation**, as well as the development of new raw materials such as plastics. The USA led the world in new technology.

Source B US exports, 1914–17

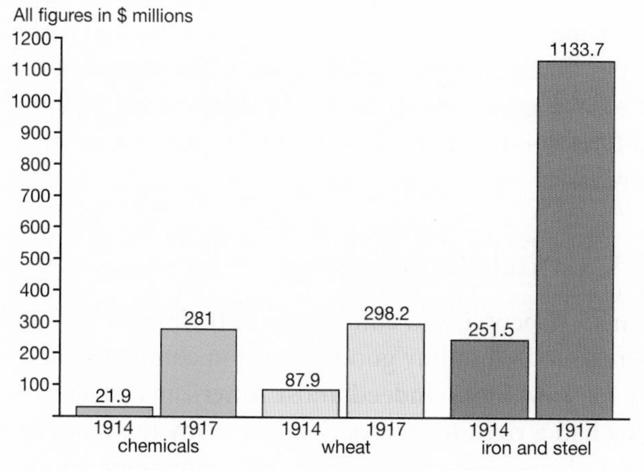

The spread of electricity

Electricity had developed slowly before the war but in the 1920s the electrical industry really boomed.

- By 1929 most homes in the cities had electricity.
- Nearly 70 per cent of all Americans had electric lights.
- More and more factories were run by electricity.
- The amount of electricity consumed more than doubled during the 1920s.

The electrification of the USA brought about the development of a whole range of domestic goods including radios, telephones, washing machines, vacuum cleaners, cookers and refrigerators. These new industries, in turn, stimulated further growth of the American economy.

Technological change

The USA led the world in changes in technology. The development of electricity was fundamental to developments in technology. It provided a cheaper, more reliable and flexible form of power for factories and other industries. Moreover, it stimulated other associated electrical goods industries such as refrigerators, vacuum cleaners and radios.

Other key developments included the conveyor belt and **mass production** techniques adopted by the car industry (see pages 54–56) which speeded up industrial production, improved productivity and led to greater profits. These were already established in some industries, for example, in the manufacture of firearms, sewing machines and railway engines. They were later extended to the production of clocks, typewriters and bicycles.

Plastics such as Bakelite were developed and used in household products. Other innovations included glass tubing, automatic switchboards and concrete mixers. New materials enabled the construction of new types of buildings. The skylines of the great cities were transformed by skyscrapers.

Source C A photograph of New York in 1924

TASKS

1. Explain why the US economy experienced a boom in the 1920s.
2. Use the information in Source B and your own knowledge to explain why the US economy benefited from the First World War. (For guidance on how to answer this type of question, see pages 40–41.)
3. Study Source C. What does it show you about the development of New York by the mid-1920s?

Consumerism

As profits increased, so did wages (though by nothing like so much). Between 1923 and 1929, the average wage rose by eight per cent. Though this was not spectacular, it was enough to enable some workers to buy – often on credit (also called **hire purchase**) – the new consumer luxuries in Source D. The development of advertising and radio commercials in the 1920s, such as the advert in Source E, encouraged people to buy these new goods.

At the start of the 1920s, the USA experienced another industrial revolution. One reason for this was widespread use of electrical power. In 1912 only 16 per cent of the American people lived in electrically lit homes. By 1927 the number had risen to 63 per cent. The growth of electric power encouraged a much more widespread use of electrical goods. During this period, consumption of other energy sources also grew; for example, the amount of oil used doubled, and usage of gas quadrupled.

Source D Growth in sales of consumer goods

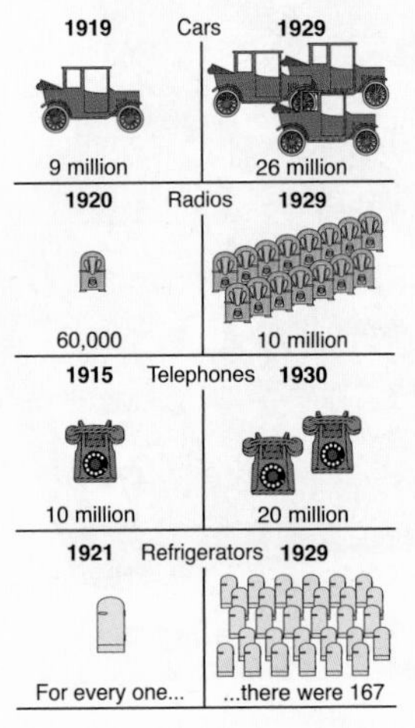

Source E Advert for a vacuum cleaner in the 1920s

Credit

The growth of credit made it much easier for people to buy goods even when they did not have enough cash to pay for them immediately. Under this system of hire purchase, goods were paid for in instalments. About half the goods sold in the 1920s were paid for by hire purchase.

Confidence

Many US people had confidence in their economy and were prepared to buy goods, invest in companies and try out new ideas. Indeed, most Americans believed they had a right to 'prosperity'. For many the main aim was to have a nice house filled with **consumer goods**. Whereas in the past people were encouraged to save and be thrifty, in the 1920s they were encouraged to 'spend, spend, spend'.

Growth of the stock market

In the 1920s, the stock market seemed to be the link to the prosperity of the USA. The values of stocks and shares rose steadily throughout the decade until they rose dramatically in 1928 and 1929. Moreover, the amount of buying and selling of shares grew substantially until it was a common occurrence for ordinary working people to become involved – the accepted image of the 1920s is that 'even the shoeshine boy' was dealing in shares.

Source F John J Raskob, a leading Democratic Party politician, speaking about the benefit of buying shares in 1928

If a man saves $15 a week, and invests in good shares ... at the end of twenty years [he] will have at least $80,000 and an income from investments of around $400 a month.

Since most companies' shares seemed to rise, people were prepared to risk their money on buying shares – after all, their value seemed likely to rise. The USA began to speculate. Even if people did not have enough money to pay the full amount, they would make a deposit, borrow to pay the rest and then sell the shares in a couple of weeks once their value had risen and a profit had been made. The speculator would then pay off their debt and still have made money on the deal. (This process was called '**buying on the margin**'.)

Source G Historian J Rublowsky describing the share-buying frenzy in his book *After the Crash* (1970)

Almost any share was gobbled up in the hope of striking it rich but many of these were worthless. The Seaboard Airline was actually a railroad and had nothing to do with aviation, yet it attracted thousands of investors because aviation shares were the glamour issue of the day.

The number of shares traded in 1926 was about 451 million. The figure increased to 577 million the following year. By 1928, with share prices rising fast, there was a **bull market** on the **Wall Street Stock Exchange** and, in 1929, there were more than 1.1 billion shares sold. Up to 25 million Americans became involved in the frenzy of share dealing in the last years of the decade. The table below illustrates how quickly sales in shares grew – and then fell.

Speculation

Advice like that offered in Source F encouraged many to invest in the stock market. Banks at the time were usually paying an annual interest rate of seven per cent on savings accounts. The difference between the return on savings and speculation made the stock market seem an attractive gamble. If a person was prepared to speculate on the market then lots of money could be made. Buying shares 'on the margin' fuelled speculation further.

Frequently, investors borrowed money to buy shares, but as long as share prices continued to rise then there was nothing to worry about. People were so confident that, by the summer of 1929, investors had borrowed $8.5 billion to buy on the margin – a figure that had risen from $3.2 billion in 1926. Source H shows how consumer confidence increased the value of shares between 1928 and 1929.

TASKS

4 Use Source H and your own knowledge to explain why there was a boom in the stock market in the 1920s. (For guidance on how to answer this type of question, see pages 40–41.)

5 What do Sources D and E suggest about the sales of consumer goods during the 1920s? (For guidance on how to answer this type of question, see pages 27–28.)

6 How useful are sources F and G to an historian studying the reasons for growth in the US stock markets during the 1920s? (For guidance on how to answer this type of question, see pages 49–50.)

7 Below is a mind map showing reasons for the increase in selling/buying shares.

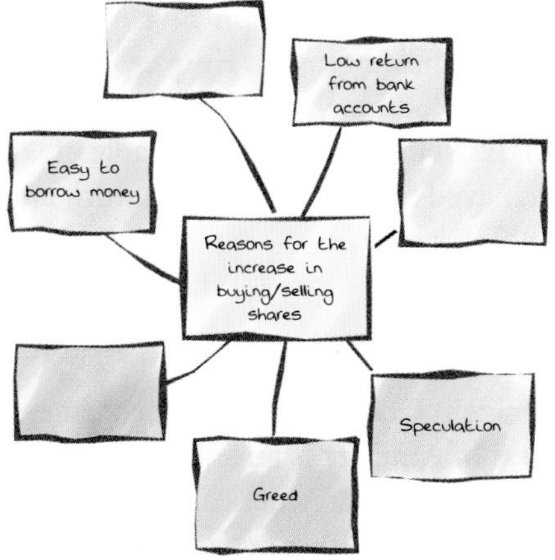

- Copy the mind map and complete the blank boxes with other reasons.
- Add new boxes or ones linked to those already there with more reasons.

Source H Selected share prices, 1927–29

Company	31 August 1928	3 September 1929	29 October 1929
American and Foreign Power	$38.00	$167.75	$73.00
AT&T	$182.00	$304.00	$230.00
Hershey Chocolate	$53.25	$128.00	$108.00
IBM	$130.86	$241.75	–
People's Gas, Chicago	$182.86	$182.86	–
Detroit Edison	$205.00	$230.00	–

How did the attitude and policies of the Republican presidents contribute to the economic boom?

In the 1920s, all the presidents of the USA were Republicans, which meant that they held similar political and economic views. They were:

- Warren Harding, 1921–23
- Calvin Coolidge, 1923–29
- Herbert Hoover, 1929–33

When Harding was elected as president, he promised that he would return the USA '**back to normalcy**'. However, he was president for only two years, dying suddenly in 1923. Directly after his death, it was revealed that he had been involved in financial scandals. Coolidge, who succeeded Harding, carried on the policy of limiting the role of government in the economy and reducing the tax burden on the rich. During Coolidge's time as president, the US economy went through a period of unparalleled growth. Hoover, the president who succeeded Coolidge, was a self-made millionaire and he was the Republicans' best example of what could be achieved in the USA by hard work and little government interference.

Laissez-faire

In 1924 President Coolidge made the comment that 'The business of America is business.' He believed, and it was a view held by many Americans, that governments should be involved as little as possible in the day-to-day running of the economy. If businessmen were left alone to make their own decisions, he thought that high profits, more jobs and good wages would be the result. This was the policy of ***laissez-faire*** – the only role for the government was to help business when it was asked to.

Under Harding and Coolidge *laissez-faire* contributed to the prosperity of the USA. Low taxes and few regulations meant that businessmen were able to chase profits without fear of interference.

Rugged individualism

Successive Republican presidents also believed in '**rugged individualism**'. This term was used by Republican presidents such as Hoover who believed that people achieved success by their own hard work. It originates with the early Americans who moved to the West and made a new life for themselves through their own efforts.

Protectionism

In the years after 1919 the USA returned to a policy of **isolationism** and refused to become involved in events abroad, particularly in Europe. Linked with this, the Republican governments put **tariffs** on imported goods in order to limit the competition from foreign imports. Imports became more expensive compared to American-made goods. This, in turn, encouraged the purchase of American goods and helped US-based producers.

However, the government of this period did act twice to intervene in the economy:

- The Fordney–McCumber Tariff (1922) raised **import duties** on goods coming into the USA to the highest level ever, thus protecting American industry and encouraging Americans to buy home-produced goods.
- A reduction of **income tax** rates left some people with more cash to spend on consumer goods. This, in turn, provided the cash to buy the home-produced goods.

TASKS

1. Describe the economic policies of the Republican governments of the 1920s.
   (For guidance on how to answer this type of question, see page 73.)
2. Were the policies of the Republican governments of the 1920s the most important reason for the economic boom in the USA?

   In your answer you should discuss the impact of the various causes of the economic boom, including the policies of the Republican presidents.

   (For guidance on how to answer this type of question, see pages 91–92.)

Examination guidance

This section provides guidance on how to answer the question which requires you to analyse and evaluate the utility of two sources. It is worth 8 marks.

How useful are Sources A and B to an historian studying the reasons why the American economy experienced a boom during the 1920s? (8 marks)

Source A Part of a speech delivered during the 1928 Presidential elections by the Republican candidate Herbert Hoover.

During the war, we turned to the government to solve every difficult economic problem. When the Republican Party came to power, it restored the government to its position of umpire instead of player. For these reasons the American people have gone forward in progress. Our opponents propose that we must thrust government into business. It would stifle initiative and invention.

Source B Neil Demarco, an historian, writing in a GCSE history textbook, *The USA: A Divided Union* (1997)

By 1929 America produced about 46 per cent of the world's industrial goods. Old values of saving money gave way to the new attitude of spending money. New methods of payment – by instalment – made it possible for many more people to buy consumer goods that previously had been out of their reach. Much of the improvement in the economy was due to more efficient methods of production, management techniques and new industries.

Tips on how to answer

This question will involve the analysis and evaluation of primary and/or secondary sources.

- In your answer you will need to **evaluate the usefulness** of the two sources in terms of their **content** value, their **authorship** and their **audience** or **purpose** or **context**.
- For each source you should aim to **write about two or three sentences commenting upon what the source says** (its **content**), putting the information into your own words and supporting it with your own knowledge of this topic.
- You should **comment upon the authors of each source**, noting **when the source was produced**.
- You should then consider **why each source was produced** and **under what circumstances** (the **purpose**). You need to evaluate **whether this makes the source biased**. Remember that a biased source can still be very useful to the historian so do not just dismiss it.
- To obtain maximum marks your answer must **give equal weight to each source** and it must contain **reasoned comments upon the three elements** (the **content**, the **author, when and why the source was produced**). If you only comment upon the content of each source do not expect to get more than half marks.

There is a sample answer with comments on page 50.

Now you have a go

How useful are Sources C and D to an historian studying the reasons for the growth in consumerism in America during the 1920s? (8 marks)

Source C President Calvin Coolidge commenting upon the power of advertising in a speech delivered to US business leaders in 1927.

Advertising makes new thoughts, new desires, new actions. It is the most powerful influence in adapting and changing habits and way of life, affecting what we eat, what we wear and the work and play of a whole nation.

Source D P. Barnes, R.P. Evans & P. Jones-Evans, historians, writing in a textbook, *GSCE History* (2003)

The USA's industrial expansion was only made possible through the invention of faster manufacturing techniques, particularly that of mass production, which meant that a product could be manufactured in large quantities using a standardised mechanical process. The development of electrical power enabled a new range of mass produced household electrical appliances such as vacuum cleaners, refrigerators, washing machines and radios to flood the market.

Refers to the origin, purpose and content of Source A, linking it to usefulness.

Refers to the origin, purpose and content of Source B, linking it to usefulness.

Compares the usefulness of both sources, and alludes to some weaknesses.

Response by candidate

Both sources are useful to the historian because they spell out reasons why the American economy experienced a boom during the 1920s. Source A is a contemporary account and is part of a speech delivered by the Presidential candidate Herbert Hoover in 1928. Hoover was hoping to be elected President and as a Republican he is praising the policies of the previous Republican Presidents of the 1920s who had not interfered in the running of the US economy. They had followed the policy of laissez faire and Hoover is saying that this had allowed the US economy to grow unhindered by government intervention. It is a biased point of view but is still useful to the historian because it spells out the Republican view. However, it is a very narrow viewpoint which does not consider other factors for the boom. Source B is the reflection of a modern historian who would have had time to reflect and reach a more balanced conclusion. Demarco identifies a number of reasons for the boom such as the availability of easy credit, payment by instalment and new methods of mass production which made goods cheaper to buy. Source B is written for educational purposes and is likely to be balanced in its assessment, allowing the author to write with the benefit of hindsight. This makes it more useful than Source A which is biased and very narrow in focus. However, Source B has a weakness because it is just a short quotation and the reasons identified by Demarco do not cover all the factors which helped bring about the economic boom of the 1920s. There is no reference to such things as America's rich natural resources and the spread of electricity which fuelled the consumer boom. While both sources therefore provide useful information to the historian, they also have their weaknesses, Source A more than Source B.

Comment on candidate performance

This is an informed answer in which the candidate demonstrates good knowledge and understanding. The content of both sources have been explained in some detail and contextualised through the inclusion of own knowledge, elaborating upon the causes of the boom identified by each author. The origin of each source has been clearly identified and there has been an informed attempt to discuss the context under which each was composed. There is an understanding of the strengths and weaknesses of both contemporary (primary) sources and reflection (secondary) sources as pieces of evidence to be used by the historian. The candidate has reached a reasoned and substantiated conclusion regarding the utility of both pieces of evidence and is worthy of receiving a mark within the top level of performance (8 marks).

5 How did this prosperity affect American society?

Source A An advertisement from 1928 for a Lincoln car in the magazine *Vogue*

TASK

Study Source A. What does it tell you about life in America in the late 1920s?

The economic boom of the 1920s was very much influenced by the growth of the car industry, especially the Ford Motor Company. New household gadgets and the influence of advertising turned the USA into a consumer society. However, not all groups and sectors shared in this increasing prosperity. Farmers, black Americans, immigrants and older industries experienced mixed fortunes in the USA of the 1920s.

This chapter answers the following questions:

- What were the features of the new consumer society?
- What was the influence of the car industry?
- Which other industries experienced a boom?
- Which groups and sectors did not prosper?

Examination guidance

Throughout this chapter you will be given the opportunity to practise different exam-style questions and detailed guidance on how to answer question 2(c). This requires you to discuss different historical interpretations. It is worth 10 marks.

What were the features of the new consumer society?

The growth in female employment (see page 87) also increased the need for labour-saving devices such as washing machines and vacuum cleaners.

Hire purchase schemes (see page 46) made it easier to buy goods on credit.

The popularity of entertainment meant more and more Americans bought radios and gramophones.

By 1927 two-thirds of US homes had electricity. This stimulated the demand for electrical goods.

For the majority of workers in industry, wages increased. Between 1923 and 1929, the average wage rose by eight per cent. In other words, workers had more spare money to spend on consumer goods.

The economic boom of the 1920s was partly encouraged by the growth of consumerism. This meant the growing demand by many Americans for everyday, often household, goods.

Reasons for consumerism

Increased demand for consumer goods was due to several factors as the diagram above shows.

Source A An advert for a refrigerator, 1929

Advertising

The advertising industry also grew rapidly as more and more firms realised the potential of the advert for increasing sales and profits. The industry used quite sophisticated techniques with more colourful adverts and the use of catchphrases. Although magazines and newspapers remained the most important method, the radio and cinema provided a whole range of new opportunities.

The people who designed the advertisements studied the psychology of the consumer and devised methods that they believed would encourage people to buy their products. Women were not only used to advertise many goods, they were also targets for the advertisers.

Source B The manager of an advertising firm explained how to appeal to women. He made these comments in 1926

Nine-tenths of the goods bought annually are bought by women. Woman is a creature of the imagination. We pay her a compliment when we say this, for imagination comes from the feelings and feelings come from the heart. And so the advertising appeal, to reach women, must not ignore the first great quality of the heart, which is love. Most advertisers do not ignore the quality of love. There, in almost every advertisement, is a reference, in word or picture, to mother love, to the home, to children, to sentiment.

Household appliances and electrical goods

Electricity usage had developed slowly before the war but grew rapidly in the 1920s. By 1929 most homes in US cities had electricity. This stimulated industrial growth as electricity provided a far more flexible and efficient form of power for factories and workshops. Moreover, it encouraged the development of a whole range of electrical goods such as vacuum cleaners, radios, **gramophones**, telephones, washing machines and refrigerators. For example:

- In 1926 Hoover introduced the famous 'beats-as-it-sweeps-as-it-cleans' vacuum cleaner, which cleverly incorporated the three established methods of cleaning carpets: beating, sweeping and suction cleaning. This innovation set the standard for the rest of the market to follow.
- By 1900 half of American houses were using an icebox to keep food cold. The ice used for storage was expensive so the remaining households had very little in the way of cooled storage. That all changed when General Electric developed the first Moniter-Top unit in 1927. This was the first refrigerator to be used over a large area.

Source C Table showing the growth of electrical goods in the 1920s

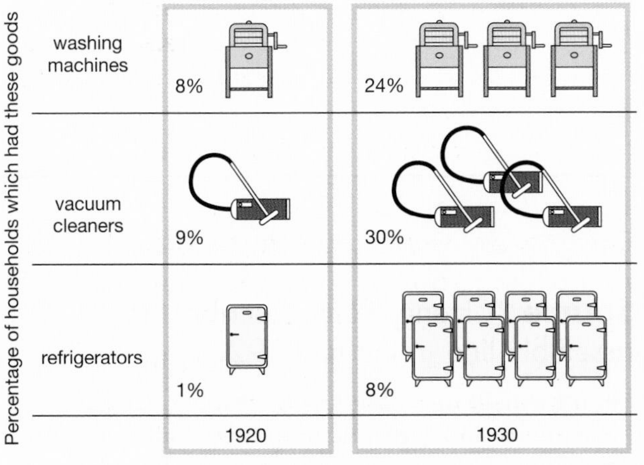

Department stores

The 1920s also saw the growth of department stores as more and more people bought consumer goods, especially electrical appliances. In the cities, chain stores stocked the new range of goods now available. In addition, the USA was the first country to have a supermarket. JC Penney opened a chain of supermarkets known as Piggly Wiggly. The first was opened in Memphis, Tennessee, in 1916. Customers helped themselves to the goods, which were individually priced, and paid for them at the checkout as opposed to waiting to be served at the shop counter.

Source D The inside of the first Piggly Wiggly store

TASKS

1. Explain why there was a growth in consumerism in the USA in the 1920s.
2. What do Sources A and B suggest about the methods used by advertisers in the 1920s? (For guidance on how to answer this type of question, see pages 27–28.)
3. Describe the growth in ownership of electrical goods in the 1920s. (For guidance on how to answer this type of question, see page 73.)
4. Devise a suitable caption that could have been used with Source D to advertise the Piggly Wiggly store.
5. Working in pairs, devise a suitable slogan or advertisement for the Hoover vacuum cleaner.

What was the influence of the car industry?

The car industry played a very important role in the boom of the 1920s, often leading the way in technological change as well as stimulating the growth of other industries.

Henry Ford

Henry Ford was an electrical engineer who built his first car in a rented brick shed. In 1903 he founded the Ford Motor Company in Detroit. In 1908 he introduced his Model T Ford which was nicknamed the 'tin lizzie'. Existing car manufacturers built several different models in a range of colours. Ford showed the benefits (and reduced costs) of manufacturing one standard model which was 'any colour as long as it was black'.

Workforce

Ford believed in hard work and would walk round his factory each day encouraging his workers to do their job properly. However, he had quite a turnover of workers who found the assembly line boring and monotonous. Therefore, in 1914 Ford announced that he would double the wages to $5 a day, which was far more than anyone else paid for the equivalent job. Workers rushed to Detroit to work for him. He also reduced the length of the working day to eight hours and introduced a third shift, so the factory was operating a three-shift system and working 24 hours each day.

The assembly line

In 1913 Ford introduced a much more efficient method of producing the cars, the assembly line or 'magic belt'. He had seen how efficiently this was used in meat-packing factories and slaughterhouses. An electric conveyor belt carried the partly assembled car at the same speed past workers who stood at the same spot and did one job, such as fitting on the wheels or doors. This saved time as the tools and equipment were brought to the worker rather than him having to waste time walking about for these. In 1913 the Ford factory in Detroit was producing one car every three minutes. By 1920 the same factory was producing the same car every ten seconds.

Source A Henry Ford describes an assembly line in the mid-1920s

In the chassis assembly line there are 45 separate operations. Some men do only two small operations, others do more. The man who places the part does not fasten it. The man who puts the bolt in does not put the nut on and the man who puts the nut on does not tighten it. On operation 34 the motor gets its petrol. On operation 44 the radiator is filled with water and on operation 45 the car drives onto the road.

Advertising

Ford was also prepared to use modern advertising techniques to sell his cars. For example, he realised the value of using attractive women in adverts, not only because it would encourage men to buy his cars, but also to promote the idea of female drivers.

Source B An advert for a Ford motor car in 1923

Affordable cars

Ford's business methods and new technology allowed him to bring down the price of cars and so make them affordable for many more Americans. In 1914 a Model T cost $850. By 1926 the price had dropped to $295. Ford also led the way in introducing hire purchase as a method of credit.

Source C Henry Ford, speaking in 1921

It is better to sell a large number of cars at a reasonable small margin than to sell fewer cars at a larger margin of profit. I hold this because it enables a larger number of people to buy and enjoy the use of a car and because it gives a larger number of men employment at good wages.

TASKS

1. What do Sources A and B suggest about developments in the car industry during the early 1920s? (For guidance on how to answer this type of question, see pages 27–28.)
2. Describe the organisation of the workforce in a Ford factory. (For guidance on how to answer this type of question, see page 73.)
3. Use Source C and your own knowledge to explain why Ford sold so many cars in the 1920s. (For guidance on how to answer this type of question, see pages 40–41.)
4. How important was Henry Ford to developments in the car industry during the 1920s?

The impact of the Model T

Ford, more than anyone else, started an enormous growth in car ownership. By 1925 half the world's cars were Model Ts. In 1927 work was completed on a new Ford factory at Dearborn, Michigan. The River Rouge complex became the biggest factory complex in the world, employing around 80,000 workers. By the late 1920s, Ford plants had been established in Asia, Australia, Canada, South Africa and South America. His techniques were so effective that they were adopted by other US car manufacturers, as well as Citroën and Renault in France and Morris and Austin in England.

Other benefits of car industry

The car industry revolutionised American industry – indeed it revolutionised American society:

- So much steel, wood, petrol, rubber and leather were used that the car industry provided jobs for more than 5 million people. By the late 1920s, cars and the car industry were using 90 per cent of the petrol, 80 per cent of the rubber and 75 per cent of the plate glass produced in the USA.
- It transformed buying habits. Hire purchase became a way of life for most Americans because it enabled an average family to buy a car.
- It promoted road building and travel, which in turn led to motels and restaurants being built in places that had previously been considered out of the way.
- It opened up the suburbs to more and more people who were now able to use the car to travel further to their place of work.
- Car ownership also benefited rural areas as the farmer could get to the local town in less than half an hour, whilst his wife no longer felt isolated in the farmhouse.
- Owning a car was no longer just a rich person's privilege, as it was in Europe in the mid-1920s. There was one car to every five people in the USA, in comparison to one to 43 in Britain and one to 7000 in the Soviet Union.

The production of automobiles rose dramatically from 1.9 million in 1920, to 4.5 million in 1929. The three main manufacturers were the giant firms of Ford, Chrysler and General Motors.

TASKS

5 Study Source D. What does it suggest about the impact of the Model T upon life in America?

6 Explain why car ownership grew so rapidly in America during the 1920s.

7 Devise your own mind map to show how the car industry benefited other sectors of the US economy.

Source D Model Ts on a high street in the USA in the mid-1920s

Which other industries experienced a boom?

Transport and the construction industry

Although the car industry led the way, several other industries experienced a boom in the 1920s. The US transport system improved greatly during this time. More and more roads were needed as car sales soared. Bus travel also proved popular. By 1930 the total length of paved road had doubled and the number of trucks on the road increased three-fold to 3.5 million by 1929.

Moreover, aircraft flights first appeared in the 1920s. By 1929 there were 162,000 domestic and commercial flights. Lindbergh, who was the first person to fly solo nonstop across the Atlantic, used his fame to promote the rapid development of US **commercial aviation**.

Economic growth led to a greater demand for buildings of every sort, from department stores, factories and houses in the suburbs, to offices, hospitals and government buildings. There was a boom in office building as the number of banks, insurance and advertising companies, and showrooms for new cars and electrical products grew rapidly. The development of new materials enabled the construction of new types of buildings, including skyscrapers, which provided more space and transformed the skyline of major cities such as New York.

The 1920s was the new era of the skyscraper and major companies competed against each other to build themselves grand office blocks. New York saw the most spectacular growth and the Woolworth building of 1913 set the trend. Completed in 1931 the Empire State building, with its 102 storeys, stole the record of being the tallest building from the recently built Chrysler headquarters with its spectacular Art Deco design. These structures became a sign of American **capitalism** and success.

The American construction industry was busier in the 1920s than it had ever been before. Moreover, it encouraged the growth of dependent industries such as bricks, tiles, glass, furniture and electrical goods.

Source A New York construction workers eat their lunches atop a steel beam 250 metres above ground, September 1932

TASKS

1 Describe developments in the construction industry between 1910 and 1929. (For guidance on how to answer this type of question, see page 73.)

2 Explain why transport got easier in America during the 1920s.

3 Was mass production the main cause of the economic boom of the 1920s?

> In your answer you should discuss the impact of the various causes of the rise of the American economy, including the impact of mass production.

(For guidance on how to answer this type of question, see pages 91–92.)

Which groups and sectors did not prosper?

Not all industries enjoyed boom conditions in the 1920s. Indeed, some faced shrinking markets and new challenges. Moreover there was little improvement in the lifestyle of many black Americans and immigrants.

Farmers

Some 30 million people earned a living through farming, and half of Americans lived in rural areas, often making their living from selling machinery or providing services to farmers. US farming had benefited from the First World War. New machines such as the combine harvester made American farming the most efficient in the world.

However, farmers were producing far more food than Americans needed. During the war, the farmers had been able to sell their surplus to Europe. After the war, the situation changed:

- European farmers were able to grow enough to meet their own needs.
- There was stiff competition from Canadian, Australian and Argentinian farmers who were supplying a vast amount of grain to the world market.

Nevertheless, American farmers could do little else other than continue to produce more food, aided by improved mechanisation. This, in turn, drove down prices and brought ruin to many small farmers.

As their income dropped, farmers found it difficult to keep up their mortgage payments. Some were evicted whilst others had to sell up to clear their debts. Some even became **sharecroppers** (a sharecropper was a tenant farmer who gave a share of his crops as rent). In 1924 alone, more than 600,000 farmers went bankrupt.

The 1920s was the first time in US history that the total number of farm workers began to shrink. Farmers borrowed more than $2 billion in order to keep hold of their property, but borrowing was often difficult because banks did not see farmers as a good risk. In 1919 total farm income had been $22 billion. By 1928 this had fallen to $13 billion.

Source B A Fordson tractor sold by Parkway Motor Co. of Washington DC, around 1921

Source A Selected US farm prices, 1919–25

Year	Cattle per head ($)	Cotton per 500 grams (cents)	Wheat per bushel ($)
1919	54.65	35.34	2.16
1920	52.64	15.89	1.83
1921	39.07	17.00	1.03
1922	30.09	22.88	0.97
1923	31.66	28.69	0.93
1924	32.11	22.91	1.25
1925	31.72	19.61	1.44

Source C Sharecroppers in the 1920s

TASKS

1 Use Source A and your own knowledge to explain why farmers faced problems in the 1920s. (For guidance on how to answer this type of question, see pages 40–41.)

2 Study Source C. What does it show you about changes in farming during the early 1920s?

3 Study the mind map below. Suggest reasons why each problem was harmful to farmers in the 1920s.

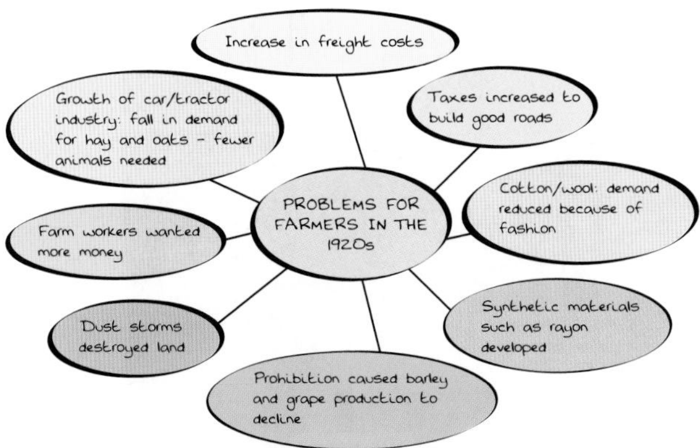

4 Study Source C. What does it show you about black sharecroppers?

5 Describe the lifestyle of black Americans in the USA in the 1920s. (For guidance on how to answer this type of question, see page 73.)

Black Americans

Black Americans were badly off during this time. They amounted to ten per cent of the population of the USA and 85 per cent still lived in the south where they were either labourers or sharecroppers. Three-quarters of a million black farm workers lost their jobs during the 1920s.

Many black Americans journeyed north to find work during the First World War. However, in the northern city of Milwaukee 60 per cent of black women worked as low-paid domestic servants in white households. Car factories would only hire blacks in small numbers and some had white-only policies. Black workers in the towns in the north were the lowest paid; the only work they found available were low-paying, menial jobs.

New York's black Harlem district was a severely overcrowded and segregated community, with more than 250,000 citizens crammed into an area 50 blocks long and eight blocks wide. Many of these people had to sleep in shifts, going to bed when others went off to work. 'Rent parties' were common on Saturday nights, to raise money to pay the landlord on Sunday.

Immigrants

New immigrants also faced discrimination. A large number worked in construction where there was a building boom, but the steady supply of cheap immigrant labour meant that wages were kept low. The unemployment rate amongst new immigrants remained high throughout the decade. In 1921 an Emergency Quota Act was passed, and in 1924 a National Origins Act reduced the quota for newer types of immigrants, especially those from Eastern Europe (see pages 9–10).

Trade unions

The 1920s marked a period of decline for **trade unions**. In 1919 more than 4 million workers (or 21 per cent of the labour force) participated in about 3600 strikes. In contrast, during 1929 about 289,000 workers (or 1.2 per cent of the labour force) staged only 900 strikes.

Union membership and activities fell sharply due to the following reasons:

- Economic prosperity of the decade led to stable prices, eliminating one major incentive to join unions.
- Employers across the nation led a successful campaign against unions known as the 'American Plan', which sought to depict unions as 'alien' to the nation's individualistic spirit. In addition, some employers, like the National Association of Manufacturers, used **Red Scare** tactics to discredit unionism by linking them to communist activities.
- The Republican governments, like businessmen, were against trade unions.
- Employers were allowed to use violence to break strikes and refuse to employ union members.
- Unions were excluded altogether from the car industry.
- Employers were able to keep wages low and working hours long, at a time when profits were increasing rapidly.

Source D A hunger march by workers in Washington in the 1920s

Older industries

There was a decline in America's traditional industries during the 1920s.

The coal industry

In the early 1920s, there were about 12,000 mines and 700,000 workers in the USA. However, the demand for coal fell in the 1920s for several reasons:

- Oil and its derivatives became more widespread.
- Gas and electricity were more widely used.
- There was more foreign competition, especially cheap coal from Poland.

A great number of mines closed down and many miners were made redundant. However, not all employers sacked their miners. One solution was to have them work for fewer hours. There were many strikes across the mining regions in order to secure decent wages and improved working conditions. These strikes were rarely successful and, in some cases, police officers and state troops were used against the strikers. For example, in 1922, 600,000 miners went on a four-month strike for better conditions. The strike failed. By 1929 the average monthly wage of a miner was $100, while a bricklayer in New York could earn more than $300 per month.

TASKS

6 Explain why trade unions declined in the 1920s.

7 What do Sources D and E suggest about life for workers in the 1920s? (For guidance on how to answer this type of question, see pages 27–28.)

8 Describe developments in the coal industry during the 1920s. (For guidance on how to answer this type of question, see page 73.)

Source E Two striking miners from Pennsylvania seek support and monetary contributions in New York in December 1927

The railroad industry

The railroad industry declined due to the huge growth of car ownership in 1920s, which led to a fall in the volume of passenger traffic on the railroads. The rapid development of a national road network, together with the availability of cheap cars and cheap petrol, presented a very serious challenge to the railroad companies. It was a challenge they could not meet. The railroad companies in some of the larger cities, where electric railways had been built before 1914, fared particularly badly.

Railroad companies did increase their carrying of freight in the 1920s by ten per cent, but this increase would have been far greater had it not been for the expansion of road traffic. Few railroad companies made large profits during this period.

The textile industry

The textile industry faced problems for several reasons:

- The lowering of the tariffs on wool and cotton in 1913 meant that the US textile industry faced stiff competition from abroad.
- It also faced the challenge of a new product – rayon. This man-made fibre was far cheaper to produce than wool, cotton or silk. Rayon required fewer workers and less processing than natural fibres. Production of rayon increased from 4.5 million kg in 1920 to 50 million kg by the end of the 1920s.
- Dramatic changes in women's fashions. By the end of the First World War, women's dresses were much shorter than they had been in 1914, and new trends in the 1920s shortened them even more. An average dress needed only a third of the material in comparison to a dress made in 1914.

Mill owners responded in various ways. Textile mills in the north, for example, in Massachusetts, either closed down or moved south, where labour was cheap. In the southern states, mill owners kept wages low by employing women or children. In the late 1920s, the average mill wage in the south was $13 for a 60-hour week. One result of low wages was an increase in the number of strikes in the industry during the 1920s.

Source F An extract from the song 'Cotton Mill Colic' by Dave McCarn (1905–64), a mill worker and folk singer from North Carolina. The song was written in 1926

When you go to work you work like the devil,
At the end of the week you're not on the level
Payday comes, you pay your rent,
When you get through you've not got a cent
To buy fat-back meat, pinto beans,
Now and then you get turnip greens.
No use to colic, we're all that way,
Can't get the money to move away.
I'm a-gonna starve, and everybody will,
'Cause you can't make a living at a cotton mill.
Twelve dollars a week is all we get,
How in the heck can we live on that?
I've got a wife and fourteen kids,
We all have to sleep on two bedsteads.
Patches on my britches, holes in my hat,
Ain't had a shave, my wife got fat.
No use to colic, everyday at noon,
The kids get to crying in a different tune.
I'm a-gonna starve, and everybody will,
'Cause you can't make a living at a cotton mill.

TASKS

9 Explain why the railroads were unable to prosper in the 1920s.

10 Use Source F and your own knowledge to explain why the textile industry went into decline during the 1920s. (For guidance on how to answer this type of question, see pages 40–41.)

11 Copy and complete the table below. Place the problems in order of importance.

Problems for the coal industry	Problems for the textile industry	Problems for the railroad industry

12 Working in groups of three or four, write a song highlighting the problems of the workers in the 'old' industries during the 1920s.

Examination guidance

This section provides guidance on how to answer the question which requires you to discuss different historical interpretations. It is worth 10 marks.

Historians have made different interpretations about the impact of the economic prosperity of the 1920s upon the lives of the American people.

These three pieces of evidence refer to the impact of the economic boom of the 1920s upon the lives of ordinary Americans.

Evidence One An interpretation written by an historian in the 1990s for a GCSE history textbook. He argues that many Americans were poor in the 1920s

If the 'Roaring Twenties' did take place, then they took place largely in the cities. In the countryside, the situation was very different. For most American farmers the 1920s was a decade of poverty and struggle. Most farmers lived in small shacks with tin roofs, no electricity, no running water and often no toilet. Faced with mounting debts many small farmers were obliged to give up their property.

Evidence Two An interpretation from an American politician who served under Herbert Hoover, speaking in a television documentary about the 1920s (1969). He argues that American people were very prosperous

In the ten years of Republican rule we had perfect contentment and permanent prosperity. Business was happy and so were all good people who supported America.

Evidence Three This evidence is a photograph of the living conditions of a poor black American family living in Harlem, New York, in the 1920s

One interpretation is that not all Americans were able to benefit from the economic boom of the 1920s. How far do you agree with this interpretation? (10 marks)

Tips on how to answer

You need to refer to three pieces of evidence, relate them to your own knowledge of this period and to the interpretation given in the question, and comment on how and why this issue has been interpreted in different ways.

- You need to read through the three pieces of evidence with care, **underlining or highlighting important details**. You can scribble some notes in the margin around the source about how it fits in with the given interpretation and your own knowledge of this period.
- Decide which piece(s) of evidence **support the interpretation** referred to in the question, and which piece(s) of evidence provide an **alternative interpretation**.
- Use your **background knowledge** of this topic area to **explain the given interpretation**, mentioning the **content** of any supporting pieces of evidence. Reference should also be made to the **authorship** of these pieces of evidence and whether the circumstances under which they were produced have **impacted upon the view they put forward**.
- You should consider any **alternative interpretations** put forward in the other piece(s)of evidence, using your **background knowledge** to explain and develop this line of argument. You must also **show how and why this alternative interpretation has been made**.
- You must provide a **clear judgement** upon the value of the given interpretation in relation to its historical context.

Response by candidate

Identifies and discusses the evidence which supports the interpretation.

Identifies and discusses the evidence which provides a counter- interpretation.

Suggests how and why these differing interpretations have been formed.

There is much evidence to support the interpretation that not all Americans were able to benefit from the economic boom of the 1920s. Evidence One shows groups of Americans who experienced hardship, which is in complete contrast to the interpretation given in Evidence Two which says that the American people prospered during the boom years and were very content with their improved lifestyle. While it is true that the economy did experience dramatic growth during the 1920s due to improved and cheaper methods of production, the impact of advertising, the availability of credit and a consumer boom, this prosperity was not available to all Americans. Evidence Two is an interpretation by an American politician of the state of the US economy during the 1920s. It is the view of a politician who supported Herbert Hoover, who was a Republican President. He comments that Americans have benefitted from this economic growth but it is a view that is biased and very narrow in focus. He is commenting in a media interview in 1969 and may be quite nostalgic about the period. The historian in Evidence One disagrees with this interpretation as he comments upon groups of Americans who did not prosper and who were not content. Evidence One is the view of a modern historian writing in a GCSE history textbook. The author is writing with the benefit of hindsight and concludes that many American farmers did not enjoy the prosperity of the 1920s. Many lived a life of poverty and struggled to exist against rising costs and falling food prices. Many were forced to abandon their farms, becoming hobos who toured the countryside in search of work. Evidence Three supports the view of the historian as it shows the poverty of a black American family living in Harlem, a poor region of New York. Black Americans generally worked in the lowest paid jobs and lived in the poorest areas of the cities. Evidence Three is a photograph taken in the mid-1920s and it confirms the interpretation of the hardship experienced by black American families. Looking at all three pieces of evidence I think that the interpretation that not all Americans benefitted from the economic boom is a valid one and is one that is confirmed by Evidence Three. The interpretation given in Evidence Two is biased but it is biased for a reason because it spells out the Republican viewpoint of the decade.

Comment on candidate performance

This is a developed answer which discusses the given interpretation and identifies and uses information from Evidence One and Three as supporting sources. The content of each source is analysed and contextualised through the inclusion of own knowledge. Attention has been paid to the attributions of both sources and how this has influenced the interpretation given. A counter-interpretation has been identified in Evidence Two and the biased nature of this source has been discussed via its content and attribution. Reasons for the biased nature of this interpretation have been suggested, and this has been linked to contextual knowledge. The answer concludes with a judgement upon the value of the given interpretation. The answer displays the characteristics of a high performing answer worthy of marks within the highest level.

6 Why did this prosperity come to a sudden end in 1929?

Source A A stockbroker trying to sell his car in late October 1929 following the events of the Wall Street Crash

TASK

Study Source A. What does it tell you about the condition of the US economy by late 1929?

In October 1929 the American stock market on Wall Street crashed. This was due to long-term problems with the US economy, especially over-production and over-speculation on the stock market. The immediate effects of the Wall Street Crash were disastrous for the USA and many other countries in Europe, especially Britain and Germany. In America, banks literally went bankrupt, leading to a depression and very high unemployment. The Roaring Twenties had come to an abrupt and, in many cases, unfortunate end.

This chapter answers the following questions:

- What were the long-term reasons for the end of prosperity?
- What were the short-term reasons for the end of prosperity?
- What were the events of the Wall Street Crash?
- What were the immediate effects of the Wall Street Crash?

Examination guidance

Throughout this chapter you will be given the opportunity to practise different exam-style questions and detailed guidance on how to answer question 2(a). This is a 'describe' question which requires you to display specific knowledge of an historical event. It is worth 4 marks.

What were the long-term reasons for the end of prosperity?

In the autumn of 1929 the prices of shares on the US stock market crashed, wiping out the fortunes of many Americans. The Crash ushered in the Great Depression of the 1930s – the worst economic decline in the history of the USA. It was a time when millions of Americans could not find work, thousands were turned out of their homes, and many roamed the land in railway wagons. Banks failed and people lost their life's savings.

There were several long-term reasons why the Crash happened in 1929, including:

- over-production
- falling demand for consumer goods
- the boom in land and property values.

Source A A statement by a leading US economist in 1928, explaining the fears that some economists had about the dramatic rise in share prices

Sooner or later, a crash is coming, and it may be terrific, factories will be shut down, men will be thrown out of work and there will be a serious business depression.

Over-production

The problems created by over-production are shown in the diagram below.

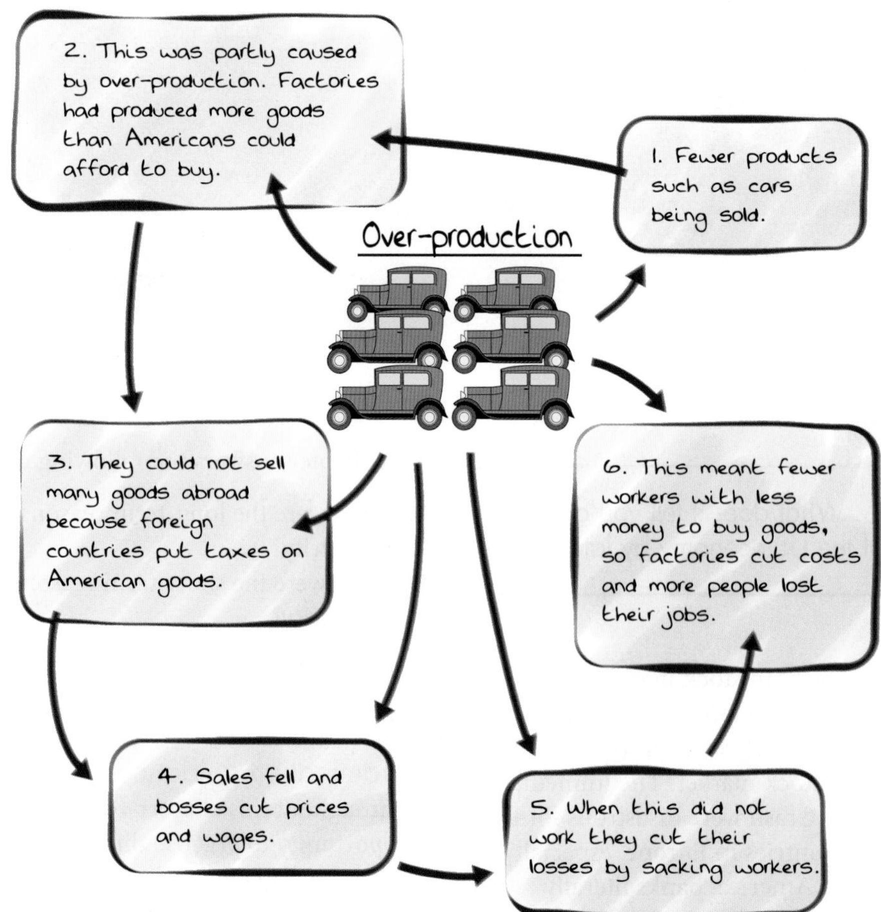

Falling demand for consumer goods

Several reasons are attributed to this fall.

- The unequal distribution of wealth. The new-found wealth of the 1920s was not shared by everyone. Almost 50 per cent of American families had an income of less than $2000 a year, the minimum needed to survive. They could not afford to buy the new consumer goods. Some manufacturers did not see that there was a limit to what could be bought, and so they continued to produce goods. The result was over-production.
- The USA could not sell its surplus products to other countries, especially those in Europe. Some European countries owed the USA huge amounts of money and were struggling with repayments. The US government had put high tariffs on foreign goods in the 1920s (see page 48). Many foreign governments responded by doing the same to American goods and consequently US businessmen found it very difficult to sell their goods abroad. Therefore, an ideal outlet for their over-production was blocked.
- During the First World War US banks had lent money to several European countries. These countries found it hard to repay these loans in the 1920s.

The boom in land and property values

One consequence of the increased wealth of the 1920s was a dramatic rise in the value of land and property. The state of Florida witnessed a sharp rise in land values with many speculators attempting to jump on the band wagon and buy property or land. Some people borrowed heavily to do so, believing that they could keep the property for a short time and then sell when it had risen in value. In 1926, however, property prices began to fall sharply in Florida and this left many homeowners in negative equity. This meant that the land or property they owned was worth substantially less than what they had originally paid for it. This was a warning that the US economy was in the process of readjustment, but it was a warning ignored by many investors.

TASKS

1. What do Sources A and B suggest about the long-term causes of the Wall Street Crash? (For guidance on how to answer this sort of question, see pages 27–28.)
2. How important was over-production in causing an end to the economic boom of the 1920s?
3. Describe the long-term causes of the Wall Street Crash. (For guidance on how to answer this type of question, see page 73.)

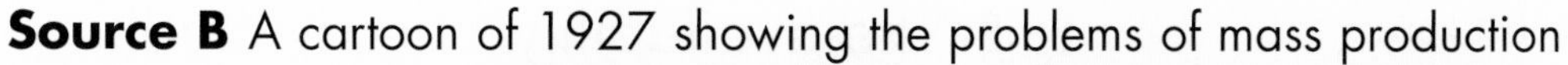

Source B A cartoon of 1927 showing the problems of mass production

What were the short-term reasons for the end of prosperity?

Short-term reasons for why prosperity came to a sudden end included:

- over-speculation on the stock market
- the availability of easy credit.

Over-speculation on the stock market

During the 1920s, more and more Americans bought shares on the stock exchange and prices kept rising. In 1928, however, shares did not rise as much as in previous years. This was because many companies were not selling as many goods, so their profits fell. Fewer people were willing to buy their shares and there was a drop in confidence in the market. This was a warning, but when share prices began rising again, greed took over and speculation recurred.

Source A A businessman warns in 1928 about the dangers of over-speculation

The number of inexperienced speculators is being increased by a great many men who have been attracted by newspaper stories. The stories tell of the big, easy profits to be made on the stock exchange. These amateurs have not learnt that markets sometimes panic and that there are large falls in prices. These suckers speculate on tips, on hunches. They buy or sell at the slightest notice.

TASKS

1. Use Source A and your own knowledge to explain why there were problems in the stock market in the later 1920s. (For guidance on how to answer this type of question, see pages 40–41.)
2. Study Source B. What does it tell you about the price of shared in the USA in the years 1925–33?

Source B A graph showing the changes in the price of shares in the USA in the years 1925–33

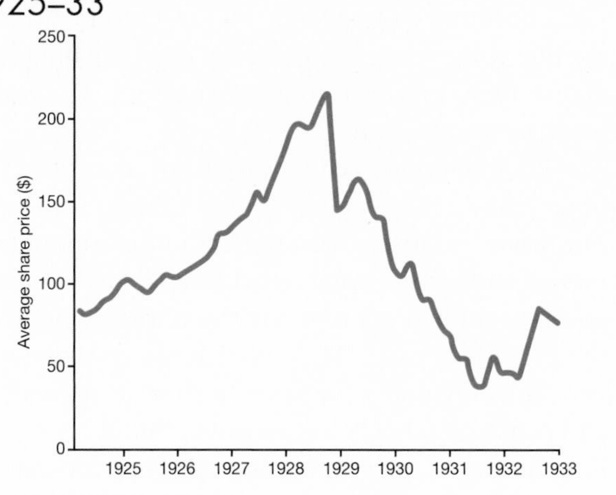

The complete lack of stock market regulation by the government or any other agency encouraged more and more speculation. Successive Republican presidents stuck to their beliefs in *laissez-faire*. In 1925 the stock market value of stocks stood at $27 billion but by October 1929 it had reached $87 billion. By the summer of 1929 there were 20 million shareholders in the USA and prices continued to rise.

The availability of easy credit

The growth of credit made it much easier for people to buy goods even though they did not have enough cash to pay for them on the spot. Firms arranged for customers to pay in instalments on hire purchase. This included the practice of buying shares on credit, 'on the margin' (see page 47). This practice was further encouraged by the easy credit policies on the part of the **Federal Reserve Board**.

This worked well as long as prices were rising. However, when the price rise started to slow down or prices fell, problems set in. Seventy-five per cent of the purchase price of shares was borrowed. This, in turn, created artificially high prices.

What were the events of the Wall Street Crash?

The boom of the 1920s ended abruptly and dramatically with the Wall Street Crash of October 1929.

Loss of confidence

When, in the autumn of 1929, some experts started to sell their shares heavily before their value fell even further, small investors panicked. They saw the fall in prices and rushed to sell their own shares – as can be seen in the bar chart below. This led to a complete collapse of prices and thousands of investors lost millions of dollars.

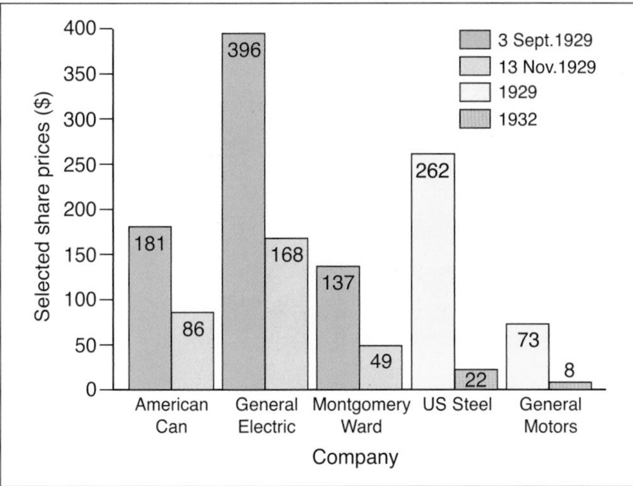

Decline in share values between 1929 and 1932.

The following headlines show the events of October 1929.

Saturday 19 October 1929

Shareholders begin to panic

Today nearly 3.5 million shares were bought and sold. Prices are beginning to fall.

Monday 21 October 1929

More heavy selling on stock market

Over 6 million shares bought and sold today. Great fluctuations in prices.

Tuesday 22 October 1929

Stock market recovers

All seems well with prices slightly recovering.

Wednesday 23 October 1929

More panic in Wall Street

Over 2.5 million shares were sold in the last hour of trading today. More and more people are trying to sell their shares and get out of the stock market.

Thursday 24 October 1929

'Black Thursday'

This has been a terrible day on Wall Street. Prices fell so quickly that people have rushed to sell their shares. Nearly 13 million shares have been traded.

Friday 25 October 1929

Bankers save the day

Bankers met at midday to support the stock market. This seems to have worked as prices have steadied.

Saturday 26 October 1929

Hoover speaks

President Hoover has assured all Americans that the panic is over and that business and banking will soon recover.

Monday 28 October 1929

Panic returns

Heavy selling again on the stock market. Almost 3 million shares were sold in the last hour of business. Dramatic falls in prices.

Tuesday 29 October 1929

'Black Tuesday'

The worst ever day on the stock market. Nearly 16.5 million shares have been traded. Shares have lost all value. Many shareholders have lost everything. Suicides reported.

Source A Depositors outside a bank in New Jersey, trying to get in to withdraw their deposits on Black Tuesday, 29 October 1929

Source B Cecil Roberts wrote about the Wall Street Crash in *The Bright Twenties*, 1938

The stock market hysteria reached its peak in 1929. Everyone was playing the market ... On my last day in New York, I went down to the barber. As he removed the sheet he said softly, 'Buy Standard Gas. I've doubled ... It's good for another double.' As I walked upstairs, I reflected that if the hysteria had reached the barber level, something must soon happen.

TASKS

1. How useful are Sources A and B to an historian studying the reasons for the Wall Street Crash? (For guidance on how to answer this type of question, see pages 49–50.)
2. Explain why share prices in the USA fell rapidly during October 1929.
3. Describe the Wall Street Crash of October 1929. (For guidance on how to answer this type of question, see page 73.)
4. Study Source A. Imagine you are a British radio reporter who witnessed this scene. Describe to your listeners what you can see.

What were the immediate effects of the Wall Street Crash?

The impact of the Crash was quite spectacular. The stock market completely collapsed.

Source A The *New York Times*, 30 October 1929

Stock prices virtually collapsed yesterday, swept downwards with gigantic losses in the most disastrous trading day in the stock market's history. Billions of dollars in market value were wiped out. The market on the rampage is no respecter of persons. It wasted fortune after fortune yesterday and financially crippled thousands of individuals in all parts of the world.

Source B American writer, Carl Sandburg, describes the collapse in share sales in *The People, Yes*, 1936

Shares in a cigar company at the time of the crash were selling for $115. The market collapsed and the share dropped to $2 and the company president jumped from his Wall Street office window.

By the end of 1929 there were about 2.5 million unemployed in the USA. However, this amounted to only five per cent of the workforce, and some felt that the country would see out the crisis. But confidence had died, and those who had money were unwilling to spend. Unemployment began to gather pace as fewer and fewer consumer goods were purchased – the amount of goods sold in retail stores halved in the years 1929–33.

Suddenly the USA became a land of unemployment, tramps, bread queues and soup kitchens. Many people were evicted from their homes and lived on the streets – children included. It was the time of the **hobo** – thousands of men travelled the country hitching rides on railcars and freight wagons.

The Depression

People were not buying goods and even the rich began to economise. Employers began to lay off employees. Servants were sacked and those who were able to find jobs worked for lower wages than they had before. The economy was spiralling downwards.

Source C From the memoirs of a young British journalist, Alistair Cooke, who had been sent to America in the late 1920s. They were published in his book *Letters from America* (1951)

Only the poor had nothing to lose. When steel stocks went from 90 to 12 the automobile companies simply let half their workers go. There were skyscrapers finished who had no tenants. There were truckers and nothing to truck, crops that went unharvested, milk that went undelivered to people who couldn't afford it. I couldn't go out in the evening without being stopped by nicely dressed men who had told their wives they were looking for night work. So they were – they were out on the streets cadging dimes and quarters.

The Depression was not caused by the Crash. The issues with the economy in the 1920s are vital in understanding what was wrong with the US at that time – look once more at pages 66–67. However, the Crash did speed up the approach of the Depression, and its effects were catastrophic for the country and the people during the next decade.

- Many stockbrokers were unable to repay their debts to the banks – many banks went bust.
- Thousands of people who had saved in banks were bankrupted.
- Workforces were laid off.
- Credit collapsed and loans were taken in.
- Those banks that survived were unwilling to make further loans – the time of speculation and risk-taking was over.

Farmers were hit terribly, and when they demonstrated in towns they carried placards attacking the president. One slogan became extremely popular: 'In Hoover we trusted, now we are busted.'

Source D Luigi Barzini, an Italian immigrant, remembers the effects of the Crash

It was Thursday 24 October, the day the dam burst on the American economy. It was a frantic day. There were two very big news stories to worry about. An anarchist had tried to kill an Italian prince in Brussels. And the price of shares had collapsed on Wall Street. Thousands of people seemed to be ruined. The Exchange had had a few slumps in the past and a few serious hiccups but had always recovered. Some of the country's most important bankers and political leaders told the people that they should not panic, and invited them not to sell America short, to trust in the country's future.

Source E Major losers in the crash

- *The Vanderbilt family lost $40 million.*
- *Rockefeller lost 80 per cent of his wealth but still had $40 million left.*
- *The British politician Winston Churchill lost $500,000.*
- *The singer Fanny Brice lost $500,000.*
- *Groucho and Harpo Marx (two of the Marx Brothers comedy team) lost $240,000 each.*

Source F A cartoon by political cartoonist, John McCutcheon, 1932, about the effects of the Wall Street Crash

Source G Suicides in the USA per 100,000 people, 1926–1941

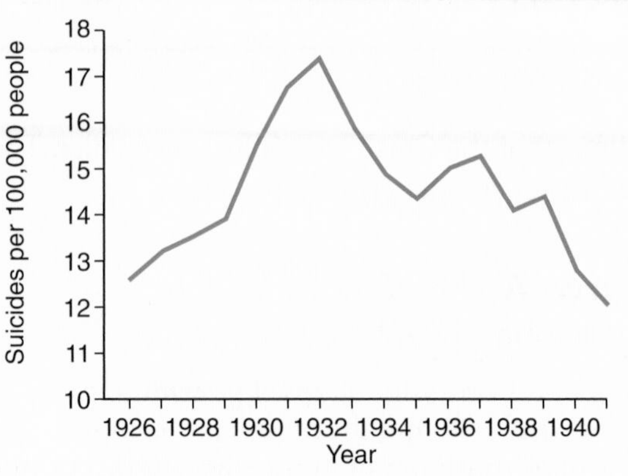

TASKS

1. How useful are Sources A and C to an historian studying the immediate effects fo the Wall Street Crash? (For further guidance on how to answer this type of question, see pages 49–50.)
2. What do Sources B and E suggest about the impact of the Wall Street Crash? (For guidance on how to answer this type of question, see pages 27–28.)
3. Why was Source F produced in 1932? (For guidance on how to answer this type of question, see page 84.)
4. Use Source D and your own knowledge to explain why the US economy went into depression after 1929. (For guidance on how to answer this type of question, see pages 40–41.)
5. Look at the information and sources on pages 71–72. Construct a pyramid/triangle to show a chronology of effects – or a fanning/rippling out of effects – so that the reader can see the chain unfold.

Examination guidance

This section provides guidance on how to answer a 'describe' question. This is worth 4 marks.

Describe the events of the Wall Street Crash. (4 marks)

Tips on how to answer

- Make sure you **only include information that is directly relevant**.
- It is a good idea to start your answer using the words from the question. For example, 'The economic boom of the 1920s came to a sudden end ....'
- Try to include **specific factual details** such as dates, events,names of key people. The more informed your description the higher the mark you will receive.
- Aim to cover at **least two key** points.

Response by candidate

The economic boom of the 1920s came to a sudden end in October 1929 with the events of the Wall Street Crash. By the summer of 1929 the prices of American stocks and shares stood at an all-time high. Many ordinary Americans had jumped onto the band wagon and bought shares, often by borrowing money to do so. Warning bells began to ring on 19 October when several big investors sold large quantities of shares. This caused prices to fall but many thought it was just a temporary fall and they would soon rise again.

However, prices continued to fall and on 24 October, nicknamed 'Black Thursday', over 12 million shares were sold. Panic now set in and many nervous investors attempted to sell their shares. This caused prices to fall even lower. Everybody wanted to sell and nobody wanted to buy. Prices continued to slide downwards. There was another huge panic on 'Black Tuesday', 29 October, when 16 million shares were sold. The market had crashed. Millions of Americans had lost their money as their shares were now worthless. Some investors committed suicide.

A number of key events are dealt with in chronological order.

A good range of specific factual detail.

Covers serveral key points and has clear links to the question.

Section C
Changes in American culture and society

Source A From a book about America in the twentieth century. The author was writing about women in the 1920s

Though a few upper middle-class women in the cities talked about throwing off the older conventions – they were the flappers – most women stuck to more traditional attitudes concerning 'their place'... most middle class women concentrated on managing the home ... Their daughters far from taking to the streets against sexual discrimination were more likely to prepare for careers as mothers and housewives. Millions of immigrant women and their daughters also clung to traditions that placed men firmly in control of the family. Most Americans concentrated on making ends meet or setting aside money to purchase the new gadgets that offered some release from household drudgery.

This section examines the key changes in American culture and society in the 1920s. An American in 1929 looking back at the previous decade would have seen huge changes in the USA. The popularity of the movies was as great as ever and the recent introduction of the 'talkies' meant that interest continued to grow. The new form of jazz music had gripped not only the USA but the world. Prosperity enabled people to become involved in many sports, either as participants or active followers. It was a decade when women pushed for greater equality and independence and the word 'flapper' entered the vocabulary (see Source A). Above all, it seemed a time when Americans made astonishing achievements, such as Lindbergh flying the Atlantic, or made bizarre records for non-stop dancing.

Each chapter within this section explains a key issue and examines important lines of enquiry as outlined below:

Chapter 7: How did popular entertainment develop during this period?

- How did movies and their influence develop?
- How did popular music and culture develop?

Chapter 8: How did the lifestyle and status of women change during this period?

- How did attitudes to women change?
- What was the flapper lifestyle?

Chapter 9: Why did sport and other leisure activities witness so much growth during this period?

- How did interest in sport grow in the 1920s?
- What were the fads, crazes and the passions for the unusual?
- Who were the American heroes of the decade?
- What was the impact of the automobile upon leisure activities?

7 How did popular entertainment develop during this period?

Source A From a newspaper article published in the Bible-Belt region of America in the mid-1920s

Jazz employs primitive rhythms which excite the baser human instincts. Jazz music also causes drunkenness. Reason and reflection are lost and the actions of the persons are directed by the stronger animal passions.

There were rapid social changes in the USA in the 1920s and the period is often referred to as the 'Roaring Twenties'. These changes included a growth in demand for **consumer goods** and a transformation in the status of some women. The radio and the cinema revolutionised entertainment and Hollywood became the centre of the film industry. More and more people watched and participated in sport. Modern forms of music, such as jazz, and dances, such as the Charleston, became popular.

TASK

Study Source A. What does it tell you about how some Americans viewed the impact of jazz?

This chapter answers the following questions:

- How did movies and their influence develop?
- How did popular music and culture develop?

Examination guidance

Throughout this chapter you will be given the opportunity to practise different exam-style questions and detailed guidance on how to answer question 2(b). This question requires you to explain the purpose behind the creation of a primary source at a particular time. It is worth 6 marks.

How did movies and their influence develop?

Source A Mary Evelyn Hults remembers the cinema in the 1920s

It was really an experience. You would be treated like a king or queen. You were issued into an enormous lobby of marble or gilt with huge stairways leading up to the balconies. All the carpets were at least an inch or two thick. Everything was done in there to make you feel comfortable, to make you feel very important.

Source B Gloria Swanson, a famous actress of this period, speaking in 1922

In the film, Rudy (Valentino) and I wore costumes of some of the most romantic periods of European history. The wardrobe department made me a gold-beaded evening gown so beautiful that movie-goers talked about it for the next year. I also wore over a million dollars' worth of jewels.

By 1910 the movie industry was well established in the USA and there were more than 8000 cinemas. This figure rose to 17,000 in 1926 and 303,000 four years later. By the time the First World War ended, movies had become the most popular form of entertainment in the USA. A visit to the cinema had become part of American life. The diagram below shows some of the reasons the cinema was so popular.

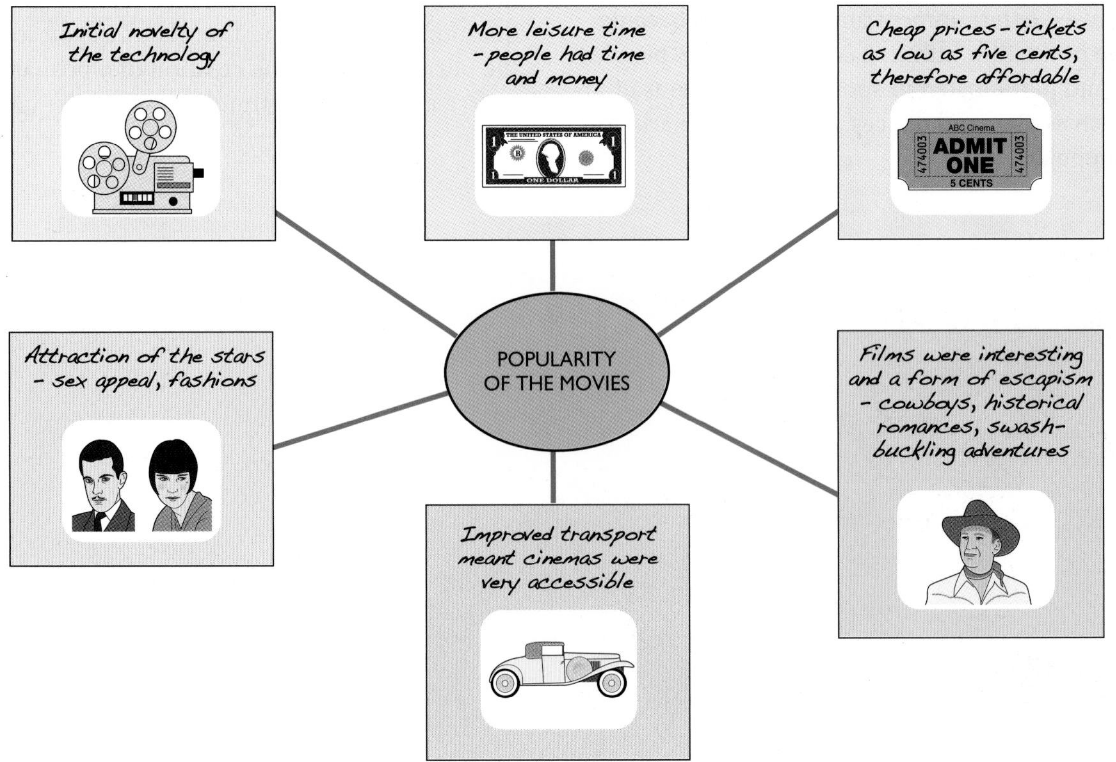

Silent movies

Until 1927 movies were silent, although they were often accompanied by live musicians and sometimes sound effects. Some even provided commentary by a cinema employee or projectionist. In most cinemas, however, a pianist played tunes while the film ran.

Fast music would be played for chase scenes and romantic music for love scenes. Gradually the cinemas (originally called nickelodeons) improved their facilities in order to attract more people. Luxurious seats were introduced and the hollow-sounding piano was replaced by mighty organs or even a full orchestra. People loved the cinema because it was a means of escapism. For a few cents people were transported out of their own humdrum lives.

Source C The Roxy cinema, New York, 1927. It could seat 6000 people

With an annual output in the 1920s of about 800 films, there was always something for the film-goer to see. The films on offer covered a wide range of subjects but the comedies of Chaplin and Buster Keaton, the romances of Clara Bow, the adventures of Douglas Fairbanks, Westerns and biblical stories were amongst the most popular.

Stars could make huge amounts of money. In 1917 Chaplin signed an eight-film contract which was worth $1 million, and in 1926 it was reported that the actress Greta Garbo earned $5000 dollars a week.

Source D From a speech to Harvard University students by J P Kennedy, an investor in the film industry, 1927

The motion picture industry has achieved a standing and a size that makes it impossible for people studying industry to overlook it. It is already the fourth largest industry in the USA. Yet, it is an industry that has developed only in the last ten or twelve years. Foreign businessmen have told me that one of the biggest trading problems that they are facing is that American films are serving as silent salesmen for other American industries.

TASKS

1. What do Sources A and B suggest about why the cinema became popular during the 1920s? (For guidance on how to answer this type of question, see pages 27–28.)
2. Use Source D and your own knowledge to explain why the film industry became so important to America. (For guidance on how to answer this type of question, see pages 40–41.)
3. Explain why the silent cinema was so popular.
4. Study Source C. What does it show about the film industry in the 1920s?

Movie stars

As the film industry developed, film producers found that movie-goers wanted to see certain stars irrespective of the film's quality. Before 1910, the names of the actors and actresses were not shown on the credits. Stars such as Charlie Chaplin, Mary Pickford, Rudolf Valentino and Greta Garbo could draw millions of people to the cinema and people began to want to know more about them. Fan magazines were published and newspapers wrote about risqué love scenes and the sex lives of the stars. Movie-makers found that sex sold tickets. Rudolf Valentino was the first male star to be sold on sex appeal. The studio publicity reported that women fainted when they saw him. He died in 1926 and more than 100,000 of his fans lined the streets during his funeral. Rioting even broke out. Several people killed themselves on hearing of his death.

The following biographies give some more information about which films the movie stars of the time starred in.

Biography Joseph 'Buster' Keaton 1895–1966

1895 Born in Piqua, Kansas
Wrote, directed and acted in his own films:
1922 *The Paleface*
1924 *The Navigator*
1926 *The General*
1927 *Steamboat Bill, Jr.*
1928 *The Cameraman*
1929 *Spite Marriage*

Biography Charlie Chaplin 1889–1977

1889 Born in London
1913 Moved permanently to the USA
1914 Made his first movie *Making a Living*
1917 Formed his own film production company.
Wrote, directed, produced and acted in his own films after this:
1921 His first full-length movie *The Kid*
1923 *A Woman of Paris*
1925 *The Gold Rush*
1928 *The Circus*

TASKS

5 How important were movie stars to the development of the film industry?

6 Describe the growth of the film industry in America between 1910 and 1930.
(For guidance on how to answer this type of question, see page 73.)

7 Use the internet to research the careers of the silent movie stars Harold Lloyd and Mary Pickford. Use your research findings to compile a biography of each star.

Biography Clara Bow 1905–1965

1905 Born in Brooklyn, New York
Starred in:
1924 *Helen's Babies*
1925 *The Plastic Age*
1926 *Dance Madness*
1926 *Mantrap*
1927 *It*
1929 *The Wild Party*
1929 *Dangerous Curves*

Biography Rudolph Valentino 1895–1926

1895 Born Rodolfo Alfonso Raffaello Piero Filiberto Guglielmi in Castellaneta, Italy
1913 Emigrated to the USA
Starred in:
1921 *The Four Horsemen of the Apocalypse* (the first film to take 1 million dollars)
1921 *The Sheik*
1921 *Camille*
1922 *Broken Blossoms*
1922 *Tried for Bigamy*
1924 *A Sainted Devil*
1926 *The Son of the Sheik*

'Talkies'

In 1927 the first 'talkie' was made (*The Jazz Singer*), which made the cinema even more popular. Unfortunately, some silent screen stars lost their jobs because their voices were not fit for the 'talkies'. By 1930 more than 100 million cinema tickets were sold every week. By the end of the 1920s there were several famous film studios such as Warner brothers, William Fox and Metro-Goldwyn-Mayer (MGM). These studios had their own publicity departments to make up and publicise stories that kept fans attached to their stars' loves, marriages and divorces. When stars like Mary Pickford or Gloria Swanson appeared in a new dress or hairstyle, millions of women would demand the same look.

Hollywood

Until 1913 most American film production was based around New York. However, many film companies were taken to court by Thomas Edison's film company, claiming they used its patented technology. To avoid the lawsuits, many film companies relocated 3000 miles to Hollywood, California.

However, it was only after the start of the First World War that the film industry in the USA became dominant across the world. The war in Europe interrupted the powerful French and Italian film industries and, after 1918, the developments in Hollywood had left the rest of the world behind.

The first film shot in the Hollywood area was called *In Old California* (1910). The following year the first studio was opened by the New Jersey-based Centaur Company, which wanted to make Western films in California. By 1915 the majority of American films were being made in the Los Angeles area. Four major film companies – Paramount, Warner Bros, RKO and Columbia – had studios in Hollywood. Five years later thousands of people were employed in the Hollywood film industry.

Movie stars themselves then moved to the Los Angeles area and began building themselves luxury homes. Gloria Swanson, for example, had a 22-room mansion in Beverly Hills. Charlie Chaplin and Buster Keaton both lived in the area.

Hollywood and the film industry in general did provoke criticism from those who believed that the movies were lowering the morals of American society. Many Americans blamed Hollywood for the blatant use of sex symbols, such as Clara Bow and Rudolph Valentino. Clara Bow was given the nickname 'The It Girl', having starred in the film of the same name. The 'It' clearly meant sex. They were also shocked by the morality of some Hollywood films. Hollywood eventually responded by setting up the Hays Code (see Source E).

Source E Extracts from the Hays Code

- *No screen nudity.*
- *Screen kisses must not last.*
- *Adultery must not be presented as attractive.*
- *Producers must avoid low, disgusting, unpleasant, though not necessarily evil, subjects.*
- *Members of the clergy cannot be comic characters or villains.*
- *Murder, arson and smuggling must be shown as evil.*

TASK

8 Use Source E and your own knowledge to explain how the film industry reacted to the claim that it had caused a decline in moral standards.
(For guidance on how to answer this type of question, see pages 40–41.)

9 Explain why Hollywood developed as the centre of the American film industry?

How did popular music and culture develop?

The impact and development of jazz in the 1920s

The 1920s is known as the 'jazz age' because the popular music of the time was jazz. The writer F Scott Fitzgerald coined the phrase in his book *The Beautiful and the Damned.*

Jazz was not new. It had originated with black slaves who were encouraged to sing in order to increase production. They used washboards, cans, pickaxes and percussion to produce their own distinctive brand of music. By changing the beat and creating particular rhythms, it became jazz. As many black musicians could not read music scores they improvised and made it up as they went along. This was one of the attractions of this new brand of music. Originally, the music had various names including 'blues', 'rag' and 'boogie-woogie'. However, these words were taken from black sexual slang terms and white people disapproved of their use. Therefore, the music was renamed jazz.

Despite its African American origins, in the 1920s jazz became popular with young middle-class whites, especially the **flappers** (see page 89). Some condemned jazz as another sign of a decline in moral standards. In 1921, for example, the *Ladies' Home Journal* published an article with the title 'Does Jazz put the Sin in Syncopation?' (Syncopation refers to the off-beat rhythms that characterise jazz music.)

Source A From an interview with a jazz musician in the early 1920s

Jazz players make their instruments do entirely new things, things trained musicians are taught to avoid. Jazz has come to stay because it is an expression of the times – the breathless, energetic, superactive times in which we are living.

Source B From *The Ladies' Home Journal,* 1922, a magazine written for American women

Jazz was originally the accompaniment of the voodoo dancer, stimulating the half-crazed barbarian to the vilest deeds. The weird chant had been employed by other barbaric people to stimulate brutality and sensuality. That this has a demoralising effect on the human brain has been demonstrated by many scientists. Jazz is harmful and dangerous and its influences are wholly bad.

Some cities, including New York and Cleveland, prohibited the public performance of jazz in dance halls. However, this only made it more exciting to the young. Jazz became the great attraction of the night clubs and speakeasies and was brought into homes through radio broadcasts. As the popularity of jazz spread, white musicians imitated the style and such bands led by Paul Whiteman and Bix Beiderbecke became famous. Perhaps the most famous jazz venue was the Cotton Club in Harlem, New York.

Biography Duke Ellington 1899–1974

He was born in Washington DC in 1899 and became a composer and pianist. In the 1920s he moved to New York, where he assembled a ten-piece band. He became popular because of recordings such as *Choo Choo* and *Chocolate Kiddies.*

Biography Louis Armstrong 1901–1971

He was born in New Orleans in 1901 and became famous as a trumpeter there. In 1922 he moved to Chicago, known as the jazz capital of the USA. By 1925 he had his own band and was known nationwide. Some of his famous recordings included *Ain't Misbehavin'* and *Tiger Rag.*

Source C 'King' Oliver's jazz band, Chicago, 1922. Louis Armstrong is the musician kneeling in the foreground

TASKS

1. Use Source B and your own knowledge to explain why some Americans disliked jazz music.
   (For guidance on how to answer this type of question, see pages 40–41.)
2. Study Source C. What does it show you about jazz music in the 1920s?
3. Explain why jazz music became so popular in America during the 1920s.

The impact of the radio

The radio had a massive influence on many Americans. The first radio station, Station KDKA, began in 1920 and by 1930 there were more than 600 radio stations in the USA and 40 per cent of US homes had a radio set. Many families bought radios on weekly instalments and **mass production** helped to lower the cost of buying them.

Radio enabled people to listen to sporting events, music, for example, jazz, as well as advertisements. News, sport and entertainment were easily relayed into millions of homes. The first national radio network, the National Broadcasting Company (NBC), was set up in 1926, followed a year later by the Columbia Broadcasting System (CBS). Indeed, radio became the main source of family entertainment. It created sporting heroes such as the boxer, Jack Dempsey, and the baseball player, Babe Ruth. It made events accessible to many people who could not afford to attend. As radio reached more than 50 million people by the end of the 1920s, there was a dramatic increase in political and social awareness among the population at large, for people no longer had to be literate to follow the news.

Source D From a US newspaper article in 1929

From the feeble wireless telegraph service in 1920, radio has grown swiftly into the billion dollar industry it is today. Advertising has made broadcasting an industry. The broadcasters discovered they could boost the car industry or the ginger beer industry. And then time on the air becomes something that people want to buy.

The impact of the gramophone

The **gramophone** industry grew rapidly after 1900, peaking in 1921 with sales of $106 million. However, by 1922, radio had destroyed the market with the free music it offered over the airwaves. Sales fell throughout the entire decade, and when the **stock market** crashed in 1929, most of the smaller companies either went out of business or were bought by larger companies.

Speakeasies

The introduction of **Prohibition** in 1920 resulted in an increase in drinking clubs (known as speakeasies, see page 33), which were run by gangsters. The entertainment in the speakeasies was often provided by groups of black Americans playing jazz. The speakeasies allowed whites and blacks to mingle socially for the first time and they drew young audiences from all social classes. Young people were attracted to both the music and the increasingly suggestive jazz dances. Both the mixing of the races and the widespread belief that jazz incited sexual activity caused large numbers of people to oppose jazz whenever possible.

Source E F Scott Fitzgerald, a contemporary novelist, describes changes in cultural activity in the early 1920s in *Tales of the Jazz Age* (1922)

The parties were bigger – the pace was faster – the shows were broader, the buildings were higher, the morals were looser and the liquor was cheaper.

Gang bosses opened fancy clubs with dancers and the hottest bands as the cabaret. At Small's Paradise in Harlem, New York, waiters danced the Charleston, carrying trays loaded down with cocktails. Popular stars like Fred and Adele Astaire entertained at The Trocadero, and at the Cotton Club Duke Ellington led the house band and tap dancer Bojangles Robinson and jazz singer Ethel Waters were the other main attractions.

Dancing

One of the biggest changes in popular culture during this period was in dancing. Dances before the First World War were slow and rather formal, but there was

Source F Reverend Burke Culpepper, a **Fundamentalist** preacher, delivering a sermon at Mount Vernon Methodist Episcopal Church, 1925

Dancing is a divorce feeder. It is heathen, animalistic and damnable. It degrades womanhood and manhood. Now is the time to say plainly that it is one of the most pernicious of all modern customs.

a more carefree approach in the 1920s. One of the most well-known dances of the time was the Charleston, which had a breathtaking pace and sudden shifting rhythms. Other popular dances were the black bottom, the vampire, shimmy, turkey trot, buzzard lope, chicken scratch, monkey glide and the bunny hug. The Charleston and other modern dances shocked the older generation and many people considered them immoral and scandalous. During this time a craze for dance marathons grew (see page 97).

Source G Dancers performing the Black Bottom, 1926

TASKS

4 Use Source D and your own knowledge to explain why radio had a big impact on the USA.
(For guidance on how to answer this type of question, see pages 40–41.)

5 Describe the new speakeasy club culture of the 1920s. (For guidance on how to answer this type of question, see page 73.)

6 Use Source F and your own knowledge to explain why some Americans disliked the new jazz culture. (For guidance on how to answer this type of question, see pages 40–41.)

7 What do Sources E and G suggest about the jazz culture of the 1920s? (For guidance on how to answer this type of question, see pages 27–28.)

8 Was the radio the most important change in popular entertainment in the USA during the 1920s?

> In your answer you should discuss the impact of the various developments in popular entertainment, including the impact of the radio.

(For guidance on how to answer this type of question, see pages 91–92.)

Examination guidance

This section provides guidance on how to answer the question which requires you to explain the reasons for the creation of a primary source at a particular time. It is worth 6 marks.

Why was this source produced in 1927? (6 marks)

Source A An advertisement from 1927 for the film *The Jazz Singer*. It was the first full-length 'talkie' film.

Tips on how to answer

- Use your **knowledge of this topic area** to consider **the content of the source** and **what it shows**
- Make use of the **information provided in the attribution** of the source – this can provide specific details such as publication date and the name of the newspaper, book or magazine in which the source first appeared. These details can help you to **identify motive** – why the source was produced at that time.
- You must support your reasoning with a reference to what was happening at the time that the source was produced. This is called **context**. You should spell out a **range of reasons** which address the key issue of **'why'** the source was produced at that time.

Response by candidate

The advertisement dates from 1927 and refers to the showing of a film called 'The Jazz Singer' which stared Al Jolson. This film made history because it was the first 'talking' picture and Al Jolson became the first actor to speak on film. Up to this time all films were silent ones. The cinema had developed during the 1920s into one of the most popular forms of entertainment in America, with a large percentage of the population making regular visits. 'The Jazz Singer' contained sound, allowing the audience to hear what the actors were saying and this helped to make the cinema even more popular in the late 1920s. This new technology marked the end of the silent era and the birth of the 'talkie' film industry. The advertisement signalled a key change in the history of the cinema. It was produced to advertise the new development of sound in films. It helped to make the cinema even more popular as a form of entertainment.

Use of own knowledge to develop the content of the source and to provide context.

Develops the attribution to help explain why the poster was produced.

Comment on candidate performance

The candidate has successfully developed the content of the source and used their knowledge of this topic area to provide historical context, spelling out the importance of posters in advertising new films. Reference has been made to the advertised film marking a key change in the history of the cinema, the move away from the silent to the talking motion picture. A range of detailed reasons have been given to help explain why the poster was issued in 1927 and these have been supported with reference to good historical context. This is a developed answer which displays the characteristics required to qualify for a mark (6) in the top level of response.

8 How did the lifestyle and status of women change during this period?

Source A An article called 'Flapper Jane' from a fashionable US magazine, 1925

Jane's a flapper. Let us take a look at the young person as she strolls across the lawn of her parents' suburban home, having just put the car away after driving sixty miles in two hours. She is, for one thing, a pretty girl. Beauty is the fashion in 1925. She is frankly, heavily made up with poisonously scarlet lips and richly ringed eyes. As for her clothes, Jane isn't wearing much this summer. Her dress is brief. It is cut low. The skirt comes just below the knees. The bra has been abandoned since 1924.

Source B From a school textbook by J T Patterson, *America in the Twentieth Century*, 1999

Though a few upper middle-class women in the cities talked about throwing off the older conventions – they were the flappers – most women stuck to more traditional attitudes concerning 'their place'. Most middle-class women concentrated on managing the home. Their daughters, far from taking to the streets against sexual discrimination, were more likely to prepare for careers as mothers and housewives. Millions of immigrant women and their daughters also clung to traditions that placed men firmly in control of the family.

TASK

How useful are Sources A and B to an historian studying the lifestyle of Flappers in the 1920s? (For guidance on how to answer this type of question, see pages 49–50.)

Women played an important role in helping the US war effort in the years 1917–18 and were rewarded with the vote in 1920. For some women, the 1920s was a period of great change, especially in their social position and appearance. These were known as flappers. For many, however, there was little change in their status or employment opportunities.

This chapter answers the following questions:

- How did attitudes to women change?
- What was the flapper lifestyle?

Examination guidance

Throughout this chapter you will be given the opportunity to practise different exam-style questions and detailed guidance on how to answer question 3. This is an essay question which requires you to evaluate two sides of an argument. It is worth 12 marks, with an additional 3 marks for SPaG.

How did attitudes to women change?

The position of women before 1917

POLITICAL POSITION
Women played no part in politics. They did not have the vote.

SOCIAL POSITION
It was thought to be unladylike to smoke or drink in public. A woman would be accompanied by a chaperone if she went out during the day or evening. Divorce and sex before marriage were rare.

EMPLOYMENT OPPORTUNITIES
These were limited and most middle- and upper-class women did not go out to work as this interfered with their domestic role as a mother and housewife. Most working women were in low-paid jobs such as cleaning, dress-making and secretarial work.

APPEARANCE
Women were expected to wear tight-waisted, ankle-length dresses, have long hair, which was tied back, and not to wear make-up.

Changes after 1917

The US entry into the First World War in 1917 provided greater opportunities for women:

- Around 2.8 million men had been drafted into the armed forces by the end of the war and more than a million women helped with the war effort.
- Approximately 90,000 women served in the US armed forces in Europe. The Navy and Marine Corps enlisted women as clerks, radio electricians, chemists, accountants and nurses. Others joined the Young Women's and Young Men's Christian Associations, the American Red Cross and the Salvation Army. The army, unlike its sister services, was more conservative in the jobs it permitted women to fill its ranks, enlisting more than 21,000 as clerks, fingerprint experts, journalists and translators.
- Women also worked in jobs traditionally done by men, such as heavy industry, engineering works and transport.

The war proved women could do the jobs just as well as men and encouraged greater freedom, especially in social habits such as smoking and drinking in public, and going out un-chaperoned. Their participation also made a powerful argument for women's voting rights, weighing heavily in the passing of the 19th Amendment, which gave American women the right to vote in 1920. This gave them greater political power and encouraged some to campaign for further change.

TASKS

1. Describe the position of women in the USA in the early twentieth century. (For guidance on how to answer this type of question, see page 73.)
2. How important was the First World War in helping to change the position of women in American society?

Changing attitudes to social etiquette and the jazz culture

The 1920s saw a series of changes to the position of women. These were influenced by:

- The consumer **boom** of the 1920s, which provided exciting opportunities for women. Labour-saving devices, such as vacuum cleaners and washing machines released women from some of the time spent on domestic chores. This enabled some to go into employment and provided others with more opportunity for leisure and recreational activities.

Source A American magazine advertisement in 1926 for the Maytag electric washing machine

- The 'Jazz Age', which brought changes in entertainment and leisure. The popularity of the cinema, radio and dance halls provided further opportunities for women. For example, Mary Pickford and Clara Bow became stars of silent movies and were so successful that they joined two other stars in setting up their own film company. Mae West, Gloria Swanson and Jean Harlow became stars of the 'talkies' and role models for many younger girls.

Employment

There were other changes in the position of women. There was certainly progress in the numbers of women in employment. By 1930 around 2 million more women were employed than had been ten years earlier. However, these tended to be in unskilled low-paid jobs. Despite the fact that a third of university degrees were awarded to women in 1930, only four per cent of university professors were women. Medical schools allocated only five per cent of places to women. Consequently, the number of female doctors actually declined in the 1920s.

Men were still paid a lot more than women for doing the same job. Women received no support from the **Supreme Court**, which banned all attempts to set **minimum wages** for women. In 1927 the government took the side of the employers when female textile workers in Tennessee went on strike for better pay. The strikers were arrested by the local police. There were some new career opportunities for women but this was in so-called 'women's jobs', such as librarians and nurses.

Source B A table showing the percentage of women in certain jobs in the years 1900–30

Jobs	1900	1930
Professional and technical workers	8	14
Managers and officials	1	3
Clerical and sales workers	8	28
Skilled craftspeople	1	1
Workers and labourers	26	19
Domestic servants	29	18
Other service workers	7	10
Farmers	6	2

More women worked and with more money of their own, they increasingly made the decisions about whether to buy new items for the home. Even women who did not earn their own money were often seen as the ones who took these purchasing decisions. Advertising was aimed specifically at women for this reason. It has even been suggested that it was pressure from women that convinced Ford to offer other colours, apart from black, for their cars.

TASKS

3 Why was Source A produced in the mid-1920s? (For guidance on how to answer this type of question, see page 84.)

4 Study Source B. What does this tell you about changes in employment opportunities for women by 1930?

Marriage

The media, and especially magazines, reminded women that they should marry and have children. Once women married they generally gave up work. Nevertheless, married women in the 1920s tended to have fewer children and lived longer than their mothers and grandmothers. In 1900, the average lifespan was 51 years. By 1925 this figure had increased to 63. In 1900, American women had an average of 3.6 children. This figure had fallen to 2.6 by 1930.

Women were less likely to remain in unhappy marriages in the 1920s. In 1914 there were 100,000 divorces. There were twice as many in 1929.

Politics

Women were given the vote in 1920. A few women did make progress in gaining political power. For example, in 1924 Nellie Tayloe Ross of Wyoming became the first woman to be elected **governor** of a state. Two years later, Bertha Knight Landes became the first female mayor of an American city, Seattle.

However, these were the exceptions and women made little progress in politics itself. Political parties wanted their vote but did not see them as realistic candidates for political office. By 1920, there were still only a handful of female politicians. Most women, in any case, had little interest in politics. The **women's movement** failed in its attempt to get the Equal Rights Amendment Act passed, which would have given them equality in law with men.

Moves towards feminism

In the years after 1900 there were a number of women's associations involved in a variety of campaigns. Some campaigned for greater employment opportunities and equal pay. Others were more concerned with improved political rights, especially the vote. This feminist movement achieved success when, in 1920, women were allowed to vote for the first time in presidential elections. However, during the 1920s, in spite of or even because of, the flapper image, the feminist movement weakened. The majority of women were uninterested in politics.

Real change?

There was still a strong conservative element in US society, especially in rural areas where religion and traditional attitudes prevented any real change.

Many married women could not afford the new labour-saving devices. A survey in 1932 of 10,000 farmhouses found that only 32 per cent had any running water at all, with 57 per cent owning a washing machine. Only 47 per cent had carpet sweepers. These women not only spent a considerable time on housework and looking after the children, but had to milk the cows and work in the fields. They experienced little change and few benefits from the Roaring Twenties.

Source C From *America as Americans See It*, by the feminist American writer Doris E Fleischman, 1932

It is wholly confusing to read the advertisements in the magazines that feature the enticing qualities of vacuum cleaners, refrigerators and hundreds of other devices which should lighten the chores of women in the home. On the whole these large middle classes do their own housework with few of the mechanical aids. Women who live on farms do a great deal of work besides caring for their children, washing the clothes and caring for the home and cooking. Thousands still work in the fields and help milk the cows.

TASKS

5 Use Source C and your own knowledge to explain why some American women were unable to make changes in their lifestyle. (For guidance on how to answer this type of question, see pages 40–41.)

6 Working in pairs, make a copy of the set of scales on the right.

PROGRESS
LACK OF PROGRESS

Using evidence from pages 86–88:
- one person should write examples of progress on the left-hand scale
- the other should write examples of lack of progress on right-hand scale.

7 Overall, do you think women made progress in their position in US society in the 1920s? Give reasons for your answer.

What was the flapper lifestyle?

The greatest change in the position of females was experienced by women known as the flappers.

In the 1920s a number of women, generally from middle- and upper-class families living in the northern states, decided to challenge the traditional attitudes towards women. They became known as the flappers. Their aim was to become more independent in their social life and to take a freer approach to their behaviour and appearance.

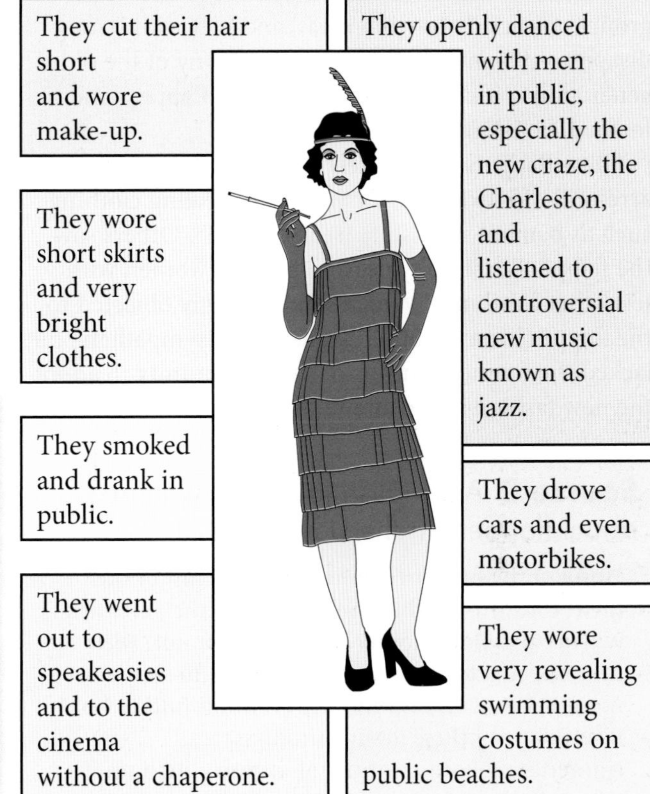

Source A A view of flappers from the *New York Times*, 1922

A flapper is shameless, selfish and honest but at the same time she thinks of these things as good. Why not? She takes a man's point of view as her mother never could. When she loses she is not afraid to admit defeat, whether it be a lover or $20 at an auction. She will never make you a husband or knit you a necktie, but she'll drive you from the station on hot summer nights in her own sports car. She'll put on trousers and go skiing with you or, if it happens to be summertime, go swimming.

Source B From a letter written to the *Daily Illini* newspaper in 1922

The word 'flapper' to us means not a female that smokes, swears and kisses her gentlemen friends goodnight, although there is no harm in any of that. We think of the flapper as the independent young woman who feels like punching someone when called the 'weaker sex', who resents being put on a pedestal and who is responsible for the advancement of women's condition in the world.

Flapper icons and role models

Actress Joan Crawford was the most famous flapper of them all. She kissed, drank, smoked and danced the Charleston in films such as *Our Modern Maidens* (1929). Girls loved it and tried to copy her. The silent film star Louise Brooks was another flapper icon. Her first on-screen role as a flapper was in the 1926 film *A Social Celebrity*. Brooks would also play flapper-like characters in *Love 'Em and Leave 'Em* (1926) and *Rolled Stockings* (1927). Other popular flappers included Colleen Moore and Clara Bow, the so-called 'It Girl' due to her flapper role in the film *It* (1927).

Source C F Scott Fitzgerald was a famous American author who wrote about the roaring twenties. In 1920 he married Zelda Zayre, who was a typical flapper

Flirting, kissing, viewing life lightly, saying damn without a blush, playing along the danger line in an immature way – a sort of mental baby vamp.

Opposition to the flapper lifestyle

However, in some respects, the flappers did not further the cause of women's rights in the 1920s. They were seen as too extreme by many traditional groups, especially in rural areas, and met with strong disapproval from religious societies. Many of the older generation criticised the lifestyle of the flappers and formed Anti-Flirt Leagues.

Some flappers deliberately flouted the law and were arrested – for example, for wearing revealing clothing such as banned swimsuits (see Source E). Others saw the flappers as simply pleasure-seeking women with few other attributes. Whilst some strongly objected to the flapper lifestyle, other women were sympathetic but lacked the financial means or the opportunity to adopt the new fashions or to attend the new social events.

Source D An English journalist writing about flappers in the USA in 1921

Think of the modern young American girl of this great country. Do they ever think? Do they ever ask whence they have come? It would seem not. Their aim appears to be to attract men and to secure money. What can a man with a mind find to hold him in one of these lovely, brainless, cigarette-smoking creatures of undisciplined sex whom he meets continually?

TASKS

1 Describe the flapper movement. (For guidance on how to answer this type of question, see page 73.)

2 What do Sources B and E suggest about the lifestyle of flappers in the 1920s? (For guidance on how to answer this type of question, see pages 27–28.)

3 Explain why some people opposed the flappers.

4 Study all the sources on pages 89 and 90 and copy and complete the following table. An example has been done for you.

Source	Positive features of flappers	Negative features
B		Pleasure-seeking

Source E A group of flappers in Chicago being arrested for wearing banned one-piece bathing suits, which were seen as too figure-hugging

Examination guidance

This section provides guidance on how to answer an essay question. The question carries 12 marks and up to an additional 3 marks will be awarded for spelling, grammar and punctuation.

Was jazz music the most important development in American culture and society during the 1920s? (12 marks)

In your answer you should discuss the impact of the main developments in American culture and society including the impact of jazz music.

A sample answer to this question is given on page 92.

Tips on how to answer

- You need to **develop a two-sided answer** which has balance and good support.
- You should **start by discussing the factor mentioned in the question**, using your factual knowledge to explain why this factor is important.
- You then need to **consider the counter-argument** by using your knowledge to examine other relevant factors.
- These points need to be discussed in some detail, starting a new paragraph for each point.
- Aim to link the paragraphs by using words such as 'other factors include', 'also important', 'in addition to', 'however'.
- **Avoid generalised comments** – the more specific your observations the higher mark you will get, providing the factual information is relevant to the question.
- **Conclude your answer with a link back to the question, making a judgement** about the importance of the factor listed in the question when ranked against the other factors you have discussed.
- You should aim to write between one and two sides of a page. See page 92 for an example answer to the question opposite.

Now you have a go

To what extent was the growing popularity of sport the most important development in American culture and society during the 1920s? (12 marks)

In your answer you should discuss the impact of the main developments in American culture and society, including the influence of sport.

Introduction which links to the question.

Deals with the key factor mentioned in the question.

Provides precise details to support the argument.

Begins the counter-argument. Using the term 'however' makes it clear you are now looking at other factors.

Other factors are discussed such as the cinema, sport, the radio and gramophone, and the changing role and status of women.

A new paragraph is started for each new factor.

A good reasoned conclusion which provides a clear judgement linked back to the question.

Response by candidate

Jazz music played a significant part in the development of American culture and society during the 1920s. Jazz developed in the Deep South out of traditional forms of black music such as blues and ragtime. By the early 1920s jazz was popular in the new clubs and speakeasies not just in the south but also in the northern cities. It allowed black people to express themselves through music and it allowed them to become more accepted into society. Jazz musicians like Louis Armstrong and Duke Ellington became household names …

However, jazz was not the only cultural and social development to affect American society during the 1920s. This was the decade of the silent cinema which attracted ever larger audiences. Hollywood stars like Charlie Chaplin and …

Organised sport also grew in popularity during the 1920s and became an important part in the social life of many Americans as they had more free time and more money to engage in leisure activities. Baseball grew in popularity due to …

Popular entertainment such as listening to the radio and gramophone, and attending the new clubs and dance halls also became fashionable during the 1920s. People went to perform the new dances such as the Charleston and the …

Women also made great social progress during the 1920s with the development of the flapper lifestyle. New modern women dressed in new fashions such as …

American culture and society underwent many changes during the 1920s. Women were afforded more freedom and adopted a more liberal lifestyle. People had more leisure time and increasingly spent it visiting the cinema, going to watch sports matches, listening to music and other cultural events on their radio. However, it was jazz music that had one of the most important impacts. People went to the new clubs to listen to the jazz musicians and to dance to the new jazz dances. They listened to jazz on the radio or on the gramophone. Jazz was therefore an important cultural and social development during the 1920s.

9 Why did sport and other leisure activities witness so much growth during this period?

Source A Adapted from *The Twenties: Fords, Flappers and Fanatics*, by George Mowry, 1963

On the battlefield, on the production line, at home in a city apartment and increasingly in the business world, the individual was becoming lost in the swarming crowd. The sporting field was one of the remaining areas of pure individual expression where success or failure depended precisely upon individual physical and intellectual prowess. And if the masses themselves could not or would not participate directly they could at least by a process of identification salute the old virtues.

TASK

Use Source A and your own knowledge to explain why there was an increased interest in sport in the USA in the 1920s. (For guidance on how to answer this type of question, see pages 40–41.)

The 1920s were years of great change for the USA. The period was, after all, named the 'Roaring Twenties'. With increasing wealth and prosperity, its citizens had more disposable income than ever before. The advent of the cheap automobile meant that people could go to more leisure activities – the cinema was not the only beneficiary. In particular, sport became a key feature of people's lives. Moreover, it seemed as though people wanted not only to watch sporting heroes but also watch individuals who pushed themselves to their limits of endurance. The names of Lindbergh, Earhart and Ederle were known in households across the USA. In addition, the USA became known for odd crazes such as dance marathons and flagpole sitting.

This chapter answers the following questions:

- How did interest in sport grow in the 1920s?
- What were the fads, crazes and the passions for the unusual?
- Who were the American heroes of the decade?
- What was the impact of the automobile upon leisure activities?

Examination guidance

Throughout this chapter you will be given the opportunity to practise different exam-style questions.

How did interest in sport grow in the 1920s?

In the early 1920s sport became a very important part of the lives of many Americans. It was made even more popular as a result of the radio. With the increasing prosperity of the USA, people had greater disposable incomes. They were able not only to watch more sport but to participate in it as well. People also had more leisure time and improved means of transportation. Indeed, the 1920s was officially named the 'Golden Age of Sport'. Baseball, football, golf, horse racing and tennis captured the imagination of many people. The number of golfers, tennis players, bowlers and amateur baseball players increased greatly. Thanks to radio broadcasts and sports journalists, athletes became larger than life and were national heroes, almost like the comic book heroes of the time.

The growth in the number of sporting heroes meant more people participated in sporting activities and cities constructed swimming pools, baseball pitches, playgrounds and recreational centres. Huge new stadia were built across the USA to cope with the explosion of interest in what became professional sports.

Baseball

Baseball became the most popular game and Babe Ruth was the most famous sportsman of the era. He became regarded as one of the greatest sports heroes in American history and has been named the greatest baseball player in history. He was a larger than life character and lived a fast life but was also known for his charity work. He has also been credited with making baseball the most popular game of the 1920s.

The New York Yankees baseball stadium, which became known as 'the house that Ruth built'.

Another great 1920s sportsperson was Oscar Charleston, who played in the Negro League. He, too, is regarded as one of the greatest players of all time, but was not allowed to play in the major leagues because of the colour of his skin. Both Ruth and Charleston were left-handed.

Biography George Herman Ruth, Jr 1895–1948

Also known as Babe Ruth, The Bambino and The Sultan of Swat.

Played baseball in the major leagues from 1914 to 1935:

- Boston Red Sox 1914–19
- New York Yankees 1920–35
- Boston Braves 1935

Career statistics:

- 714 home runs
- 2873 hits
- World Series Champion seven times
- Ruth was the first player to hit 60 home runs in one season (1927)

Biography Oscar Charleston 1896–1954

Baseball player in the Negro League:

- Indianapolis ABCs 1915–18, 1920, 1922–23
- Chicago American Giants 1919
- St Louis Giants 1921

Baseball player/manager:

- Harrisburg Giants 1924–27
- Philadelphia Hilldales 1928–29
- Various teams until 1941

Boxing

Spectators flocked to see all big sporting events, especially boxing matches. In 1921, 75,000 people paid $1.5 million to watch Jack Dempsey fight Georges Carpentier and, five years later, some 145,000 saw the boxing match between Jack Dempsey and Gene Tunney.

Biography Jack Dempsey 1895–1983

Nickname 'The Manassa mauler'
1895 Born William Dempsey in Mansassa, Colorado
1913–27 Fought 83 bouts:
Won 66 (51 KOs)
Lost 6 (1 KO)
Drew 11
1919 Became world champion heavyweight boxer, defeating Jess Willard
1926 Lost heavyweight title to Gene Tunney

Biography Gene Tunney 1897–1978

1897 Born James Tunney in New York
1919–28 Fought 86 bouts:
Won 80 (48 KOs)
Lost 1
Drew 5
1926 Won heavyweight title from Jack Dempsey
1928 Retired as undefeated champion

The heavyweight boxing champion Gene Tunney knocking down Jack Dempsey in the eighth round of the 1927 title bout in Chicago. This bout became known as the 'Long Count' fight.

Source A From *Only Yesterday, A History of the 1920s*, written by F L Allen in 1975

130,000 people watched Gene Tunney outbox a weary Jack Dempsey at Philadelphia and paid nearly a million dollars for the privilege: 145,000 watched the return match at Chicago and the receipts reached the incredible sum of $2.6 million. Compare that sum with the trifling $452,000 taken when Dempsey regained his title from Willard in 1919 and you have a measure of what happened in a few years. So enormous was the amphitheatre at Chicago that two-thirds of people in the outermost seats did not know who had won when the fight was over. Nor was the audience limited to the throng of Chicago, for millions more – 40 millions, the radio stations claimed – heard the breathless story of it, blow by blow over the radio.

TASKS

1. Describe the sporting career of **either** Babe Ruth **or** Jack Dempsey. (For guidance on how to answer this type of question, see page 73.)
2. Use Source A and your own knowledge to explain why boxing became a popular sport in the 1920s. (For guidance on how to answer this type of question, see pages 40–41.)

Games

There was also a craze for games. The Chinese game of Mah Jongg suddenly became extremely fashionable. Crosswords were introduced. In fact, in 1924 the *New York Times* noted the craze with alarm and called solving crosswords a 'sinful waste in the utterly futile finding of words the letters of which will fit into a prearranged pattern, more or less complex. This is not a game at all.'

Flagpole sitting

Perhaps the oddest craze of the 1920s was flagpole sitting. For a period of about five years in the 1920s, people tried to outdo each other by staying as long as possible on a pole. Alvin 'Shipwreck' Kelly was the most well known of these figures. In 1929 Kelly held the record for flagpole sitting – 49 days at Atlantic City. One of the biggest competitions was in Baltimore in 1929, which had eighteen boys and three girls taking part.

Newspapers and magazines

More and more people bought newspapers and magazines. In 1919 the first tabloid newspaper, the *New York Daily News*, was published. This encouraged other newspapers, which concentrated on crime, strip-cartoons and fashion. Advertisers were keen to use magazines and newspapers to sell their goods. In 1922 ten magazines claimed a circulation of more than 2.5 million.

The newspapers sponsored events like beauty contests, which really took off in the 1920s, and the short-lived craze of live goldfish eating competitions. Readers wanted to find out about sporting and cinema heroes and heroines and anyone who did something out of the ordinary. Figures such as Gertrude Ederle and Charles Lindbergh became household names (see pages 99 and 100).

TASKS

2 Use Source B and your own knowledge to explain why the 1920s has been described as a decade of 'fads and crazes'. (For guidance on how to answer this type of question, see pages 40–41.)

3 Write an article for an American magazine describing the various fads and crazes that became so popular during the 1920s.

Source B Flappers playing Mah Jongg, December 1922

Who were the American heroes of the decade?

Charles Lindbergh with his plane *Spirit of St Louis*.

Charles Lindbergh

On 20 May 1927, Charles Lindbergh took off alone from New York in a single-engine monoplane, the *Spirit of St Louis*. His aim was to fly across the Atlantic Ocean and his journey took 33 hours and 39 minutes. He flew 3633 miles with no map, no radio and no parachute. For food during his flight, he took only five sandwiches – two ham, two roast beef and one hard-boiled egg. He had two canteens of water.

The event created huge interest in the USA and for many Americans Lindbergh symbolised the growing strength of their country. Many also viewed his feat as the triumph of the individual, a clear indication of the spirit of the USA.

Lindbergh became a national hero and was awarded the Distinguished Flying Cross. He was given a tickertape parade when he returned to New York and it was estimated that 1800 tons of paper had been thrown out of windows during the celebrations. He received more than 55,000 telegrams and for many became the symbol of the USA. The older generation was especially impressed by Lindbergh because he seemed to represent something of the pioneering spirit and did not reflect some of the behaviour of the young during the 1920s.

Source A A report of Lindbergh's landing in Paris, which appeared in the *New York Times* on 22 May 1927

PARIS, May 21. Lindbergh did it. Twenty minutes after 10 o'clock tonight suddenly and softly there slipped out of the darkness a gray-white airplane as 25,000 pairs of eyes strained toward it. At 10:24 the Spirit of St Louis landed and lines of soldiers, ranks of policemen and stout steel fences went down before a mad rush as irresistible as the tides of the ocean.

TASK

Use Source A and your own knowledge to explain why Charles Lindbergh became so famous. (For guidance on how to answer this type of question, see pages 40–41.)

Gertrude Ederle

In 1926, Ederle was the first woman to swim the English Channel in a time of 14 hours and 30 minutes. In doing so, she also beat the existing men's cross-Channel record. She was given a huge welcome in New York on her return, as was Charles Lindbergh, the first man to fly solo non-stop across the Atlantic in 1927.

Gertrude Ederle, prepared for her cross-Channel swim.

Amelia Earhart

In 1929 Amelia Earhart accompanied two pilots to become the first female to fly across the Atlantic, making the journey from Trepassey Harbor in Newfoundland to Llanelli in Wales in 20 hours and 40 minutes. When she qualified to fly in 1923, she became only the sixteenth woman to be granted a pilot's licence.

Amelia Earhart, 1929.

What was the impact of the automobile upon leisure activities?

Henry Ford's mass production techniques led to a dramatic fall in the price of motor cars, making them affordable to the average American. The subsequent increase in car ownership caused improvements to be made in the US's infrastructure, resulting in the building of new roads and the construction of garages, motels and roadside restaurants. Cheap affordable transport meant it was easier for ordinary Americans to travel to visit friends and family, to attend sporting fixtures, dance marathons, or to travel to the cities to participate in the celebration of record-breaking achievements, such as those of Lindbergh and Earhart. The motor car allowed families to explore the countryside, undertake holidays and short-break vacations. The result was a more mobile society and it was the beginning of America's 'love affair' with the motor car.

TASK

How useful are Sources A and B to an historian studying the impact the motor car had upon the lifestyle of many Americans?

(For guidance on how to answer this type of question, see pages 49–50.)

Source A An account by a modern historian of how the motor car helped to change American society during the 1920s

The impact of the car on life in the USA cannot be exaggerated. It gave people great freedom to travel, whether to visit friends or to take day trips to the cities. Many people moved out to live in the suburbs during the 1920s because they could drive to work. The car meant that young people could escape their parents and go off to cinemas or clubs. Not everybody was in favour of the car: some thought it was leading to a moral decline in young people; others blamed it for making crime easier.

Source B A photograph, taken in the mid-1920s, showing Model Ts parked in a high street in the USA

Examination guidance

Here is an opportunity for you to practise some the questions that have been explained in previous chapters. The questions cover all the questions that appear on the Unit One examination paper and are worth 53 marks in total.

Question 1

This question is focused on changes in American culture and society.

Source A A baseball game being played at the stadium belonging to the New York Yankees in 1925

Source B An extract from a school textbook (1999)

America fell in love with organised sport during the 1920s. Sports stars became American heroes. Working hours were changing and more people had leisure time. They could visit the new stadiums or listen to games on the radio. They could also play sport themselves.

(a) What do Sources A and B suggest about the growth of organised sport in the USA in the 1920s? (4 marks)

- Remember to pick out at least two facts from each source.
- You may be able to make use of the information provided in the caption.
- For further guidance, see pages 27–28.

Source C From a website

The 1920s was a decade of freedom for American women. They received the right to vote. They took part in activities usually associated with men. Driving motorbikes and cars, flying aeroplanes and smoking cigarettes became female activities.

(b) Use Source C and your own knowledge to explain why life changed for some American women during the 1920s. (6 marks)

- You will need to pick out at least two facts from the source and explain them in your own words.
- You must demonstrate your knowledge of this topic by providing at least one additional factor not mentioned in the source.
- For further guidance, see pages 40–41.

Source D A photograph taken in the late 1920s showing young Americans enjoying dancing to jazz music.

Source E From an advertisement for the cinema published in an American newspaper, *Saturday Evening Post* (June 1929)

Go to a motion picture and let yourself go. Before you know it, you are living in the story, laughing, hating, struggling, winning! All the adventure, all the romance, all the excitement you lack in your daily life is in the pictures. They take you completely out of yourself into a wonderful new world.

(c) How useful are Sources D and E to an historian studying popular entertainment in the USA in the 1920s? (8 marks)

- Aim to concentrate upon three focus areas – what information do the sources provide (their content), who was their author (their origin), why were they produced (their purpose)?
- Remember to make references to the usefulness of both sources to the historian.
- For further guidance, see pages 49–50.

Question 2

This question is based on political and social challenges in the USA in this period.

(a) Describe the work and importance of the NACCP (4 marks)

- You will need to describe at least two key features.
- Be specific, avoid generalised comments.
- For further guidance, see page 73.

Source F A cartoon about Prohibition published in a New York magazine in the early 1920s.

(b) Why was this cartoon published in the early 1920s? (6 marks)

- You should use your knowledge of this topic area to discuss the content of the source and its attribution.
- You must suggest a variety of reasons to explain why this source was published at that time.
- For further guidance, see page 84.

Historians have made different interpretations about gangsters in the USA in the 1920s.

These three pieces of evidence refer to the activities of gangsters in the USA in the 1920s. Study these and answer the question that follows.

Evidence one An interpretation written by an historian in the 1990s for a GCSE school history textbook. She argues that the gangsters upset the American people

Rival gangs fought each other for control of the bootlegging industry. The American people were angered by the level of violence associated with bootlegging. The most notorious gangster was Al Capone. He bribed the police, judges and local politicians to keep his illegal activities of bootlegging, gambling and prostitution going. Gangsters like Capone terrified ordinary Americans.

Evidence two An interpretation by a gangster interviewed about true-life American crime for a magazine in the 1940s. He argues that many Americans were happy with the way the gangsters worked

We made our money by supplying a public demand. If I was supposed to have broken the law, my customers, who numbered hundreds of the best people in Chicago, were as guilty as I am. The only difference between me and them was that I sold and they bought. Many people called me a gangster and bootlegger. Others saw me as a businessman supplying their needs.

Evidence three This evidence is a photograph from a Chicago newspaper covering the St Valentine's Day Massacre, published in February 1929

(c) One interpretation is that the American people were greatly angered by the activities of the gangsters in the 1920s. How far do you agree with this interpretation? (10 marks)

- You need to identify which pieces of evidence support the given interpretation and which provide an alternative interpretation.
- You should use your knowledge of this topic area to discuss how and why this issue has been interpreted in different ways.
- Remember to provide a judgement upon the value of the given interpretation.
- For further guidance, see pages 63–64.

Question 3

This question is focused on the American economy.

(a) Was the panic selling of shares the main cause of the Wall Street Crash in October 1929? (12 marks & 3 marks for SPaG)

- Remember that your answer needs to debate the topic, examining both sides to the argument.
- Aim to link your paragraphs, covering a variety of key issues.
- You should provide a conclusion with contains a judgement which is linked back to the question.
- Remember that you will be awarded marks for good spelling, punctuation and grammar.
- For further guidance, see pages 91–92.

Section A
The rise of the Nazi Party and its consolidation of power, 1919–34

Source A From *Weimar and the Rise of Hitler*, A Nicholls

Much more important than the fairness or unfairness of the treaty was its impact on the new German Republic. How far is it true that the Versailles Treaty wrecked German democracy/that Germany's economy was ruined by reparations and her security undermined? Much more serious was the political demoralisation which the treaty caused within Germany. The real damage the treaty did to Germany was to disillusion more moderate men who might otherwise have supported their new republic. The peace settlement continued to poison the political atmosphere in Germany for many years.

This section examines the key developments in the rise of the Nazi Party from the problems of the Weimar Republic, including the impact of the Treaty of Versailles (see Source A), and its economic problems in the 1920s to the consolidation of Nazi power during 1933–34.

By the end of the 1920s, Germany was experiencing political and economic turmoil. The early 1930s saw unemployment rise to 6 million and extreme political parties such as the Nazis and Communists began to have successes in local, general and presidential elections. The Weimar Republic seemed unable to cope with the serious issues facing Germany and the extreme parties seemed to offer quick and simple solutions. In 1932 the Nazis became the largest party in Germany and its leader, Adolf Hitler, became Chancellor in January 1933. By August 1934 the Nazis had established a one-party state.

Each chapter explores a key question and examines important lines of enquiry as outlined below:

Chapter 10: How did developments in Germany from 1919–1929 affect the rise of the Nazis?

- What were the political and economic problems of the Weimar Republic?
- How did the Nazi Party develop, 1920–23?
- What were the consequences of the Munich *Putsch*, November 1923?
- How did the Nazi Party change, 1924–29?

Chapter 11: How and why did Hitler get appointed Chancellor in January 1933?

- What was the impact of the **Wall Street Crash** and the Great **Depression**?
- Why was the Nazi Party successful after 1930?
- What was the role of Hitler in increasing support for the Nazis?
- How did the events of July 1932 to January 1933 bring Hitler to power?

Chapter 12: How did the Nazis consolidate their power, 1933–34?

- What was the significance of the *Reichstag* Fire?
- Why was the Enabling Act important for Hitler?
- How did the Nazis remove opposition to their regime?
- What was the importance of the Night of the Long Knives?
- Why was the support of the army important for Hitler?

10 How did developments in Germany from 1919–29 affect the rise of the Nazis?

Source A From *Weimar Culture* by the US historian P Gay, written in 1974

The German people had had little practice in politics ... By 1919 there was democracy and the Weimar Republic opened the door to real politics, the Germans stood at the door, gaping, like peasants asked to a palace, hardly knowing how to behave themselves.

TASK

Study Source A. What does it tell you about politics in Germany in 1919?

On 11 November 1918, the **armistice** was signed bringing an end to fighting in the First World War (1914–18) and Germany became a **republic**. The five years after the war were chaotic and Germany experienced an attempted Communist revolution, political assassinations, *Putsches* (armed uprisings) and massive **inflation**. Above all, Germans had to accept what they felt was a vindictive peace settlement – the Treaty of Versailles. Many Germans said that all the problems of the post-war years were the result of the decisions that had been made by the politicians of the new Weimar Republic. By the end of 1923, under the guidance of Gustav Stresemann, political and economic stability was being restored to Germany. However, an economic crisis in the USA in 1929 destroyed that stability and, within four years, the Nazi Party were in control of Germany.

This chapter answers the following questions:

- What were the political and economic problems of the Weimar Republic?
- How did the Nazi Party develop, 1920–23?
- What were the consequences of the Munich *Putsch*, November 1923?
- How did the Nazi Party change, 1924–29?

Examination guidance

Throughout this chapter you will be given the opportunity to practise different exam-style questions.

What were the political and economic problems of the Weimar Republic?

On 11 November 1918 the First World War came to an end with Germany signing an armistice. This was signed by politicians of the new republic, which had been established after the abdication of the ***Kaiser*** on 9 November 1918 due to his waning support.

Many Germans saw the ending of the war as a betrayal of the German army (*Reichswehr*). The notion was that the army had not been defeated by the **Allies** – it had been forced to surrender by the new government. The army had been 'stabbed in the back' (*Dolchstoss*) by the politicians who signed the armistice. These politicians became known as the 'November Criminals'.

From its very beginning, therefore, many Germans, especially those in the army, despised the new republic. In the final weeks of 1918 there were attacks on the new German government from the left and the right. After the elections for the **Constituent Assembly** in January 1919, it was decided that Berlin was too dangerous a place for the members to meet. Therefore, the decision was taken to meet in the more peaceful surroundings of the town of Weimar. Hence the eventual name of the new republic.

Source A Key articles of the Weimar Constitution

Article 1	The German ***Reich*** is a republic. Political authority derives from the people.
Article 22	The *Reichstag* delegates are elected by universal, equal, direct and secret suffrage by all men and women over 20 years of age, in accordance with the principles of proportional representation.
Article 41	The *Reich* President is chosen by the whole of the German electorate.
Article 48	If public safety and order in the *Reich* is materially disturbed or endangered, the *Reich* President may take the necessary measures to restore public safety and order.

The most important result of the January election was that because of **proportional representation** and a large number of parties, no single party won a majority of seats. Therefore, there would have to be a **coalition government**. This was to be a problem for the Weimar Republic throughout its life. For example, from 1923 to 1930, there were ten coalition governments.

Following the abdication of the *Kaiser*, a new constitution had to be drawn up and this was finalised in August 1919. This was the first time that Germany had experienced democracy. There were many flaws in the constitution and when things did not go well for Germany in the early post-war years, politicians were criticised for creating a weak system of government.

Source B Some flaws of the Weimar Constitution

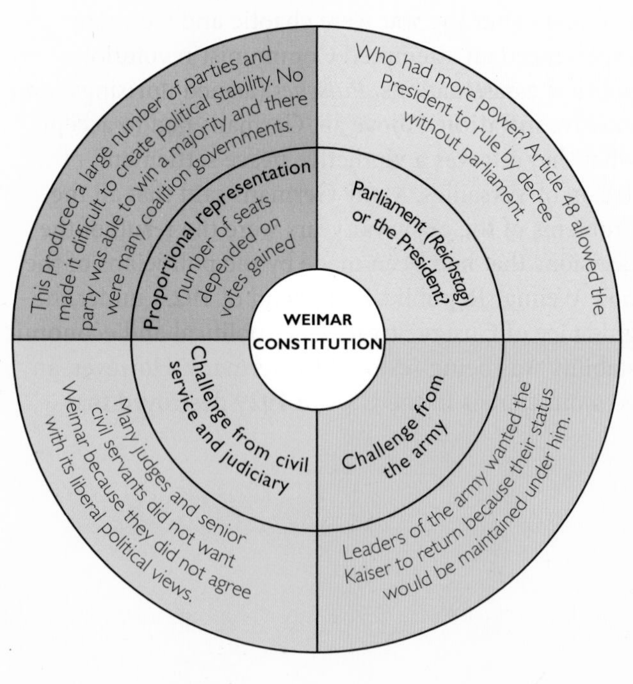

TASK

1 What do the terms 'stabbed in the back' and 'November Criminals' mean?

Unrest in Germany, 1918–23

The Weimar government was initially unpopular among many Germans because it had surrendered, established a weak constitution and failed to end food shortages. Weimar was hated by **communists**, **socialists**, nationalists, army leaders and those who had run Germany before 1918. It seemed to have a bleak future.

Because of the fear of a revolution in the chaos of the post-war period, the Weimar government made a deal with the new army leader, Groener. It was agreed that the army would support the new government against revolution and the government would support and supply the army. Thus Weimar became dependent on the army.

For some Germans this dependency on the army weakened the authority of the Weimar Republic. In 1919 there was an attempted communist revolution (also known as the Spartacist Rising) in Berlin. In the following year there was also an attempted right-wing takeover (the Kapp *Putsch*) in Berlin. The map below shows the extent and duration of the unrest in post-war Germany.

TASKS

2 Explain why the Weimar Republic was so named.

3 Explain why the Weimar Republic had so many coalitions. Suggest reasons why coalitions are often weak.

4 Use Source B and your own knowledge to explain why there were problems with the Weimar Constitution. (For guidance on how to answer this type of question, see page 141.)

5 Write a newspaper article attacking the Weimar Constitution. Try to write a short but witty headline.

6 Study the map below. Describe the political violence in Germany between 1919 and 1923.

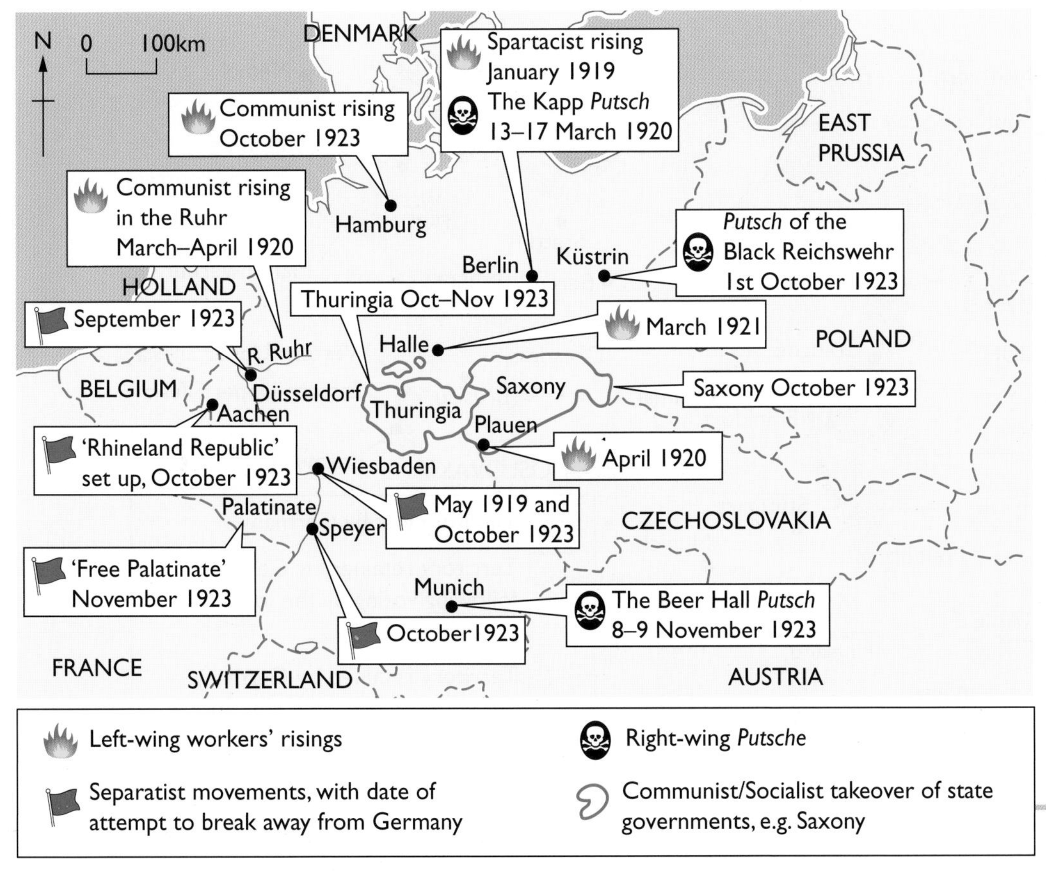

Political violence in Germany, 1919–23.

The Treaty of Versailles

Although the Germans signed the armistice on 11 November 1918, it was not until 28 June 1919 that the treaty ending the war was signed. When the terms of the settlement were published huge numbers of Germans were horrified.

The Treaty of Versailles imposed extremely severe terms on Germany (see Source E). Germany lost 13 per cent of its land, 48 per cent of its iron production and more than 6 million citizens were absorbed into other countries. Perhaps the harshest term for Germany was Article 231 – the War Guilt Clause. This stated that Germany had to accept blame for starting the war in 1914, and had to agree to pay compensation for the damage she had caused to the Allied powers. This was compounded when entry to the **League of Nations** was denied, thus showing that Germany was a pariah.

For most Germans the Treaty stoked the fire of shame and humiliation. To them Versailles was nothing more than a dictated peace (*Diktat*). A scapegoat was needed – and the Weimar government and its politicians fitted the bill.

The Weimar cabinet initially rejected the terms of the peace settlement and on 19 June Chancellor Scheidemann resigned in disgust. Leading politicians called the terms a *Gewaltfrieden* (an enforced peace). Nevertheless, from this point, criticism of the Weimar government began to grow and the idea that the politicians had stabbed the army in the back (*Dolchstoss*) continued to gain currency.

Source D An extract from a German newspaper

Vengeance! German nation! Today in the Hall of Mirrors [Versailles] the disgraceful treaty is being signed. Do not forget it. The German people will, with unceasing work, press forward to reconquer the place among nations to which it is entitled. Then will come vengeance for the shame of 1919.

Source C Map showing the territorial terms of the Treaty of Versailles

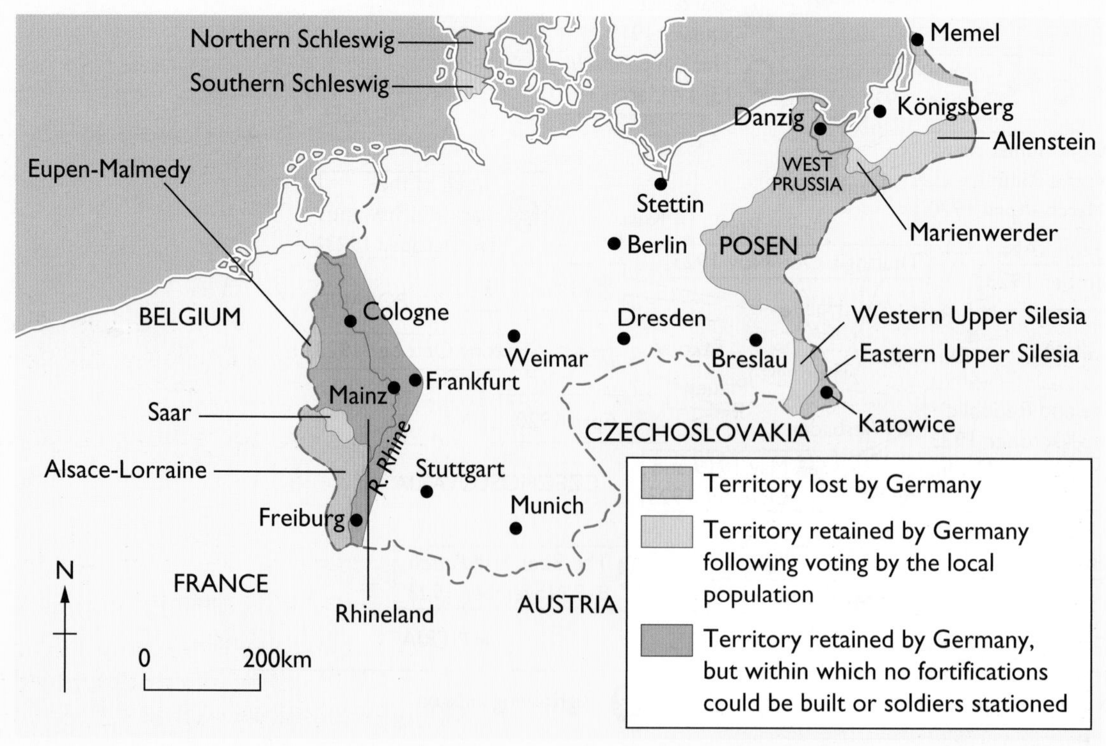

Source E Table showing some of the most important terms of the Treaty of Versailles

Territorial terms	Military terms	Financial terms
All **colonies** to be given to the Allied Powers.	Army not to exceed 100,000.	Coal to be mined in the Saar by France.
Alsace-Lorraine returned to France.	No tanks, armoured cars and heavy military permitted.	**Reparations** fixed at £6600 million.
Eupen-Malmedy given to Belgium after a **plebiscite**.	No military aircraft permitted.	Cattle and sheep to be given to Belgium and France as reparations.
Saar to be administered by the League of Nations.	No naval vessel to be greater than 10,000 tons.	Germany to build merchant ships to replace Allied ships sunk by U-boats.
Posen and West Prussia given to Poland, and Eastern Upper Silesia given to Poland after a plebiscite.	No submarines permitted.	
Danzig created a **Free City**.	Rhineland **demilitarised**.	
Memel to be administered by the League of Nations.		
No union (*Anschluss*) with Austria.		
Northern Schleswig given to Denmark after a plebiscite.		

Source F A cartoon entitled 'Clemenceau the Vampire' from the German right-wing satirical magazine, *Kladderadatsch*, published in July 1919. Clemenceau was the leader of France

TASKS

7 Study Source D. What does it tell you about German attitudes towards the signing of the Treaty of Versailles?

8 Use Source C and your own knowledge to explain why the Treaty of Versailles caused territorial problems for Germany. (For guidance on how to answer this type of question, see page 141.)

9 Explain why Article 231 was hated by most Germans.

10 Why was Source F published in July 1919? (For guidance on how to answer this type of question, see page 188.)

11 Work in groups of three or four. Choose either territorial, military or financial terms of the Treaty of Versailles. Present a case for the class indicating that your choice has the most important consequences for Germany.

Economic instability

When the Allies announced the reparations – £6600 million – the Weimar government claimed that it could not pay. Moreover, the loss of wealth-making industrial areas exaggerated the problem. Germany experienced a period of inflation and the Weimar government began to print more money in order to pay France and Belgium as well as its own workers. The value of the German currency started to fall rapidly and Germany failed to meet reparations payments. As a result French and Belgian forces occupied the Ruhr in 1923.

Source G Table showing the decreasing value of the German mark against the British pound, 1914–23

Jan 1919	£1 = 35 marks
Jan 1920	£1 = 256 marks
Jan 1921	£1 = 256 marks
Jan 1922	£1 = 764 marks
Jan 1923	£1 = 71,888 marks
July 1923	£1 = 1,413,648 marks
Sept 1923	£1 = 3,954,408,000 marks
Oct 1923	£1 = 1,010,408,000,000 marks
Nov 1923	£1 = 1,680,800,000,000,000 marks

When international confidence in the mark collapsed, what was already inflation became hyperinflation (see Source G). This was yet another humiliation for the Weimar government. However, in the summer of 1923, Gustav Stresemann became Chancellor and he began to steady things. He introduced a new currency called the *Rentenmark*, which was later converted into the *Reichsmark*. The following year, the new currency and loans from the USA enabled an economic recovery. It seemed as if the Weimar Republic had weathered the storms and could look forward to a period of stability and prosperity.

The recovery of the Weimar Republic, 1924–29

The recovery seemed to encourage greater support for the Weimar Republic and less support for extremist parties such as the Nazis and Communists. Stresemann was aware that Germany could still not afford the reparations payments and persuaded the French, British and Americans to lower them through the **Dawes Plan**, which was agreed in August 1924. The Dawes Plan made the payments more manageable and the USA agreed to give loans to Germany to help their economic recovery.

Further changes to the reparations came with the **Young Plan** in 1929 when payments were reduced by three-quarters and the length of time Germany had to pay was extended to 59 years.

The period 1924–29 saw greater political stability. Stresemann had been able to resolve many of the economic problems and, after the 1928 election, a new coalition was formed. It seemed as if the Weimar Republic could look forward to a period of prolonged stability. Moreover, in 1925 Hindenburg was elected President. He had been one of Germany's war leaders between 1914 and 1918, and his election seemed to show that the old conservative order now accepted the Republic. However, Germany's recovery depended on the prosperity of the USA.

TASKS

12 Study Source E. What does it tell you about inflation in Germany during the years 1919–23?

13 Explain why reparations were such a problem for Germany in the 1920s.

14 How successful was Gustav Stresemann in solving Germany's economic problems?

How did the Nazi Party develop, 1920–23?

The German Workers' Party

In 1919, in the atmosphere of political chaos (see page 107), Anton Drexler founded the German Workers' Party (*Deutsche Arbeiter Partei*, DAP) in Munich, Bavaria. This was a right-wing, nationalistic party, which stressed the *völkisch* idea – the notion of a pure German people. But DAP also had some socialist ideas, such as wanting a classless society and the restriction of company profits. It had only about 50 members by the end of 1919.

While working for the army intelligence unit, Adolf Hitler attended a meeting in September 1919 and became so angered by the comments made by one of the speakers that he made a powerful speech in reply. Drexler was so impressed by Hitler that he asked him to join the party.

In the DAP, Hitler discovered that he was good at public speaking. His enthusiasm was soon rewarded within the party by being made responsible for recruitment and propaganda.

Source A From a letter written by Hitler in 1921

During the Communist attempt to take over in Munich, I remained in the army ... In my talks as an education officer, I attacked the bloodthirsty Red dictatorship ... In 1919, I joined the German Workers' Party which then had seven members and I believed that I had found a political movement in keeping with my own ideas.

TASKS

1. What were the main ideas of the DAP?
2. Study Source A. What does it tell us about Hitler's political ideas in 1919?
3. Look at the speech bubbles around Hitler's head below. Copy these and then add two or three sentences explaining why Hitler chose to speak about each one.
4. Research: create a timeline of Hitler's life from 1889 to 1919. Select no more than ten important events.

The 25 Point Programme

In February 1920 Hitler and Drexler wrote what became known as the 25 Point Programme. It was a political manifesto and Hitler kept to most of the ideas throughout the rest of his life. The Programme was announced at a meeting in Munich and shortly after the words 'National Socialist' were added to the party's name, and it became **NSDAP**. The party grew rapidly in 1920 and Hitler was largely responsible for this – his public speaking attracted hundreds to meetings of the NSDAP. Increased membership meant the party was able to buy up and publish its own newspaper – the *Völkischer Beobachter* (People's Observer).

Hitler spoke at several meetings and his standard themes are shown in the illustration below.

Hitler's influence on the party was such that he became its leader in July 1921. He began to develop his ideas on how he should lead the party. He had the title '*Führer*' (leader) but he gradually developed the word to have a much more powerful meaning. For him, it meant that he had to have absolute power and authority in the party and he was answerable to no one. This was the ***Führerprinzip*** (the leadership principle) and became a cornerstone of the party organisation.

No. 1	The union of all Germans to form a Greater Germany.
No. 2	The scrapping of the Treaty of Versailles.
No. 4	Citizenship of the state to be granted only to people of German blood. Therefore no Jew was to be citizen of the nation.
No. 6	The right to vote in elections to be allowed only to German citizens.
No. 7	Foreign nationals to be deported if it became impossible to feed the entire population.
No. 8	All non-Germans who entered the country after 1914 to leave.
No. 13	The government to **nationalise** all businesses that had been formed into corporations.
No. 14	The government to profit-share in major industries.
No. 17	An end to all speculation in land and any land needed for communal purposes would be seized. There would be no compensation.
No. 23	All newspaper editors and contributors to be German, and non-German papers to appear only with permission of the government.
No. 24	Religious freedom for all – providing the views expressed did not threaten or offend German people.
No. 25	The creation of a strong central government for the *Reich* to put the new programme into effect.

Key features of the 25 Point Programme.

TASKS

5 Explain what is meant by the *Führerprinzip.*

6 Study the key features of the 25 Point Programme above. Copy the table below and insert which parts of the Programme relate to the particular area.

Treaty of Versailles	Race	Religion	Civil rights	Industry

7 Work in pairs. What does the 25 Point Programme tell you about the ideology of the early Nazi Party?

The *Sturmabteilung*

As leader of the Nazi Party, Hitler began to make some changes. He adopted the **swastika** as the emblem of the party, and the use of the raised arm salute. The political meetings in Munich at this time generated much violence and, in order to protect Nazi speakers, protection squads were used. These men were organised into the Gymnastic and Sports Section, which was developed into the *Sturmabteilung* (SA) in 1921, led by Ernst Röhm. The members of the SA were more commonly known as the 'Brownshirts' because of the colour of their uniform.

Early growth of the Nazi Party

During the period 1921–23 the SA was used to disrupt the meetings of the Social Democratic and Communist Parties. Hitler ensured that there was maximum publicity for his party and membership grew from about 1100 in June 1920 to about 55,000 in November 1923.

His speeches had the usual anti-Weimar criticisms, but also contained growing references to the purity of the German (or **Aryan**) race and vitriolic comments about Jews. For Hitler and his followers, the Jews were becoming the scapegoat for all Germany's problems. Although at this point the Nazi Party was essentially a regional organisation with its main support in Bavaria, this did not stop Hitler having national political aims.

When the economic and political crises of 1923 hit Germany, Hitler decided that the Nazi Party was in a position to overthrow the regional government in Munich and could then march on Berlin. Hitler detested the Weimar Republic and, following the invasion of the Ruhr by the French and the onset of hyperinflation, he felt that Weimar was now so disgraced it could easily be toppled. As the Nazi Party had grown in strength and popularity in Munich and Bavaria, Hitler decided his first step would be to seize control of Bavaria and then march on Berlin. He would then remove the weak Weimar politicians and form his own Nazi government.

Source B A member of the Nazi Party describing one of Hitler's speeches in 1922

My critical faculty was swept away. Leaning forward as if he were trying to force his inner self into the consciousness of all these thousands, he was holding the masses, and me with them, under a hypnotic spell by the sheer force of his belief … I forgot everything but the man; then glancing around, I saw that his magnetism was holding these thousands as one.

TASKS

8 How important were the SA to the Nazi Party?

9 Use Source B and your own knowledge to explain why support for Hitler increased during the early 1920s. (For guidance on how to answer this type of question, see page 141.)

It is believed that Hitler chose to depict the swastika in a white circle on a red background because white stood for nationalism and red for the worker. The swastika was chosen possibly because it was anti-Semitic and stood for the victory of the Aryan man

What were the consequences of the Munich *Putsch*, November 1923?

Reasons for the Munich *Putsch*, November 1923

As membership of the Nazi Party grew, and as he became a well-known figure in Bavarian politics, Hitler began to consider the idea of launching himself on to the national scene. He had been impressed by the seizure of power by Benito Mussolini in Italy in 1922. Mussolini, leader of the Italian National Fascist Party, had used his private army (the Blackshirts) to seize power after marching on the capital. Hitler saw that Mussolini had the support of the regular army and knew that he would have to win over the German army and navy (*Reichswehr*) if a march on Berlin took place.

The government of Bavaria, headed by Gustav von Kahr, along with the army chief von Lossow and police chief Seisser, had never fully supported Weimar. Hitler knew that if he could win the support of these three important men then an attack on Berlin was feasible.

The diagram below looks at the reasons for the *Putsch*.

Map showing Germany and Bavaria.

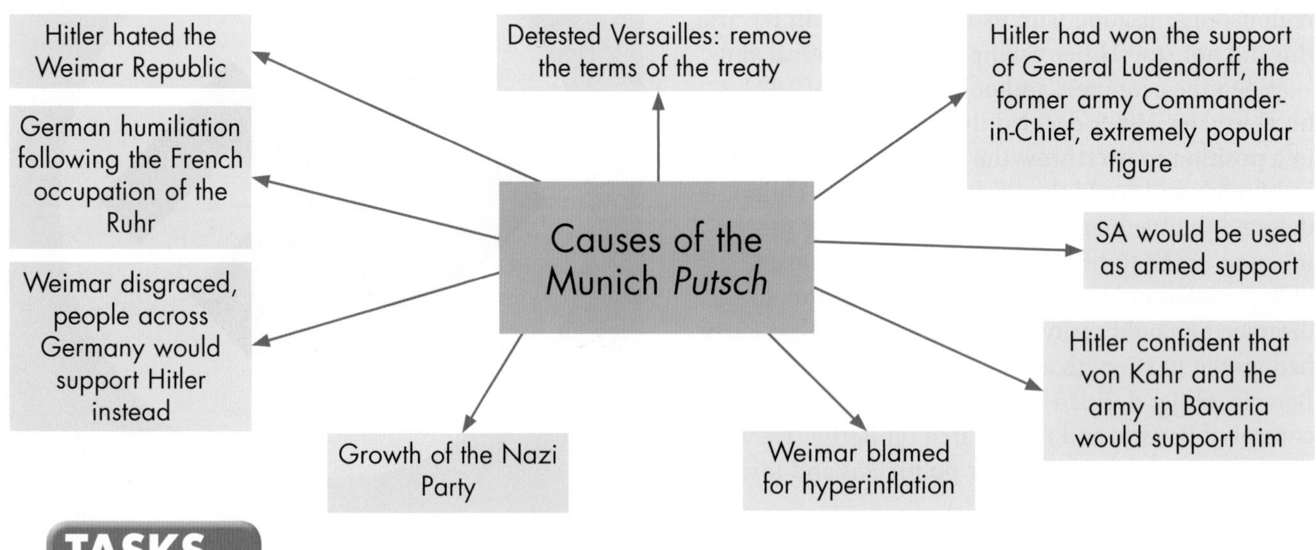

TASKS

1 Explain why Hitler thought he could secure national support in his attempt to seize power in 1923.

2 Study the diagram of the causes of the Munich *Putsch* above. Work in pairs to decide the rank order of importance of the causes. Explain the reasons behind your choice.

The events of the Munich *Putsch*

On the evening of 8 November 1923, Hitler and 600 Nazis seized the Burgerbräu Keller where von Kahr, von Seisser and von Lossow were attending a meeting. Hitler placed the three leaders in a room and won promises of support for his planned takeover from them after they had been held at gunpoint. This and the events that followed are known as the Munich *Putsch*. Remarkably, the three were allowed to leave the building. However, the following day von Seisser and von Lossow changed their minds and organised troops and police to resist Hitler's planned armed march through Munich.

Source A Hitler's announcement at the beginning of the *Putsch* on 9 November 1923

Proclamation to the German people! The Government of the November Criminals in Berlin has today been deposed. A provisional [temporary] German National Government has been formed, this consists of General Ludendorff, Adolf Hitler and Colonel von Seisser.

Source B Armed SA men at a barricade in Munich, 9 November 1923. The future leader of the SS, Heinrich Himmler, is holding the Second Reich flag (pre-1918) in the middle of the photograph

Despite his plans having fallen apart, Hitler continued with the march through Munich. However, the Nazis had only about 2000 rifles and when they were challenged they were no match for the well-armed police force. As the two opposing forces met, shots were fired and sixteen Nazis and four policemen were killed. The incident was soon over and the Nazis scattered. Hitler disappeared but was arrested two days later, the same day that the Nazi Party was banned.

TASKS

3 What do Sources A and B suggest about the Munich *Putsch*? (For guidance on how to answer this type of question, see page 132.)

4 Describe the events of the Munich *Putsch*. (For guidance on how to answer this type of question, see page 175.)

5 How successful was the Munich *Putsch*?

Hitler's trial and imprisonment

Hitler was arrested along with his main supporter General Ludendorff and was tried for treason. The trial began in February 1924 and lasted almost one month. The trial gave Hitler nationwide publicity and introduced him to the German public via the national press. He denied the charge of treason. He insisted that he was simply attempting to restore Germany's greatness and was resisting the weak and feeble Weimar government. He poured scorn on the November Criminals, the Treaty of Versailles and those Jewish **Bolshevists** who had betrayed Germany. He attacked Weimar at every available opportunity and used the trial to put forward his political views. The sympathetic judges allowed him to make long speeches which were then reported in national newspapers. Hitler became famous in Germany.

Hitler was found guilty of treason but the judges treated him leniently and sentenced him to five years in prison, the minimum sentence. Ludendorff was not charged.

On 1 April, Hitler was sentenced to five years to be served in Landsberg prison. He served only nine months. Whilst there he completed his autobiography *Mein Kampf* (My Struggle), which also contained his political views (see diagram below). The sentence allowed him time to reflect on the *Putsch* and his future in politics. Historians now believe it was in Landsberg that Hitler came to the conclusion that he was the leader needed to make Germany great again. He had a relatively easy time in jail and was permitted as many visitors as he wanted. He received large amounts of mail and was able to access whatever books he wanted.

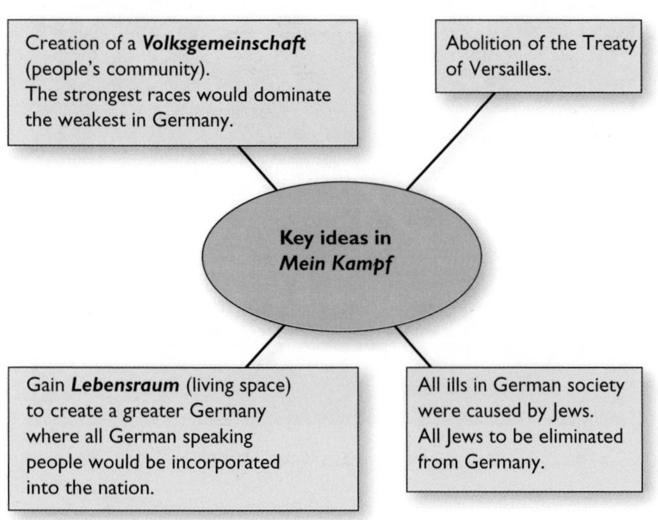

Source C The main defendants in the trial following the *Putsch*. Left to right – H Pernet, F Weber, Wilhelm Frick, H Kriebel, General Ludendorff, Adolf Hitler, W Bruckner, Ernst Röhm, R Wagner

Source D From the *Rise and Fall of the Third Reich* by William Shirer, an American journalist who lived in Berlin in the 1930s

Hitler was shrewd enough to see that his trial would provide a new platform from which he could for the first time make his name known far beyond Bavaria and indeed Germany ... By the time it ended ... Hitler had transformed defeat into triumph ... impressed the German people by his eloquence and the fervour of his nationalism, and emblazoned his name on the front pages of the world.

Source E Comments made by Hitler as a prisoner in Landsberg. He was speaking to a fellow Nazi inmate

When I resume active work, it will be necessary to follow a new policy. Instead of working to achieve power by armed conspiracy, we shall have to hold our noses and enter parliament against the Catholic and Communist members. If outvoting them takes longer than out-shooting them, at least the results will be guaranteed by their own Constitution. Sooner or later, we shall have a majority in parliament ...

TASKS

6 Study Source C. What does it show you about who was involved in the Munich Putsch?

7 Use Source D and your own knowledge to explain why the trial was so important for Hitler. (For guidance on how to answer this type of question, see page 141.)

8 Study Source E. What does it tell us about Hitler's attitude towards the failure at the Putsch?

9 Design an advertisement for *Mein Kampf*. Focus on why it is important for Germans to read, how it shows Hitler's ideas and how it will change people's opinions.

How did the Nazi Party change, 1924–29?

The fortunes of the Nazi Party declined when Hitler was in prison. It had been banned but survived secretly. The replacement leader, Alfred Rosenberg, had few leadership qualities and the party split into rival groups. On release from prison, Hitler was able to persuade the President of Bavaria to lift the ban on the Nazi Party. In February 1924, the Nazi Party was relaunched and Hitler slowly began to take control once again. This meant making changes to the party and its structure. Hitler made sure that only his closest associates helped run the party from Munich and these people and the *Gauleiter* (local party leaders) pushed the idea of the *Führerprinzip* (see page 112).

At the Bamberg Party Conference in 1926, Hitler continued to strengthen his position as leader of the party. Possible rivals to Hitler's leadership such as Gregor Strasser and Josef Goebbels were won over. Strasser was appointed Party Propaganda Leader and Goebbels was made *Gauleiter* of Berlin. Other opponents were removed. For example, Hitler forced Röhm to resign as leader of the SA because he was concerned that the SA would continue to be a violent group. He could not guarantee that Röhm would follow his orders. The new leader of the SA was Ernst von Salomon. Hitler then created his own bodyguard, the *Schutzstaffel*, which became more well known as the SS. One further change at this time was the introduction of the HitlerJugend (**Hitler Youth**), which was set up to rival other youth groups.

Hitler was now the undisputed leader – *'Der Führer'* – and his message was to use endless propaganda to win over the voters. The 25 Point Programme of 1920 was accepted as the cornerstone of Nazi Party policy. However, in 1928, Point 17 (see page 112) was amended to say that privately owned land would be confiscated only if it was owned by a Jew. Before 1928, Hitler had tried to win the support of the urban voters but now he decided that the rural voters should be targeted also. This came at the time when farmers began to experience economic problems and found Nazism attractive.

Hitler's leadership and reorganisation of the party paid dividends. The party had only 27,000 members in 1925 but this figure exceeded 100,000 by the end of 1928. It was a nationwide party which had begun to attract all classes. Yet, despite the changes, the Nazis won only 12 seats in parliament in the 1928 elections, having held 32 in 1924.

There were further changes within the Nazi Party in the late 1920s when Hitler began to target the peasants as a key electoral group. He also replaced Strasser as Party Propaganda Leader with Goebbels.

However, it was events in the USA which propelled the Nazi Party to the forefront of politics in Germany. The Wall Street Crash in 1929 (see page 120) created an economic blizzard and as unemployment began to rise in Germany, so did the fortunes of the Nazi Party. The 'lean years' were at an end. Hitler and the Nazis were in power only four years after the Crash.

TASKS

1 Explain why the Bamberg Conference was important for Hitler.

2 Describe the development of the Nazi Party between 1924 and 1929. (For guidance on how to answer this type of question, see page 175.)

3 Create an election poster for the Nazi Party for 1928, showing that it has changed since the Munich *Putsch*.

4 To what extent was hatred of the Treaty of Versailles the most important problem facing the Weimar government in the 1920s?

> In your answer you should discuss the seriousness of the many problems facing the Weimar government including the hatred of the Treaty of Versailles.

(For guidance on how to answer this type of question, see pages 195–96.)

Examination guidance

Here is an opportunity for you to practise some of the questions that have appeared in this and the following chapters. The questions cover all the questions that appear on the Unit One examination paper and are worth 53 marks in total. The first question is here, the other two are on page 210.

Question 1

This question is focused on the rise to power of the Nazis.

Source A A photograph of Hitler addressing a mass rally of Nazi Party members in 1932

Source B A report written by a member of the Social Democratic Party in Berlin (February 1932)

Several of the meetings have been disrupted and a considerable section of the audience had to be taken away badly injured. I urgently request the cancellation of the meeting with me as speaker. As things are, there is obviously no longer any police protection able to stop the aggressive actions of the SA.

(a) What do Sources A and B suggest about the methods used by the Nazis in their rise to power? (4 marks)

● For guidance, see page 132.

(b) Use Source C and your own knowledge to explain why the Great Depression had a serious impact on life in Germany in the early 1930s. (6 marks)

● For guidance, see page 141.

Source C From a school history textbook

After 1929 there was a terrible economic crisis in Germany which developed into the Great Depression. Unemployment soared and prices of agricultural products and consumer goods fell sharply causing financial hardship for farmers, small businesses and the self-employed. The Great Depression brought misery to millions of Germans. This explains why so many people started to vote for the extremist parties.

Source D An election poster from July 1932. It shows a National Socialist German worker towering over his political enemies – Jews and Communists

Source E Josef Goebbels, a leading Nazi, writing in his diary (24 March, 1933)

Today, the Leader (Adolf Hitler) delivered an address to the German Reichstag. He was in good form. His speech was that of an expert statesman. Many in the House saw him for the first time, and were much impressed by him. The Leader spoke freely and well. The House was in an uproar of applause, laughter, and enthusiasm. He was an incredible success!

(c) How useful are Sources D and E to an historian studying the reasons why the Nazi Party gained support in Germany? (8 marks)

● For guidance, see pages 155–56

How and why did Hitler get appointed Chancellor in January 1933?

Source A From 'A Fairytale of Christmas' by Rudolf Leonhard (1931), a member of the **KPD** (Communist Party). Leonhard was writing about the unemployed in Germany

No one knew how many of them there were. They completely filled the streets ... They stood or lay about in the streets as if they had taken root there. The streets were grey, their faces were grey, and even the hair on their heads and the stubble on the cheeks of the youngest there were grey with dust and their adversity.

TASK

Study Source A. What does it tell us about unemployment in Germany in 1931?.

Germany was able to recover under Stresemann and for many citizens there were five years of prosperity. Nevertheless, some were experiencing problems by 1928, namely farmers. Even Stresemann realised that the German economy was 'dancing on a volcano'. However, the Wall Street Crash in October of 1929 was to have immediate and far-reaching consequences. The Crash led to the Great Depression in the USA, which then spread around the world. US loans to Germany were called in and unemployment in Germany began to rise as companies collapsed. By 1932, there were about 6 million unemployed and the Weimar government had had to invoke Article 48 of the constitution (see page 106). The economic problems led to political discontent and extreme parties were able to secure support in the elections. By 1932, the Nazi Party had become the largest party in Germany and, following endless political scheming amongst leading politicians such as Brüning, von Papen, von Schleicher and Hindenburg, Hitler became Chancellor of Germany in January 1933.

This chapter answers the following questions:

- What was the impact of the Wall Street Crash and the Great Depression?
- Why was the Nazi Party successful after 1930?
- What was the role of Hitler in increasing support for the Nazis?
- How did the events of July 1932 to January 1933 bring Hitler to power?

Examination guidance

Throughout this chapter you will be given the opportunity to practise different exam-style questions and detailed guidance on how to answer question 1(a). This requires you to select and organise relevant information from two sources. It is worth 4 marks.

What was the impact of the Wall Street Crash and the Great Depression?

Source A From *Slump! A Study of Stricken Europe Today* written by H H Tiltman, a US journalist, 1932

Where two Englishmen will, in nine cases out of ten, begin a conversation by discussing sport, two Germans will ask each other why they and their families should go hungry in a world stuffed with food ... This explains the keen interest which all classes in Germany are taking in politics ... When men and women in their tens of thousands will sit for hours listening to National Socialists, Socialists and Communists, it means that politics have become a matter of bread and butter.

TASK

1 Study Source A. What does it suggest about the political situation in Germany in 1932?

The impact of the economic crisis on the German people

By 1929, much of Germany had experienced five years of prosperity. The loans from the USA had helped to remove inflation and there had been much investment in industry. However, the prosperity depended on the USA and when its **stock market** collapsed in October 1929, the problems created there had huge consequences for the German economy. The death of Stresemann that year also added to the crisis. Many Germans had thought that he was the only person who would be able to steer Germany through troubled times again.

Bankers and financiers in the USA now withdrew the loans made under the Dawes Plan to Germany in 1924. International trade began to contract and German exports fell rapidly in the years after 1929. The Great **Depression** had arrived in Germany. Unemployment began to rise as employers sacked workers and factories closed. German farmers had already been experiencing problems and the continued fall in food prices worsened their plight. Some Germans were unable to pay their rents and found themselves living on the streets.

The government financed unemployment relief, but as its revenue began to shrink, the threat of benefit cuts loomed large. The unemployed and hungry wanted solutions and looked to political parties such as the Nazis, which they believed would be able to relieve their suffering.

Source B Graph showing unemployment in Germany, 1928–32

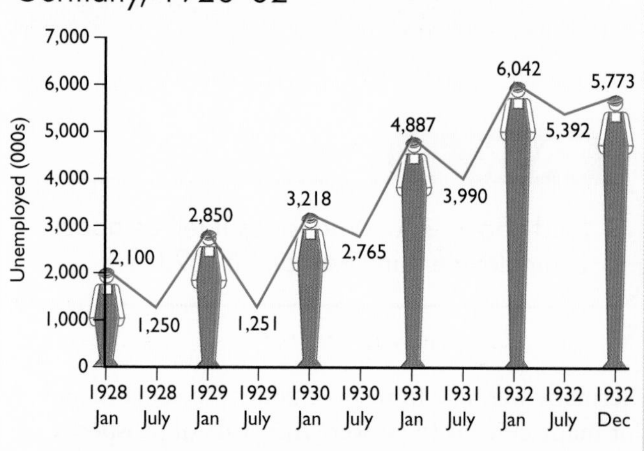

Unemployment continued to rise in the early 1930s and by early 1932 the total figure exceeded 6 million. This meant that four out of every ten German workers were without jobs. Unlike 1923 the fear in Germany this time was not inflation, it was unemployment. If a political party could offer clear and simple solutions to the economic problems, it would readily win votes. The workers wanted jobs and the middle classes feared a communist revolution like the one that had occurred in Russia in 1917. The German Communist Party (KPD) was growing and, like the Nazis, promised a way out of the Depression.

Source C Unemployed in Hanover, queuing for their benefits 1932. Note the writing on the wall of the building. Translated it says 'Vote Hitler'

TASKS

2 What do Sources B and C suggest about the situation in Germany in 1932? (For guidance on how to answer this type of question, see page 132.)

3 Describe the impact of the economic crisis of the early 1930s upon the German people. (For guidance on how to answer this type of question, see page 175.)

4 Construct a mind map to show the effects of the Depression on Germany.

5 Study Source D. What does it tell you about democracy in Weimar Germany in the years 1930–32?

The impact of the economic crisis on the Weimar government

The economic crisis created problems for the Weimar government and there was little agreement about how to tackle unemployment and poverty. In March 1930, Chancellor Muller was replaced by Heinrich Brüning of the Centre Party. Brüning did not have a majority as the Weimar Constitution demanded, and he had to rely on President Hindenburg using Article 48 (see page 106). From this point on, the *Reichstag* (parliament) was used less frequently. Many historians view this as the death of Weimar and the end of parliamentary democracy.

Source D The role of the *Reichstag* and the President, 1930–32

	1930	1931	1932
Presidential decrees	5	44	66
Reichstag laws	98	34	5
Reichstag: days sitting	94	42	13

Because Brüning did not have a majority in the *Reichstag*, he called a general election in September 1930. It was this election that gave the Nazis their breakthrough. They won 107 seats and became the second biggest party in Germany after the Social Democrats (SPD) who won 143 seats. Brüning could still not rely on having his policies accepted in the *Reichstag* and he came to depend more and more on President Hindenburg (see Source D, page 121).

Brüning's reduction of government spending only served to lose him support of the unemployed and led to him being nicknamed the 'hunger Chancellor'. The people of Germany were extremely tired of shortages of food – and were now experiencing shortages for the third time in sixteen years. Brüning was also blamed for foreign investors withdrawing assets from Germany. Moreover, during the banking crisis of 1931 when some German banks collapsed, potential investors were frightened off. Some foreign governments were willing to loan money to Germany but their terms were unacceptable. The only encouraging consequence of the economic crisis was the suspension of reparations payments, but this did not come until 1931. The economic situation remained bleak.

Brüning was unable to win support for his policies and so he resigned in May 1932. During his time as Chancellor, the right-wing Nazi Party had had successes in the regional and general elections. Moreover, during the next eight months there was continued political and economic turmoil which saw the extreme parties become more violent. Some of the changes brought in by Brüning had made some improvements but it was too little, too late.

The Depression seemed to have unleashed chaos across Germany, resulting in Hitler becoming Chancellor in January 1933.

Source E A German Communist Party (KPD) election poster from 1932. Translated, it reads 'Away with the system'

Source F From *The Past is Myself* written in 1968 by Christabel Bielenberg, an Englishwoman who lived in Germany under the Nazis. Here, she is remembering a conversation with Herr Neisse, her gardener

Then came 1929 and economic trouble, and a huge wave rolled over Europe and America leaving a trail of bankruptcies. Herr Neisse lost the chance to own a vegetable stall and he lost his job. He joined an army of 6 million unemployed ... **Communism** *did not appeal to him ... he just wanted to belong somewhere. National Socialism was more like it. He began to go to Nazi Party meetings ... he was told that the Jews were the evil root of all Germany's problems. Although he knew of the corruption of party members he believed Hitler knew nothing of it. Neisse said 'Hitler loves children and dogs too.'*

TASKS

6 Explain why some Germans opposed Brüning's economic policies.

7 Study Source E. Explain why the KPD was attractive to many Germans.

8 Use Source F and your own knowledge to explain why Some German people were attracted to the Nazi Party. (For guidance on how to answer this type of question, see page 141.)

9 Work as a group of three or four. Imagine you are setting up a political party in Germany in 1932. Make a list of the key points you would highlight in order to appeal to as many German citizens as possible. Design posters:
a) to show your political beliefs
b) to attack Chancellor Brüning.

Why was the Nazi Party successful after 1930?

The role of Josef Goebbels

During the years 1929–33 the Nazis increased their support through propaganda. They did this in a variety of ways, such as having mass rallies, placing posters in prominent places and displaying banners wherever possible so that the Nazis appeared to be everywhere.

The Nazis were most fortunate in having a person who understood how to use the mass media and also manipulate huge audiences. Josef Goebbels ensured that the Nazi message was simple and frequently repeated. By the early 1930s, the Nazis owned 120 daily or weekly newspapers that were regularly read by hundreds of thousands of people across the country. As Germany descended into political chaos in 1930–32, Goebbels was able to present the Nazi Party in local, regional, national and presidential elections. The Nazi message was heard everywhere, especially on the radio.

Source A Nazi election poster, 1932. The text reads 'Work and Bread'. The poster shows all the kinds of tools being given out, showing the Nazis would help all kinds of workers

Source B Nazi Party election poster, 1930. The words at the top read 'List 9 National Socialist German Workers' Party'. Some of the words coming from the snake are: money-lending, Versailles, unemployment, war guilt lie, Bolshevism, inflation and terror

TASK

1 Study Sources A and B. Explain:
- **a)** Which groups of people would be attracted to the Nazis by these posters.
- **b)** The reasons why the Nazis were attractive.
- **c)** How useful are the sources as evidence of the reasons why people voted for the Nazis?

Success in the elections

When Chancellor Brüning called a general election in 1930, he was hoping to secure a clear majority for his Centre Party. However, the impact of the Wall Street Crash and the developing Depression disrupted the political situation. Unemployment had hit all classes and thus Hitler and the Nazis tried to appeal to all sections of society. The Nazi message was that Weimar had caused the economic crisis and the weak coalition governments had no real solutions to offer. The Nazis alone could unite Germany in a time of economic crisis.

The Nazis then played on the resentment of the Treaty of Versailles. The old wounds were reopened and Germany's problems were blamed on the November Criminals and the Weimar Republic. Only the Nazis could restore Germany to its former glory.

If there were any who doubted the simple Nazi messages, then Hitler ensured that another scapegoat could be offered. He blamed the Jews for Germany's problems saying they:

- were involved not only with communism but also the evils of capitalism
- had helped to cause unemployment
- had conspired in Germany's defeat in the Great War
- had been involved in the Bolshevik Revolution
- were preparing to cause a revolution in Germany, which would mean that all private property and wealth would be seized by the state.

Source C An extract from *Mein Kampf*, Hitler's autobiography written in 1924

Propaganda must confine itself to a very few points and repeat them endlessly. Here, as with so many things in this world, persistence is the first and foremost condition of success.

The 1930 election proved to be the breakthrough for Hitler and the Nazi Party (see Source D). For Brüning, the election meant that he still had to rely on other parties and, moreover, he continued to rely on Hindenburg and Article 48 (see page 106).

TASKS

2 Use Source C and your own knowledge to explain why the use of propaganda was important to the Nazi Party. (For guidance on how to answer this type of question, see page 141.)

3 Study Source D. Describe how the Nazi Party had increased its support by September 1930.

Source D Table showing *Reichstag* seats after the elections of May 1928 and September 1930

Political party	May 1928	September 1930
Social Democratic Party (SPD)	153	143
National Party (DNVP)	73	41
Nazi Party (NSDAP)	12	107
Centre Party (ZP)	62	68
Communist Party (KPD)	54	77
People's Party (DVP)	45	30
Democratic Party (DDP)	25	20

The presidential election 1932

During the presidential election of 1932, when Hitler stood against Hindenburg, the Nazis were quick to use modern technology. For example, by using the aeroplane Hitler was able to speak at as many as five cities on the same day, flying from one venue to the next. Goebbels ensured that there were mass rallies and that not only was the Nazi message being spread, but also that Hitler was being recognised as a national political figure. The message was put over in films, on the radio and even on records. Goebbels mastered the art of propaganda in these years. President Hindenburg did not campaign.

Hindenburg just failed to win more than 50 per cent of the votes in the election and so there had to be a second round of voting. Hitler was quite successful in winning a large number of votes in each round, though he himself was quite disappointed at his showing. Goebbels presented the presidential defeat as a victory because of the huge vote for Hitler and the overall percentage of votes won.

The tactics used by Hitler and Goebbels were paying off and there was greater success in the *Reichstag* elections in July 1932 (see page 130). Goebbels ensured that the German people were given positive images of Hitler and the Nazis. He also continued to play on their fears, particularly their fear of communism.

Source E The cover photograph of the book *'Hitler über Deutschland'* (Hitler over Germany), published in Germany in 1932

Source F A Nazi election poster of 1932. It says 'Our last hope – Hitler'

Candidate	First round	Second round
Hindenburg	18,650,000	19,360,000
Hitler (NSDAP)	11,340,000	13,420,000
Thälmann (KPD)	4,968,000	3,710,000

Results of the presidential election.

Source G A Nazi poster of 1932. It says 'We farmers are getting rid of the dung – we are voting Nazi'. The dung represents Jews and socialists

Source H From a Nazi election leaflet of 1932

The German farmer stands in between two great dangers today – one is the American capitalist system and the other is the Marxist economic system of **BOLSHEVISM.** Capitalism and Bolshevism work hand in hand; they are born of Jewish thought and serve the master plan of Jews all over the world. Who alone can save the farmer from these dangers?

NATIONAL SOCIALISM

TASKS

4 Describe the methods used by Goebbels to win people over to Nazism. (For guidance on how to answer this question, see page 175.)

5 Study Source E. What does it show you about Hitler's campaigning methods in the early 1930s?

6 Study Sources F, G and H. In each case:
  a) explain who the target audience is
  b) describe the methods being used to attract their support
  c) explain how the sources support each other about the reasons why people voted for Hitler.

7 Re-read pages 123–126, then look at the table below. Complete the boxes, giving at least one reason to show how the Nazis could appeal to different groups of society at the same time.

Working classes	
Farmers	
Middle classes	
Upper classes	

Financial support for the Nazis

Hitler and the Nazis could not have conducted their campaigns without financial backers. One example of how funds were crucial came in 1932, when 600,000 copies of the economic programme were produced and distributed in the July *Reichstag* election. The Nazi Party received funds from leading industrialists such as Thyssen, Krupp and Bosch. These **industrialists** were terrified of the communist threat and were also concerned at the growth of **trade union** power. They knew that Hitler hated communism and that he would reduce the influence of the unions.

Furthermore, by 1932 the Nazis had begun to develop close links with the National Party (DNVP). The DNVP leader, Alfred Hugenberg, was a newspaper tycoon, and permitted the Nazis to publish articles which attacked Chancellor Brüning. Hence, Goebbels was able to continue the nationwide campaign against Weimar and keep the Nazis in the forefront of people's minds.

Source I An anti-Hitler poster by a communist, John Heartfield. Born Helmut Herzfeld, he changed his name as a protest against the Nazis. He fled Germany in 1933. The caption reads 'The meaning of the Hitler salute. Motto: millions stand behind me! Little man asks for big gifts'

The *Sturmabteilung* (SA)

In his speeches, Hitler claimed that parliamentary democracy did not work and said that only he and the NSDAP could provide the strong government that Germany needed. The Nazis used their private army, *Sturmabteilung* (SA), not only to provide protection for their meetings but also to disrupt the meetings of their opponents, especially the Communists. Hitler reappointed Ernst Röhm as leader of the SA in January 1931 and within a year its membership had increased by 100,000 to 170,000. These men were the 'bully boy thugs' of the Party who loved to engage in street fights with the political opposition.

The Communists had their own private army (*Die Rotfrontkämpfer* – Red Front Fighters) and there were countless fights between them and the SA. On many occasions, there were fatalities. Hitler sought to show the German people that he could stamp out the Communist violence and their threat of revolution. The SA also attacked and intimidated any overt opponents of the Nazis.

Source K A battle between SA members and Communist Red Front Fighters in 1932. The signs read 'Up the Revolution' and 'Free the political prisoners'

Source J Results of the July 1932 general election

Political party	Number of *Reichstag* seats	Percentage of vote
Nazis (NSDAP)	230	37.4
Social Democrats (SPD)	133	21.6
Communist Party (KPD)	89	14.3
Centre Party (ZP)	75	12.5
National Party (DNVP)	37	5.9
People's Party (DVP)	7	1.2
Democratic Party (DDP)	4	1.0

TASKS

8 Why was Source I produced in 1932? (For guidance on how to answer this type of question, see page 188.)

9 Explain why the Nazi Party increased its financial support before the 1932 election.

10 Use Source K and your own knowledge to explain why the political scene in Germany was becoming more violent during the early 1930s. (For guidance on how to answer this type of question, see page 141.)

11 How important were the SA in Hitler's rise to power?

12 Study Source D on page 124 and Source J opposite. What were the main voting trends over the three general elections?

What was the role of Hitler in increasing support for the Nazis?

Hitler had developed the art of public speaking in the early days of the NSDAP and his speeches always attracted many people and helped increase the membership of the Nazi Party. He helped to draw up the 25 Point Programme (see page 112) and he was fully aware that after the *Putsch* he had to present himself and his party as law abiding and democratic. He also knew that he had to be able to offer something to all groups in German society if he was to be successful in any elections. He never lost sight of these points during the two years before he became leader of Germany.

Hitler could be all things to all people. He was the war hero, the saviour and the ordinary man in the street. The image created was that his whole existence was given over to Germany and there were no distractions to prevent him achieving his goals. He had created a philosophy that all could comprehend. Furthermore, his vision of the future revolved around making Germany the strongest nation in the world. Hitler had the one characteristic which most other politicians lacked – charisma.

Source A Part of a speech made by Hitler in Munich, August 1923

The day must come when a German government will summon up the courage to say to the foreign powers: 'The Treaty of Versailles is founded on a monstrous lie. We refuse to carry out its terms any longer. Do what you will! If you want war, go and get it! Then we shall see if you can turn 70 million Germans into slaves!' Either Germany sinks ... or else we dare to enter on the fight against death and the devil ...

Source B Nazi Party rally in Nuremberg, 1927

Source C From *Inside the Third Reich* by Albert Speer, written in 1970. Speer was recalling a meeting in Berlin in 1930 at which Hitler spoke. Speer was a university lecturer and later became Minister of Armaments in Nazi Germany

I was carried away on a wave of enthusiasm (by the speech) … the speech swept away any scepticism, any reservations. Opponents were given no chance to speak … Here, it seemed to me, was hope. Here were new ideals, a new understanding, new tasks. The peril of communism, which seemed inevitably on its way, could be stopped, Hitler persuaded us, and instead of hopeless unemployment, Germany could move to economic recovery.

Source D Adapted from the diary of Luise Solmitz, 23 March 1932. A schoolteacher, Solmitz was writing about attending a meeting in Hamburg at which Hitler spoke

There stood Hitler in a simple black coat, looking over the crowd of 120,000 people of all classes and ages … a forest of swastika flags unfurled, the joy of this moment showed itself in a roaring salute … The crowd looked up to Hitler with touching faith, as their helper, their saviour, their deliverer from unbearable distress … He is the rescuer of the scholar, the farmer, the worker and the unemployed.

TASKS

1 Use Source A and your own knowledge to explain why many Germans decided to vote for the Nazi Party. (For guidance on how to answer this type of question, see page 141.)

2 How useful are Sources C and D to an historian studying why people were attracted into voting for the Nazi Party? (For guidance on how to answer this type of question, see pages 155–56.)

3 Study Sources B and F. What do these sources show you about Hitler and the Nazi Party?

4 Study Source E. Why would the Nazi Party want this to be shown all over Germany?

5 Construct a mind map to show why the Nazis had become so popular by July 1932.

Source E A photograph taken to show Hitler's love of children

Source F A portrait of Hitler painted in 1933 by B Von Jacobs

How did the events of July 1932 to January 1933 bring Hitler to power?

Hitler had been quite successful in the presidential elections in March and April 1932. He was now the leader of the second largest party in the *Reichstag* and was well known across Germany. When a general election was called for 31 July 1932, the Nazis were optimistic about improving on the number of votes they had won in the previous election of September 1930.

There was much violence in the run-up to the election. About 100 people were killed and more than 1125 wounded in clashes between the political parties. On 17 July there were at least nineteen people killed in Hamburg.

More people voted in July than in any previous Weimar election. The Nazis won 230 seats and were now the largest party in the *Reichstag* (see Source K, page 127). However, Chancellor von Papen of the Centre Party, despite not having won the most seats, did not relinquish his post and began to scheme with President Hindenburg. Hitler demanded the post of Chancellor and, at a meeting with Hitler in August, Hindenburg refused to contemplate Hitler as Chancellor, even if he did lead the largest party in the *Reichstag*.

Source A From the book *Hitler, 1889–1936: Hubris* by Professor I Kershaw, a specialist historian writing in 1998

At the meeting in August, Hindenburg refused Hitler the Chancellorship. He could not answer, he said, before God, his conscience and the Fatherland if he handed over the entire power of the government to a single party and one which was so intolerant towards those with different views.

It was not possible for any party to command a majority in the *Reichstag* and it was impossible to maintain a coalition. Von Papen dissolved the *Reichstag* in September 1932 and new elections were set for early November the same year. Von Papen held the opinion that the Nazis were losing momentum and if he held on they would slowly disappear from the scene. He was correct about them losing momentum, as the results of the November general election showed.

Biography Paul von Hindenburg 1846–1934

1846 Born in Posen
1866 Joined the Prussian army
1870–71 Fought in the Franco-Prussian War
1903 Reached the rank of general
1914 Commanded German armies in East Prussia. Victorious at the Battles of Tannenberg and Masurian Lakes
1916 Made Chief of General Staff
1918 Retired from the army
1919 Put forward the *Dolchstoss* theory (see page 108)
1925–34 President of the Weimar Republic

Political scheming

However, von Papen still could not secure a majority in the *Reichstag*. At the same time, Hitler continued to demand the post of Chancellor on the grounds that the Nazi Party was the biggest in the *Reichstag*. When von Papen suggested abolishing the Weimar Constitution, von Schleicher, the Minister of Defence, persuaded Hindenburg that if this happened there might be civil war.

Source B November 1932 *Reichstag* election results

Political party	Number of seats	Percentage of vote
Nazis (NSDAP)	196	33.1
Social Democrats (SPD)	121	20.4
Communist Party (KPD)	100	16.9
Centre Party (ZP)	70	11.9
National Party (DNVP)	52	8.8
People's Party (DVP)	11	1.9
Democratic Party (DDP)	2	1.0

Von Papen lost Hindenburg's confidence and resigned. He was succeeded by von Schleicher. Von Schleicher hoped to attain a majority in the *Reichstag* by forming a so-called *Querfront*, meaning 'cross-front', whereby he would bring together different strands from left and right parties.

Von Papen was determined to regain power and so he met with Hitler in early January 1933. It was decided that Hitler should lead a **Nazi-Nationalist government** with von Papen as the Vice-Chancellor. Scheming and plotting now took the place of considered open political debate. The army, major landowners and leaders of industry were convinced that von Papen and Hitler were saving Germany from Schleicher's plans and a possible Communist takeover. The idea that von Schleicher's government might include some socialists was appalling to them.

Source C Cartoon from the British magazine, *Punch*, January 1933, which shows Hitler being carried on the shoulders of Hindenburg and von Papen

Von Papen was able to convince President Hindenburg that a coalition government with Hitler as Chancellor would save Germany and bring stability to the country. Von Papen said that he would be able to control Hitler – 'he would make Hitler squeak'.

On 30 January 1933, Adolf Hitler became Chancellor of Germany. He was the leader of the largest party and he had been invited to be leader by the president. He had achieved his aim of becoming Chancellor by legal and democratic means.

TASKS

1. Use Source A and your own knowledge to explain why Hindenburg refused to appoint Hitler Chancellor in 1932. (For guidance on how to answer this type of question, see page 141.)
2. Compare the results of the July and November 1932 elections. Explain how and why they differ. (The results of the July elections are on page 127.)
3. Why was the cartoon (Source C) published in January 1933? (For guidance on how to answer this type of question, see page 188.)
4. Re-read pages 130–31. The events of 1932 are complex. To simplify things, complete the table below. In each box write the main actions of the individual from mid-1932 to 1933.

Hitler	von Papen	von Schleicher	Hindenburg

5. To what extent was political scheming in 1932–33 the most important reason for Hitler becoming Chancellor of Germany?

In your answer you should discuss the importance of various reasons which helped Hitler to become Chancellor, including the political scheming of 1932–33.

(For guidance on how to answer this type of question, see pages 195–96.)

Examination guidance

This section provides guidance on how to answer a source comprehension question. This requires you to select and organise relevant information from two sources. It is worth 4 marks.

What do Source A [Source F on page 125] and Source B suggest about why support for the Nazis increased after 1929? (4 marks)

Source B An extract from a school textbook (2003)

After 1929 unemployment figures began to rise sharply, reaching a peak of just over 6 million by 1932. The result was social misery on a large scale, which affected people of all classes. In desperation people increasingly began to turn to the extreme parties and support for the communists and Nazis greatly increased.

Comment on candidate performance

The candidate has made a number of valid observations based upon both sources and has displayed an understanding of how the worsening economic situation helped to achieve a growth in support for the extreme parties like the Nazis. Historical context is provided through reference to the failure of the Brüning government to put forward effective plans to cut the rapid rise in unemployment. At least two relevant points are extracted from each source and discussed in some detail. Both sources are afforded equal weighting and this, together with an informed discussion, makes the answer worthy of maximum (4) marks.

Tips on how to answer

- In the case of a **visual source** you will need to **look into the picture** and **extract relevant details**.
- You will need to **pick out at least two relevant points** which are well developed and supported.
- You should **make use of the written statement attached to the source** which is intended to provide you with additional information.
- In the case of a **written source** you will need to **read the extract carefully, underlining** or **highlighting** key points.
- You should then **try to rephrase and explain these points** in your own words, making sure you discuss **at least two key points**.
- Aim to bring in your own **background knowledge** to expand upon these points.
- To obtain maximum marks you need to ensure that you have **referred to both sources in equal measure**.
- An **imbalanced answer** which concentrates too much on one source will not score you top marks.

Identifies the key theme of both sources and provides historical context.

Picks out and develops at least two points from Source A.

Picks out and develops at least two points from Source B.

Response by candidate

Both sources show how Germany was affected by the effects of the Great Depression after1929. Source A is an election poster which shows a mass of unemployed German workers who are desperate for a job. The caption of the poster suggests that their only hope of getting a job is by voting for the Nazi Party. Hitler was promising to create jobs and put people back to work. This is also the message of Source B. It says that unemployment had reached a high of over 6 million by 1932 and this had caused hardship for millions of Germans from all social classes. The Bruning government seemed unable to deal with Germany's economic problems and so people began to vote for the extreme parties like the Nazis who promised to take action to put people back to work. The Nazi Party seemed to offer answers to the unemployment problem and this is one reason why its support grew after 1929.

12 How did the Nazis consolidate their power, 1933–34?

Source A An extract from Hitler's 'Appeal to the German people' made on 31 January 1933, the day after he had been appointed Chancellor of Germany

In the last fourteen years the November parties have created an army of millions of unemployed. Germany must not and will not sink into Communist anarchy … We have unbounded confidence, for we believe in our nation and in its eternal values … In place of our turbulent instincts, the new government will make national discipline govern our life … We do not recognise classes, only the German people with its millions of farmers, citizens and workers who together will either overcome this distress or give in to it. Now, German people, give us four years and then judge us.

TASK

Study Source A. What does it tell us about Hitler's intentions upon being appointed Chancellor in 1933?

In the period January 1933 to August 1934, Hitler and the Nazis secured control of all aspects of the German state. By August 1934, Hitler had combined the posts of Chancellor and President and was safe in the knowledge that the army supported him. Moreover, the banning of political parties, the control of the media, trade unions and police ensured that there was little or no opposition to the Nazi regime. Once more Hitler pointed out that his actions were always within the legal framework of the time.

This chapter answers the following questions:

- What was the importance of the *Reichstag* Fire?
- Why was the Enabling Act important for Hitler?
- How did the Nazis remove opposition to their regime?
- What was the importance of the Night of the Long Knives?
- Why was the support of the army important for Hitler?

Examination guidance

Throughout this chapter you will be given the opportunity to practise different exam-style questions and detailed guidance on how to answer question 1(b). This requires you to use source material and your own knowledge to explain a development. It is worth 6 marks.

What was the significance of the *Reichstag* Fire?

The end of parliamentary democracy

When Hitler became Chancellor, there were only two other Nazis in the cabinet of 12 – Wilhelm Frick and Hermann Goering. Hitler's position was not strong because the Nazis and his allies, the **Nationalist Party**, did not have a majority in the *Reichstag*. Furthermore, President Hindenburg detested him. However, it was soon clear that von Papen's claim that he would be able to control Hitler was utterly wrong.

Hitler immediately called a general election for 5 March, hoping it would give him a clear majority in the *Reichstag*. If he controlled parliament then he would be able to make the laws needed to tighten his grip on the nation. It would all be done by the rule of law – Nazi law. Violence and terror were again seen in this election campaign and there were about 70 deaths in the weeks leading up to voting day. Once again, Hitler received large amounts of money from leading industrialists to assist his campaign. With access to the media, he knew that Goebbels would be able to put the Nazi message over unceasingly.

One week before the election, on 27 February, the *Reichstag* building was set on fire (see Source A, page 141). It is not known who started the fire, but the Nazis arrested Marinus van der Lubbe, a Dutch Communist. This was a wonderful opportunity for Hitler and Goebbels to exploit. They claimed that the Communists were about to stage a takeover.

Source B From the memoirs of Rudolf Diels, Head of the Prussian Police in 1933. He was writing about Hitler's reaction to the *Reichstag* Fire. Diels was writing in 1950

Hitler was standing on a balcony gazing at the red ocean of fire. He swung round towards us … his face had turned quite scarlet with the excitement … Suddenly he started screaming at the top of his voice: 'Now we'll show them! Anyone who stands in our way will be mown down. The German people have been too soft for too long. Every Communist official must be shot. All friends of the Communists must be locked up. And that goes for the Social Democrats too.'

Source A The trial of Marinus van der Lubbe. Van der Lubbe is wearing a striped jacket

Source C Berlin police burn red flags after raiding the homes of Communists, 26 March 1933

Biography Franz von Papen 1879–1969

Career to 1933

1879 Born in Werl, Westphalia

1913 Entered the diplomatic service as a military attaché to the German ambassador in Washington DC

1917 German army adviser to Turkey and also served as a major in the Turkish army in Palestine

1918 Left the German army. He entered politics and joined the Catholic Centre Party

1922 Elected to the *Reichstag*

1932 Appointed Chancellor in June. Schemed with Hindenburg, thinking Hitler and the Nazis could be manipulated

1933 Appointed Vice-Chancellor under Hitler. Assumed Hitler could be dominated

TASKS

1. Explain why von Papen thought he could control Hitler.
2. Use Source B and your own knowledge to explain why the Reichstag fire was useful to the Nazi Party. (For guidance on how to answer this type of question, see page 141.)
3. What impression do you gain about van der Lubbe from Source A?
4. Devise a caption for Source A for publication in a Nazi newspaper.
5. Research: find out more about the background and trial of Marinus van der Lubbe.
6. How far does Source C support the view that parliamentary democracy had ended in Germany by March 1933?

Why was the Enabling Act important for Hitler?

Source A Table of election results, March 1933

Political party	Seats won	Percentage of vote
Nazi Party (NSDAP)	288	43.9
National Party (DNVP)	52	8.0
People's Party (DVP)	2	1.1
Centre Party (ZP)	92	13.9
Democratic Party (DDP)	5	0.9
Social Democratic Party (SPD)	120	18.3
Communist Party (KPD)	81	12.3
Others	7	1.6

Following the *Reichstag* Fire, Hitler persuaded Hindenburg to sign the 'Decree for the Protection of People and State'. This suspended basic civil rights and allowed the Nazis to imprison large numbers of their political opponents. The Communist and Socialist newspapers were banned.

At the election in March 1933, the Nazis won 288 seats. Despite imprisoning many Socialists and Communists and having all the advantages of media control, the Nazis did not win a majority of votes. Therefore, a coalition was formed with the National Party, ensuring a majority in the *Reichstag*. Even though he had a majority, Hitler was disappointed because he needed two-thirds of the seats in order to be able to change the constitution.

His next step was to pass the Enabling Bill. This would give him and his government full powers for the next four years and would mean that the *Reichstag* would become a rubber stamp for Nazi activities. The Bill was passed – but by devious means (see diagram).

The Enabling Bill was passed on 23 March 1933 and was the end of the Weimar Constitution and democracy. It is regarded as the 'foundation stone' of the Third Reich and allowed Hitler to secure closer control of the nation. It quickly resulted in the suspension of civil liberties, the imposition of censorship and control of the press, the abolition of trade unions and the disbanding of all political parties apart from the Nazi Party. By such means Hitler created a 'dictatorship'.

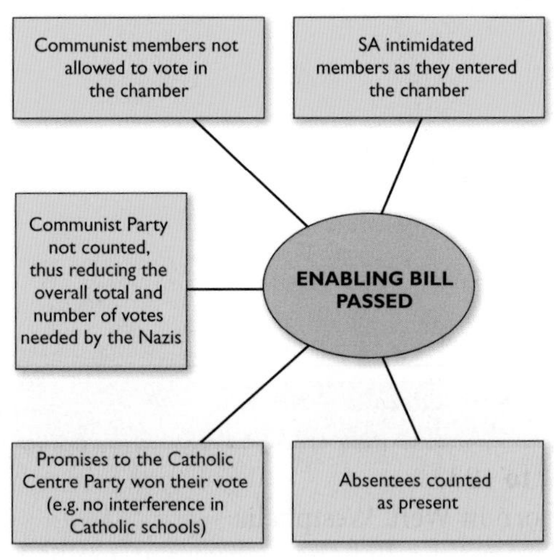

TASKS

1 Work in pairs. You are investigative journalists in Germany 1933. Write an article exposing the links between the *Reichstag* Fire (page 134) and how the Enabling Law was able to be passed.

2 How important was the Enabling Act in increasing Hitler's power?

How did the Nazis remove opposition to their regime?

With the new Enabling Law, Hitler was now in a position to bring German society into line with Nazi philosophy. This policy was called ***Gleichschaltung***. It would create a truly National Socialist state and would mean that every aspect of the social, political and economic life of a German citizen was controlled and monitored by the Nazis.

Trade unions

On 2 May 1933, all trade unions were banned. The Nazis said that a national community had been created, therefore such organisations were no longer needed. The Nazi Labour Front was set up to replace not only trade unions but also employers' groups. Wages were decided by the Labour Front (*Deutsche Arbeitsfront* – DAF) and workers received work books which recorded the record of employment. Employment depended on ownership of the work book. Strikes were outlawed and any dissenters would be sent to the new prisons – concentration camps for political re-education. Some union leaders were sent immediately to the new concentration camps. The first concentration camp opened at Dachau in March 1933. There could be no challenge to the Nazi state.

The work book of a German worker recording his places of employment between 1932 and 1940. This shows the depth of Nazi control.

Political parties

The Communist Party (KPD) had been banned after the *Reichstag* Fire and its property had been confiscated. On 10 May, the Social Democratic Party had its headquarters, property and newspapers seized. The remaining political parties disbanded themselves voluntarily at the end of June and beginning of July. On 14 July 1933 the Law Against the Formation of Parties was passed, which made the Nazi Party the sole legal political party in Germany. Thus within a few months Hitler had achieved political control of the country.

In the November 1933 general election, 95.2 per cent of the electorate voted and the Nazis won 39,638,000 votes. (There was some protest against the Nazis – about 3 million ballot papers were spoilt.)

Control of state government (*Länder*)

Hitler also broke down the **federal structure** of Germany. There were eighteen ***Länder*** and each had its own parliament. On occasions in the Weimar period, some of the *Länder* had caused problems for the President because their political makeup differed and they refused to accept decisions made in the *Reichstag*. President Ebert had issued more than 130 emergency decrees to overrule some of the *Länder*. Hitler decided that the *Länder* were to be run by Reich governors and their parliaments were abolished in January 1934. Thus he centralised the country for the first time since its creation in 1871.

TASKS

1 What is meant by the term *Gleichschaltung*?

2 Describe how Hitler increased his control over the German workforce. (For guidance on how to answer this type of question, see page 175.)

3 Explain why Hitler wanted to disband the political parties.

What was the importance of the Night of the Long Knives?

Source A Hitler and Röhm with SA troops

The Night of the Long Knives (also known as 'Operation Hummingbird' or 'the Blood Purge') was the purging of Hitler's political and military rivals in the SA *Sturmabteilung*. One cause of the removal of leaders of the SA was the need to win the support of the army (see page 140). However, in the first months of his Chancellorship, Hitler saw the SA as quite a major threat.

The SA had been a key part in the growth of the Nazis and by 1933 they were well known across Germany. Most of the SA were working-class people who favoured the socialist views of the Nazi programme. They were hoping that Hitler would introduce reforms to help the workers.

Moreover, Röhm, the leader of the SA, wanted to incorporate the army into the SA and was disappointed by Hitler's close relations with industrialists and the army leaders. Röhm wanted more government interference in the running of the country in order to help the ordinary citizens. He wanted to move away from Germany's class structure and bring greater equality. In effect, he wanted a social revolution. There was further tension for Hitler because his personal bodyguard, the SS (*Schutzstaffel*), led by Heinrich Himmler, wished to break away from the SA. Goering (Head of the **Gestapo**) wanted to lead the armed forces and hence saw an opponent in Röhm.

Source B From *Hitler Speaks* by H Rauschning, 1940. Rauschning was a Nazi official who left Germany in 1934 to live in the USA. Here he is describing a conversation with Röhm in 1934. Röhm was drunk

'Adolf's a swine ... He only associates with those on the right ... His old friends aren't good enough for him. Adolf is turning into a gentleman. What he wants is to sit on the hill top and pretend he is God. He knows exactly what I want ... The generals are a lot of old fogeys ... I'm the nucleus of the new army.'

Hitler took action in June, following information from Himmler that Röhm was about to seize power. On 30 June 1934, Röhm and the main leaders of the SA were shot by members of the SS. Hitler also took the opportunity to settle some old scores – von Schleicher was murdered, as was Gregor Strasser, a key figure amongst those Nazis with socialist views, similar to Röhm. About 400 people were murdered in the purge.

Source C An extract from a school textbook *GCSE History* by P. Barnes, R.P. Evans, P. Jones-Evans (2003)

By 1934 the SA was very powerful and its leader Ernst Röhm felt that Hitler was introducing change too slowly and rumours circulated that Röhm wanted the SA to take over the army. Hitler now had to make a choice between the SA and the army. He chose the army and on the night of 30 June 1934 he carried out a purge against the SA leadership.

Source D From Hitler's speech to the *Reichstag* on 13 July 1934, justifying his actions concerning the SA

In the circumstances I had to make but one decision. If disaster was to be prevented at all, action had to be taken with lightning speed. Only a ruthless and bloody intervention might still perhaps stifle the spread of revolt. If anyone reproaches me and asks why I did not resort to the regular courts of justice for conviction of the offenders, then all I can say is – 'In this hour I was responsible for the fate of the German people and therefore I became the supreme judge of the German people.'

The impact of the Night of the Long Knives

The Night of the Long Knives is often seen as the turning point for Hitler's rule in Germany. He eradicated would-be opponents and secured the support of the army. The SA was relegated to a minor role and, if there had been any doubt about Hitler's rule, it was now clear that fear and terror would play significant roles.

Source E A cartoon by David Low which appeared in the *London Evening Standard*, 3 July 1934. The caption reads: 'They salute with both hands now.' Goering is standing to Hitler's right, dressed as a Viking hero, and Goebbels is on his knees behind Hitler. The words 'Unkept promises' appeared on the paper in front of the SA and 'the double cross' above and below Hitler's armband

THEY SALUTE WITH BOTH HANDS NOW.

TASKS

1. Study Source A. What does it show you about Hitler and the SA?
2. Explain why Hitler was becoming concerned about the role of the SA.
3. How useful are Sources C and D to an historian studying the reasons why Hitler ordered the Night of the Long Knives? (For guidance on how to answer this type of question, see pages 155–56.)
4. Use Source B and your own knowledge to explain why Röhm became critical of Hitler's leadership. (For guidance on how to answer this type of question, see page 141.)
5. How important was the Night of the Long Knives in increasing Hitler's power?
6. Why was the cartoon (Source E) produced in July 1934? (For guidance on how to answer this type of question, see page 188.)
7. What were the results of the Night of the Long Knives? Construct a circle with the 'Night of the Long Knives' at the centre. Look at the points below and consider the results of the purge for each, working out who gained most from the Night of the Long Knives and who gained the least, or lost. Then place them around the circle, starting with the one who benefited most at the top, and work in a clockwise direction.
   - The army
   - The SA
   - Hitler's rivals
   - The SS
   - Hitler's own position
   - Himmler and Goering

Why was the support of the army important for Hitler?

Hitler was keen to secure the support of the army. By early 1934, there were some in the Nazi Party, such as Röhm, the leader of the SA, who wished to incorporate it into the SA. However, Hitler knew that there would be opposition from the generals and this could mean a challenge to his own position. Furthermore, if he removed the SA, he could win the support of the army in his bid for the presidency. The army felt threatened by the SA and many of the army leaders did not like the socialist nature of the SA. President Hindenburg was becoming very frail and Hitler sought to combine his own post and that of president. The support of the army was gained following the Night of the Long Knives when the leaders of the SA were assassinated.

Source A The army's oath of allegiance to Hitler, August 1934

I swear before God to give my unconditional obedience to Adolf Hitler, Führer of the Reich and of the German people, and I pledge my word as a brave soldier to observe this oath always, even at the peril of my life.

Source B Hitler Youth on the occasion of the Referendum on the Merging of the Offices of Reich President and Reich Chancellor (19 August 1934). The words on the side of the lorry read 'The *Führer* commands, we follow! Everyone say Yes!'

Following the death of Hindenburg in August 1934, the army swore allegiance to Hitler who, having combined the roles of Chancellor and President, was now their *Führer.* He became the Commander-in-Chief of the Armed Forces. Hitler decided he needed to seek the approval of the German people when he combined the posts. In the referendum of 19 August, more than 90 per cent of the voters (38 million) agreed with his action. Only 4.5 million voted against him and 870,000 spoiled their ballot papers.

TASKS

1 What do Sources A and B suggest about support for Hitler in August 1934? (For guidance on how to answer this type of question, see page 132.)

2 Describe how Hitler increased his control over Germany after the death of President Hindenburg. (For guidance on how to answer this type of question, see page 175.)

3 Explain why Hitler needed the support of the army.

4 Was the Night of the Long Knives the most important event in helping Hitler achieve control over Germany?

> In your answer you should discuss the importance of the various events that helped Hitler achieve control over Germany, including the Night of the Long Knives.

(For guidance on how to answer this type of question, see pages 195–96.)

Examination guidance

This section provides guidance on how to answer a question which requires you to use source material and your own knowledge to explain a development. It is worth 6 marks.

Use Source A and your own knowledge to explain why the Night of the Long Knives took place.

(6 marks)

Source A [From a school textbook]

By 1934, the SA had become enormously powerful with more than two million members. Its leader, Ernst Röhm, had particular ideas about the direction he thought the Nazis should be taking. He urged Hitler to adopt more socialist policies and to act against industrialists and big business. Hitler rejected these ideas and was persuaded by Goebbels that Röhm was plotting against him. He acted swiftly against Röhm and on 30th June 1934 he ordered the arrest of the top SA leaders in an event called the Night of the Long Knives.

Tips on how to answer

- Read through the source, **underlining or highlighting** the key points.
- In your answer you should **try to rephrase and explain these points** in your own words.
- Aim to bring in your own **background knowledge** to expand upon these points.
- Think about any **other relevant factors** which are not included in the source and bring them into your answer.
- To obtain maximum marks **you need to do two things** – refer to information from the source and add to this with information from your own knowledge of this topic area.
- You should try to **explain and develop** at least **three points**.

Response by candidate

The Night of the Long Knives took place on 30th June 1934 and was ordered by Hitler. He had become increasingly concerned that Röhm and the SA were growing too powerful. The SA numbered over 2 million and their violent activities on the streets against Communists and Jews was causing criticism of the Nazi Party to grow. Hitler wanted to make the Party more respectable and he disliked Röhm's criticism of his leadership and his demands for a Second Revolution. Hitler could not afford to anger the industrialists and big business as he needed their support to expand the German economy. Hitler came to see Röhm as a threat to his power, especially as the SA leader was demanding that he be allowed to take charge of the German army. Hitler needed the support of the army Generals and they hated Röhm. Hitler decided that the support of the army was more important than the support of the SA and so he ordered that Röhm and the other SA leaders be arrested and shot.

Use of own knowledge to develop points in the source.

Refers to other reasons not mentioned in the source.

Section B
Changing life for the German people, 1933–39

Source A Part of a speech delivered by Hitler in 1939, in which he outlines his aims for the youth of Germany

In my great educative work I am beginning with the young. We older ones are used up. We are rotten to the marrow. But my magnificent youngsters! Are there finer ones in the world? With them I can make a new world. My teaching is hard. Weakness has to be knocked out of them. A violently, active, dominating, determined, brutal youth, that is what I want.

Source B Robert Ley, the leader of the Labour Front, spells out the hold of the Nazi Party over the German people

We start our work when the child is three. As soon as it begins to think, a little flag is put in its hand. Then comes school, the Hitler Youth Movement, the Storm Troop. We never let a single soul go, and when they have gone through all that, there is the Labour Front, which takes them when they are grown up and never lets hold of them, whether they like it or not.

This section examines the domestic policies introduced by the Nazis in the years 1933–39 towards women, the young, the unemployed and minority groups, especially the Jews.

The Nazis implemented policies that reflected their own beliefs about the role of various groups in Germany. Women reverted to their traditional family role. The young were indoctrinated into Nazi ideas (see Source A). The economy was reorganised to prepare Germany for war and remove unemployment (see Source B). Moreover, the Nazis ensured control of political life by censorship, propaganda and the setting up of a police state. Finally, the Jews, who had no part in Nazi racial theory, were persecuted in order to drive them out of Germany.

Each chapter explains a key issue and examines important lines of enquiry as outlined below:

Chapter 13: How did Nazi economic and social policy affect life in Germany?

- What measures were used to control the economy, reduce unemployment and control the workforce?
- What was the role of women?
- How successful were these policies?
- How did education and youth movements control the young?
- How successful were these policies?

Chapter 14: How did Nazi political policy affect life in Germany?

- What was the police state?
- How did the Nazis extend their control over central and local government?
- How were propaganda and censorship used?

Chapter 15: How did Nazi racial and religious policy affect life in Germany?

- What was Nazi racial policy?
- Why and how did the Nazis persecute the Jews?
- How did the Nazis change relations with the Catholic and Protestant Churches?

13 How did Nazi economic and social policy affect life in Germany?

Source A Nazi poster of 1937 showing the central role of women. It says 'The Nazi Party protects the national community'

The young were of particular importance to the Nazis. They were seen as the future of the Third Reich and so their education and activities needed to be carefully controlled. In addition the Nazis tried to radically change the role of women in society. They opposed the progress women had made and wanted them to revert to a traditional domestic role. To what extent did they achieve this? Hitler was determined to keep his promise to reduce unemployment but, at the same time, control the workforce. Moreover, the Nazis brought in measures to control the economy, more especially Goering's Four Year Plan, in an attempt to create *autarky* (self-sufficiency).

This chapter answers the following questions:

- What measures were used to control the economy, reduce unemployment and control the workforce?
- What was the role of women?
- How successful were these policies?
- How did education and youth movements control the young?
- How successful were these policies?

TASK

Study Source A. What does it show you about the role of women in Nazi Germany?

Examination guidance

Throughout this chapter you will be given the opportunity to practise different exam-style questions and detailed guidance on how to answer question 1(c). This requires you to analyse and evaluate the utility of the two sources. It is worth 8 marks.

What measures were used to control the economy, reduce unemployment and control the workforce?

By January 1933 when Hitler became Chancellor, Germany had experienced more than three years of **depression** with unemployment of 6 million. Hitler introduced a series of measures to reduce unemployment.

The National Labour Service Corps (RAD)

This was a scheme to provide young men with manual labour jobs. From 1935 it was compulsory for all men aged 18–25 to serve in the **RAD** for six months. Workers lived in camps, wore uniforms, received very low pay and carried out military drill as well as work.

Source A An Austrian visitor describes a labour service camp in 1938

The camps are organised on thoroughly military lines. The youths wear uniforms like soldiers. The only difference is that they carry spades instead of rifles and work in the fields.

Job creation schemes

Hitler at first spent millions on job creation schemes, rising from 18.4 billion marks in 1933 to 37.1 billion five years later. The Nazis subsidised private firms, especially in the construction industry. They also introduced a massive road-building programme to provide Germany with 7000 km of *autobahns* (motorways), as well as other public works schemes, such as the construction of hospitals, schools and houses.

TASKS

1 What do Sources A and B suggest about the methods used by the Nazis to reduce unemployment? (For guidance on how to answer this type of question, see page 132.)

2 Describe the RAD organisation. (For guidance on how to answer this type of question, see page 175.)

Source B An official photograph showing workers gathering to begin work on the first *autobahn*, September 1933

Measures to control the economy

In 1934 Hjalmar Schacht was made Economic Minister. He used **deficit spending** to boost the economy. In particular, he introduced Mefo Bills to finance increased public spending without causing **inflation**. These were credit notes issued by the *Reichsbank* and guaranteed by the government. They were to be converted into *Reichsmarks* and payable, with interest, after five years. By 1937 the government had paid out 12 billion *Reichsmarks* in Mefo Bills.

Schacht resigned as Economic Minister in 1937. The year before, Goering had drawn up the Four Year Plan for the economy. This set much higher targets for the economy and tried to ensure that Germany moved much closer to ***autarky***, or self-sufficiency, and reduced German dependence on the import of vital raw materials. Experiments were begun to try to produce artificial replacements for vital raw materials that could only be obtained from abroad. For example, the chemical company IG Farben was paid to try to develop a method of extracting oil from coal. However, these attempts were not successful in reducing the amount of goods that Germany imported.

Invisible unemployment

The Nazis used some dubious methods to keep down the unemployment figures. The official figures did not include the following:

- Jews dismissed from their jobs.
- Unmarried men under 25 who were pushed into National Labour schemes.
- Women dismissed from their jobs or who gave up work to get married.
- Opponents of the Nazi regime held in concentration camps.

The figures also listed part-time workers as being fully employed.

TASKS

3 How successful was Hitler in reducing unemployment in Germany between 1933 and 1939?

4 How accurate are Nazi claims that their policies led to a dramatic fall in the number of unemployed in Germany?

Rearmament

Hitler was determined to build up the armed forces in readiness for future war. This, in turn, greatly reduced unemployment.

- The reintroduction of **conscription** in 1935 took thousands of young men into military service. The army grew from 100,000 in 1933 to 1,400,000 by 1939.
- Heavy industry expanded to meet the needs of rearmament. Coal and chemical usage doubled in the years 1933 to 1939; oil, iron and steel usage trebled.
- Billions were spent producing tanks, aircraft and ships. In 1933, 3.5 billion marks were spent on rearmament. This figure had increased to 26 billion marks by 1939.

Controlling the workforce

The Nazis were determined to control the workforce to prevent the possibility of strikes and to ensure that industry met the needs of rearmament. This was achieved through two organisations, the Labour Front and Strength through Joy.

Strength through Joy (Kraft durch Freude – KdF)

This was an organisation set up by the German Labour Front to replace trade unions. The KdF tried to improve the leisure time of German workers by sponsoring a wide range of leisure and cultural trips. These included concerts, theatre visits, museum tours, sporting events, weekend trips, holidays and cruises. All were provided at a low cost, giving ordinary workers access to activities normally reserved for the better off.

Beauty of Work was a department of the KdF that tried to improve working conditions. It organised the building of canteens, swimming pools and sports facilities. It also installed better lighting in the workplace.

Source C Extract from the *Strength through Joy* magazine, 1936

KdF is now running weekly theatre trips to Munich from the countryside. Special theatre trains are coming to Munich on weekdays from as far away as 120 km. So a lot of our comrades who used to be in the Outdoor Club, for example, are availing themselves of the opportunity of going on trips with KdF. There is simply no other choice. Walking trips have also become very popular.

Source D Official figures from the Nazi Party showing numbers taking part in KdF activities in 1938

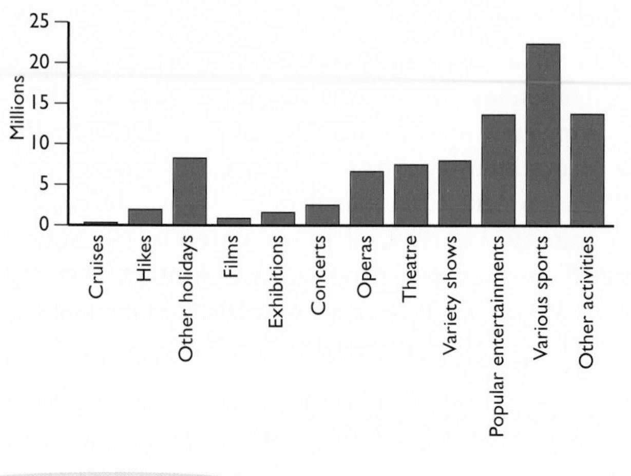

Source E A DAF log book belonging to a German worker, showing that he had worked on government schemes throughout 1935

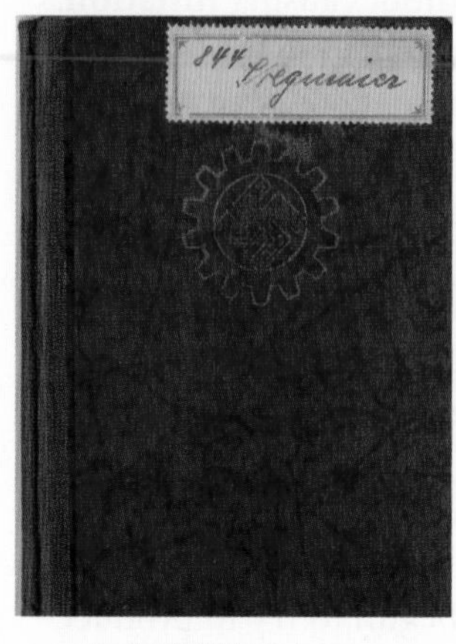

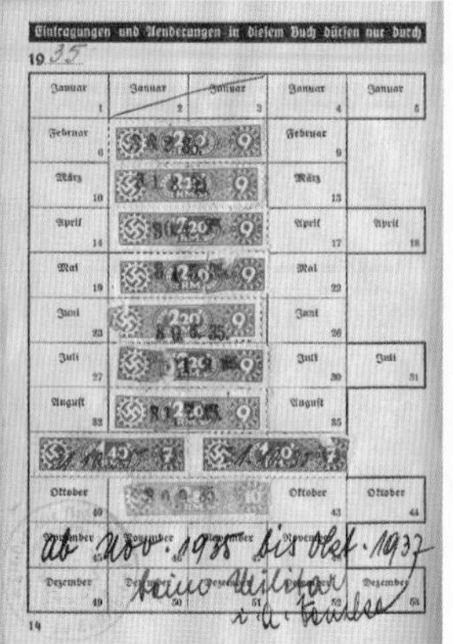

The German Labour Front (Deutsche Arbeitsfront, DAF)

On 2 May 1933, to avoid the possibility of strikes and other industrial action, the Nazis banned all trade unions. They were replaced by the German Labour Front under its leader, Robert Ley.

- DAF included employers and workers and was supposed to represent the interests of both.
- All strikes were banned and wages were decided by the Labour Front.
- Workers were given relatively high wages, job security and social and leisure programmes.
- Workers received work books which recorded the record of employment. Employment depended on ownership of a work book.
- In theory DAF membership was voluntary, but any worker in any area of German commerce or industry would have found it hard to get a job without being a member.
- Membership required a fee within the range of 15 *pfennig* to 3 *Reichsmark,* depending on the category a member fell into in a large scale of 20 membership groups.

Volkswagen scheme

In 1938 the German Labour Front organised the Volkswagen (people's car) scheme, giving workers an opportunity to subscribe five marks a week to buy their own car. This was a swindle. By the time war broke out in 1939, not a single customer had taken delivery of a car. None of the money was refunded.

TASKS

5 Describe the work of the German Labour Front (DAF). (For guidance on how to answer this type of question, see page 175.)

6 How useful are Sources C and D to an historian studying the work of the KdF? (For guidance on how to answer this type of question, see pages 155–56.)

7 How successful was the Volkswagen scheme?

8 Design your own poster to persuade German workers to participate in the Volkswagen programme.

What was the role of women?

Changes during the Weimar Republic

Political progress	Economic progress	Social progress
Women over the age of 20 were given the vote and took an increasing interest in politics. By 1933 one-tenth of the members of the *Reichstag* were female.	Many took up careers in the professions, especially the civil service, law, medicine and teaching. Those who worked in the civil service earned the same as men. By 1933 there were 100,000 women teachers and 3000 doctors.	Socially, they went out unescorted, drank and smoked in public, were slim and fashion conscious. They often wore relatively short skirts, had their hair cut short and wore make-up.

Women had made significant progress in their position in German society during the 1920s, as shown in the table above.

Source A German women in a bar, 1930

Nazi ideals

The Nazis had a very traditional view of the role of women, which was very different from women's position in society in the 1920s. The Nazis' ideal woman:

- did not wear make-up
- was blonde, heavy hipped and athletic
- wore flat shoes and a full skirt
- did not smoke
- did not go out to work
- did all the household duties, especially cooking and bringing up the children
- took no interest in politics.

Source B Goebbels describes the role of women in a speech in 1929

The mission of women is to be beautiful and to bring children into the world. The female bird pretties herself for her mate and hatches eggs for him. In exchange, the male takes care of gathering the food and stands guard and wards off the enemy.

Source C A German rhyme addressed to women

Take hold of the kettle, broom and pan,
Then you'll surely get a man!
Shop and office leave alone,
Your true life work lies at home.

TASKS

1 Study Source A. What does it show you about the position of women in Weimar Germany?

2 What do Sources B and C suggest about Nazi attitudes towards the role of women? (For guidance on how to answer this type of question, see page 132.)

Changes under Nazi policies

The Nazis brought in a series of measures to change the role of women.

Marriage and family

The Nazis were very worried by the decline in the birth rate. In 1900 there had been more than 2 million live births per year but this figure dropped to less than 1 million in 1933.

- A massive propaganda campaign was launched to promote motherhood and large families.
- In 1933 the Law for the Encouragement of Marriage was introduced. This aimed to increase Germany's falling birth rate by giving loans to help young couples to marry, provided the wife left her job. Couples were allowed to keep one-quarter of the loan for each child born, up to four children.
- On Hitler's mother's birthday (12 August) medals were awarded to women with large families.
- In 1938 the Nazis changed the divorce law – a divorce was possible if a husband or wife could not have children.
- The Nazis also set up the *Lebensborn* (Life Springs) programme whereby specially chosen unmarried women could 'donate a baby to the *Führer*' by becoming pregnant by 'racially pure' **SS** men.
- A new national organisation, the German Women's Enterprise, organised classes and radio talks on household topics and the skills of motherhood.

Jobs

Instead of going to work, women were asked to stick to the 'three Ks' – *Kinder, Küche, Kirche* – 'children, kitchen, church'. The Nazis had another incentive to get women to give up work. They had been elected partly because they promised more jobs. Every job left by a woman returning to the home became available for a man.

Women doctors, civil servants and teachers were forced to leave their jobs. Schoolgirls were trained for work at home (see page 151) and discouraged from going on to higher education.

However, from 1937 the Nazis had to reverse these policies. Germany was rearming. Men were joining the army. Now they needed more women to go out to work. They abolished the marriage loans and introduced a compulsory 'duty year' for all women entering employment. This usually meant helping on a farm or in a family home in return for bed and board but no pay. This change of policy was not very successful. By 1939 there were fewer women working than there had been under the Weimar Republic.

Appearance

Women were encouraged to keep healthy and wear their hair in a bun or plaits. They were discouraged from wearing trousers, high heels and make-up, from dyeing or styling their hair, and from slimming, as this was seen as bad for childbearing.

Source D A Nazi poster of 1937 showing the ideal image of a German woman

TASKS

3 Draw sketches of two women.

- Label the first sketch with the features of a 'modern woman' during the 1920s.
- Label the second sketch with the Nazi view of women.

4 Describe the attitude of the Nazis towards the role of women. (For guidance on how to answer this type of question, see page 175.)

Source E A German cartoon from the 1930s. The caption reads 'Introducing Frau Müller who up to now has brought 12 children into the world'

„Und hier stelle ich Euch Frau Müller vor, die bis jetzt 12 Kinder zur Welt gebracht hat!"

Source F A Nazi pamphlet sent to young German women

1. Remember that you are a German.
2. If you are genetically healthy, you should get married.
3. Keep your body pure.
4. Keep your mind and spirit pure.
5. Marry only for love.
6. As a German choose only a husband of similar or related blood.
7. In choosing a husband, ask about his ancestors.
8. Health is essential for physical beauty.
9. Don't look for a playmate but for a companion in marriage.
10. You should want to have as many children as possible.

Source G Marianne Gartner was a member of the League of German Maidens and remembers one of its meetings in 1936

At one meeting the team leader raised her voice. 'There is no greater honour for a German woman than to bear children for the Führer and for the Fatherland! The Führer has ruled that no family will be complete without at least four children. A German woman does not use make-up! A German woman does not smoke! She has a duty to keep herself fit and healthy! Any questions?' 'Why isn't the Führer married and a father himself?' I asked.

TASKS

5 How useful are Sources D and E to an historian studying the role of women in German society? (For guidance on how to answer this type of question, see pages 155–56.)

6 How far does Source E support the view that women occupied an important place in Nazi society?

7 Use Source F and your own knowledge to explain the role of women in Nazi Germany. (For guidance on how to answer this type of question, see page 141.)

8 Design a mind map like the one below to show the expectations for women living in Germany during the time of the Nazis. The first box has been completed for you.

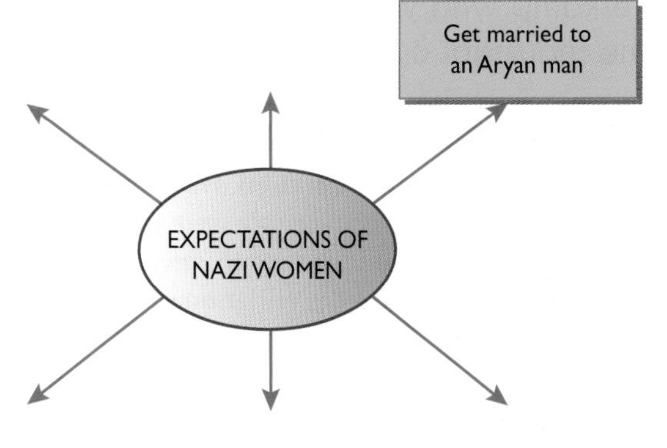

How successful were these policies?

Source A Extract from a letter from several women to a Leipzig newspaper in 1934

Today man is educated not for, but against, marriage. We see our daughters growing up in stupid aimlessness living only in a vague hope of getting a man and having children. A son, even the youngest, laughs in his mother's face. He regards her as his servant and women in general are merely willing tools of his aims.

Source B From a newspaper article by Judith Grunfeld, an American journalist, 1937

How many women workers did the Führer send home? According to the statistics of the German Department of Labour, there were in June 1936, 5,470,000 employed women, or 1,200,000 more than in January 1933. The Nazi campaign has not been successful in reducing the numbers of women employed. It has simply squeezed them out of better paid positions into the sweated trades. This type of labour with its miserable wages and long hours is extremely dangerous to the health of women and degrades the family.

Source C The memories of Wilhelmine Haferkamp who was 22 in 1933. She lived in the industrial city of Oberhausen

When one had ten children, well not ten but a pile of them, one had to join the Nazi Party. 1933 it was and I already had three children and the fourth on the way. When 'child-rich' people were in the Party the children had a great chance to advance. I got 30 marks per child from the Hitler government and 20 marks per child from the city. That was a lot of money. I sometimes got more 'child money' than my husband earned.

Source D From a newspaper article by Toni Christen, an American journalist, 1939

I talked to Mrs Schmidt, a woman of about 50, as she came out of the shop. 'You see, older women are no good in Germany,' she said. 'We are no longer capable of bearing children. We have no value to the state. They don't care for us mothers or grandmothers any more. We are worn out, discarded.'

Source E Employment of women (millions)

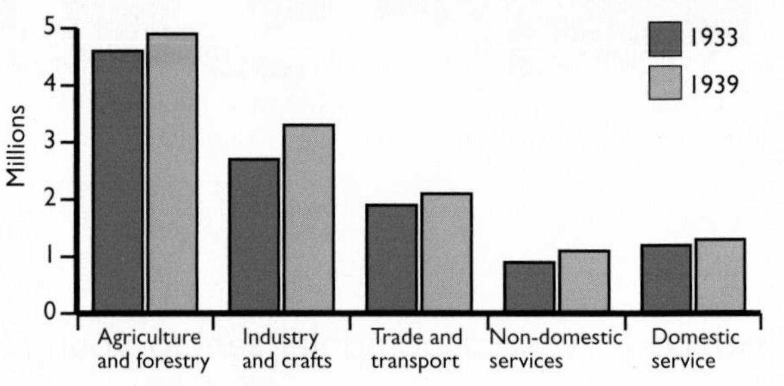

TASKS

1 Make a copy of the following table. Sort Sources A–E into successes and failures for Nazi policies in the areas of marriage/ family and jobs. Complete the table with an explanation of your choices. One has been done for you.

	Success	Failure
Marriage and family		Source B as the Nazis did not value older women
Jobs		

2 You are a British journalist who has visited Nazi Germany in 1938 to investigate the role of women. Use the work you have done on Task 1 to write an article explaining the successes and failures of Nazi policies. You will need a catchy headline. You could include imaginary interviews.

How did education and youth movements control the young?

Hitler saw the young as the future of the Third Reich. They had to be converted to Nazi ideals. This was achieved through control of education and the **Hitler Youth**.

Education

Everyone in Germany had to go to school until the age of fourteen. After that schooling was optional. Boys and girls went to separate schools.

Teachers

Teachers had to swear an oath of loyalty to Hitler and join the Nazi Teachers' League. Teachers had to promote Nazi ideals in the classroom.

Curriculum

This was changed to prepare students for their future roles. Hitler wanted healthy, fit men and women so fifteen per cent of time in school was devoted to physical education. With the boys the emphasis was on preparation for the military. Girls took needlework and home crafts, especially cookery, to become good homemakers and mothers. New subjects such as race studies (see page 168) were introduced to put across Nazi ideas on race and population control. Children were taught how to measure their skulls and to classify racial types. They were also taught that **Aryans** were superior and should not marry inferior races such as Jews.

Textbooks

These were rewritten to fit the Nazi view of history and racial purity. *Mein Kampf* became a standard text.

Lessons

These began and ended with the students saluting and saying '***Heil Hitler***'. Nazi themes were presented through every subject. Maths problems dealt with social issues. Geography lessons were used to show how Germany was surrounded by hostile neighbours. In history lessons, students were taught about the evils of **communism** and the Treaty of Versailles.

Source A A question from a Nazi maths textbook, 1933

*The Jews are aliens in Germany. In 1933 there were 66,060,000 inhabitants of the German **Reich** of whom 499,862 were Jews. What is the percentage of aliens in Germany?*

TASKS

1 Explain why the Nazis wanted to control education.

2 Study Source A. What does it show you about education in Nazi Germany?

3 Describe how the school curriculum changed under the control of the Nazis. (For guidance on how to answer this type of question, see page 175.)

The Hitler Youth

The Nazis also wanted to control the young in their spare time. This was achieved through the Hitler Youth.

- All other youth organisations were banned.
- From 1939 membership was compulsory.
- By 1939 there were 7 million members.

TASKS

4 What do Sources B and C suggest about the Hitler Youth movement? (For guidance on how to answer this type of question, see page 132.)

5 Describe the activities of the Hitler Youth Movement. (For guidance on how to answer this type of question, see page 175.)

6 You have been asked by your local Hitler Youth group to produce a poster promoting the organisation. You could use either Source B or C as the illustration for your poster and get more ideas from Source A on the next page.

Hitler Youth males	Hitler Youth females
Source B A recruiting poster for the Hitler Youth, 1933 	**Source C** A recruiting poster for the Young Girls which says 'Every ten year old to us' 
Boys joined the German Young People (Jungvolk) at the age of ten. From fourteen to eighteen they became members of the Hitler Youth (Hitler jungend). *They learned Nazi songs and ideas and took part in athletics, hiking and camping. As they got older they practised marching, map reading and military skills. Many enjoyed the comradeship. It is also possible they enjoyed the fact that their camps were often near to those of the League of German Maidens.*	*Girls joined the Young Girls (Jungmädel) at the age of ten. From fourteen to eighteen they joined the League of German Maidens (Bund Deutsche Mädchen). They did much the same as the boys except they also learned domestic skills in preparation for motherhood and marriage. There was much less emphasis on military training.*

How successful were these policies?

Although many young Germans joined the Hitler Youth, it was not popular with some of its members. Some young people challenged Nazi ideas by playing their own music, wearing their choice of clothes and growing their hair long. One such group was called the Edelweiss Pirates (see page 190).

Source A The memories of a Hitler Youth leader given during an interview in the 1980s

What I liked about the Hitler Youth was the comradeship. I was full of enthusiasm when I joined the Young People at the age of ten. I can still remember how deeply moved I was when I heard the club mottoes: 'Young People are hard. They can keep a secret. They are loyal. They are comrades.' And then there were the trips! Is anything nicer than enjoying the splendours of the homeland in the company of one's comrades?

Source B From an article on the Hitler Youth published in a British magazine in 1938

There seems little enthusiasm for the Hitler Youth, with membership falling. Many no longer want to be commanded, but wish to do as they like. Usually only a third of a group appears for roll-call. At evening meetings it is a great event if 20 turn up out of 80, but usually there are only about 10 or 12.

TASKS

1. Explain why some teenagers rebelled against the Hitler Youth Movement.
2. How useful are Sources A and B to an historian studying the Hitler Youth movement? (For guidance on how to answer this type of question, see pages 155–156.)

Source C Members of the League of German Maidens going on a hike, 1936

Source D A teacher with her pupils during a history lesson, *c.*1933

Source E A letter written by a member of the Hitler Youth to his parents in 1936

How did we live in Camp S—, which is supposed to be an example to all the camps? We practically didn't have a minute of the day to ourselves. This isn't camp life, no sir! It's military barrack life! Drill starts right after a meagre breakfast. We would like to have athletics but there isn't any. Instead we have military exercises, down in the mud, till the tongue hangs out of your mouth. And we have only one wish: sleep, sleep ...

Source F From the memoirs, written in the 1960s, of a German who was a student in the 1930s

No one in our class ever read Mein Kampf. I myself only used the book for quotations. In general we didn't do much about Nazi ideas. ***Anti-Semitism*** *wasn't mentioned much by our teachers except through Richard Wagner's essay 'The Jews in Music'. We did, however, do a lot of physical education and cookery.*

TASKS

3 Use Source E and your own knowledge to explain why the Hitler Youth movement was not popular with all young Germans. (For guidance on how to answer this type of question, see page 141.)

4 Do Sources A–F (pages 153–54) suggest that Nazi policies were popular with the young? To answer this question make a copy of and complete the following table. One example has been done for you. Give a brief explanation for each decision.

Popular	Unpopular	Undecided
		Source D because although it shows a march, the girls do not look enthusiastic.

Now write three paragraphs.

- First paragraph explaining the sources which agree that they were popular.
- Second paragraph explaining the sources that disagree.
- Third paragraph explaining the sources that agree and disagree.

Examination guidance

This section provides guidance on how to answer the question which requires you to analyse and evaluate the utility of two sources. It is worth 8 marks.

How useful are Sources A and B to an historian studying the role of women in German society between 1933 and 1939? (8 marks)

Source A An extract from a Nazi Party pamphlet published in the mid-1930s, showing Nazi attitudes towards the place of women in German society

German women wish in the main to be wives and mothers. They do not wish to be comrades [workers] ... they have no longing for the factory, no longing for the office. A cosy home, a loved husband and a multitude of happy children are closer to their hearts.

Source B Josh Brooman, an historian, writing in a history textbook, *Hitler's Germany* (1985)

Within months of Hitler coming to power, many women doctors and civil servants were sacked from their jobs. Then women lawyers and teachers were dismissed. By 1939 there were few women left in professional jobs.

Tips on how to answer

This question will involve the analysis and evaluation of primary and/or secondary sources.

- In your answer you will need to **evaluate the usefulness** of the two sources in terms of their **content** value, their **authorship** and their **audience** or **purpose** or **context**.
- For each source you should aim to **write about two or three sentences commenting upon what the source says** (its **content**), putting the information into your own words and supporting it with your own knowledge of this topic.
- You should **comment upon the authors of each source**, noting **when the source was produced**.
- You should then consider **why each source was produced** (the **purpose**) and **under what circumstances**. You need to evaluate **whether this makes the source biased**. Remember that a biased source can still be very useful to the historian so do not just dismiss it.
- To obtain maximum marks your answer must **give equal weight to each source** and it must contain **reasoned comments upon the three elements** (the **content**, the **author**, **when and why the source was produced**). If you only comment upon the content of each source do not expect to get more than half marks.

Evaluates the authorship, content and purpose of Source A, linking it to usefulness.

Evaluates the authorship, content and purpose of Source B, linking it to usefulness.

Considers the strengths and weaknesses of both sources and how this impacts upon their usefulness.

Candidate response

The two sources are useful to the historian because they provide different information about the role of women in German society between 1933 and 1939. Source A is a contemporary account and is an extract from a pamphlet produced by the Nazi Party in the mid-1930s. It comments that German women did not want to work in factories or offices and preferred to be loyal housewives and mothers spending their time bringing up the family. It is a biased source spelling out the Nazi view that all German women wanted this lifestyle. It reflects the image of the Three K's - Kinder, Küche, Kirche. Its weakness is that it only gives a very one-sided Nazi view of the role of women. However, it is still very useful to the historian because it spells out the stereotypical image of the place of women in German society that the Nazi Party wanted to spread. Source B is a secondary source produced in 1985 and is the reflection of a modern historian who was able to research his information. The source provides a different view to that given in Source A, commenting upon how German women were forced to give up their jobs as doctors, civil servants, lawyers and teachers. Women were pushed out of the professions and in Nazi society they were expected to become housewives and mothers, giving up any idea of following a career. The author Josh Brooman was writing with the benefit of hindsight and as he produced this for educational purposes it is likely to be a balanced assessment. While Source B states that women were forced to leave the professions its usefulness is limited because it does not say whether they did this willingly or resented doing so and it only gives a very narrow view, that of professional women with no mention of what happened to women working in non-professional jobs. While both sources provide useful information the historian also needs to consider their weaknesses.

Comment on candidate response

This is an informed response which considers the utility of both sources in equal measure. Discussion has taken place about the origin and purpose of each source, evaluating the authorship and how this impacts upon the utility of the information to the historian. There has been a valid attempt to discuss the context under which each source was composed. The content of both sources has been discussed and elaborated upon, using the candidates own knowledge of this topic area to provide historical context, such as the reference to the Three K's. There is an understanding of the strengths and weaknesses of both contemporary (primary) sources and reflection (secondary) sources as pieces of evidence to be used by the historian. Some consideration is also given to the weaknesses of both sources. The answer is worthy of receiving a mark within the top level of performance (8 marks).

14 How did Nazi political policy affect life in Germany?

Source A Police arresting **communists** on Hitler's orders, 1933

TASK

Study Source A. What does it show you about the Nazi police state?

A key element in maintaining a Nazi dictatorship was to create a climate of fear – to make people too frightened to actively oppose the Nazi state. This was achieved through the establishment of a police state, including a secret police, the **Gestapo**, the SS, Nazi control of the law courts and the setting up of concentration camps. Once Hitler had removed opposition, he had to create a state which believed in and supported Nazi ideals. This was achieved through skilful use of propaganda by Goebbels, whose Ministry of Propaganda controlled all aspects of the media, the arts, entertainment.

This chapter answers the following questions:

- What was the police state?
- How did the Nazis extend their control over central and local government?
- How were propaganda and censorship used?

Examination guidance

Throughout this chapter you will be given the opportunity to practise different exam-style questions and detailed guidance on how to answer question 2(c). This requires you to discuss different historical interpretations. It is worth 10 marks.

What was the police state?

The Nazi police state operated through the use of force and terror. The Nazis used their own organisations to instil fear into the German people. The **SS** (*Schutzstaffel*), **SD** (*Sicherheitsdienst,* Security Service) and Gestapo were the main organisations and in 1936 they were all brought under the control of Heinrich Himmler.

Biography Heinrich Himmler 1900–45

1900 Born near Munich
1918 Joined the army
1923 Joined the Nazi Party and participated in the Munich *Putsch*
1929 Appointed leader of the SS
1930 Elected as a member of parliament
1934 Organised the Night of the Long Knives
1936 Head of all police agencies in Germany
1945 Committed suicide

Source A An auxiliary policeman (SA drafted into the police) guarding arrested communists

The role of the SS (*Schutzstaffel*)

The SS had been formed in 1925 to act as a bodyguard unit for Hitler and was led by Heinrich Himmler after 1929. Himmler built up the SS until it had established a clear visible identity – members wore black. They showed total obedience to the *Führer*. By 1934 the SS had more than 50,000 members who were to be fine examples of the Aryan race and were expected to marry racially pure wives.

After the Night of the Long Knives, the SS became responsible for the removal of all opposition to the Nazis within Germany. Within the SS, the Security Service (SD) had the task of maintaining security within both the party and the country.

The Gestapo

The Gestapo (***Ge****heime* ***Sta****ats* ***Po****lizei* – secret state police) was set up in 1933 by Goering. In 1936 it came under the control of the SS. It was supervised by Himmler's deputy, Reinhard Heydrich. By 1939 the Gestapo was the most important police section of the Nazi state. It could arrest and imprison those suspected of opposing the state. The most likely destination for suspects would be a concentration camp run by the SS. It has been estimated that, by 1939, there were about 160,000 people under arrest for political crimes.

Source B An incident reported in the Rhineland, July 1938

In a café, a 64-year-old woman remarked to her companion at the table: 'Mussolini [leader of Italy] has more political sense in one of his boots than Hitler has in his brain.' The remark was overheard and five minutes later the woman was arrested by the Gestapo who had been alerted by telephone.

The legal system

Even though the Nazis controlled the *Reichstag* and could make laws, Hitler wanted to ensure that all laws were interpreted in a Nazi fashion. The law courts therefore had to experience ***Gleichschaltung***, just as any other part of society. Some judges were removed and all had to become members of the National Socialist League for the Maintenance of Law. This meant that Nazi views were upheld in the courts. In October 1933 the German Lawyers Front was established and there were more than 10,000 members by the end of the year.

In 1934 a new People's Court was established to try cases of treason. The judges were loyal Nazis. Judges knew that the Minister of Justice would check to see if they had been lenient and sometimes Hitler would alter sentences if he felt that they were too soft.

Source C Judge Roland Freisler, State Secretary of the Reich Ministry of Justice. Here, he is presiding over a People's Court

Source D An explanation of the judge's role, put forward by Nazi legal expert Professor Karl Eckhardt in 1936

The judge is to safeguard the order of the racial community, to prosecute all acts harmful to the community and to arbitrate in disagreements. The National Socialist ideology, especially as expressed in the party programme and in the speeches of our Führer, is the basis for interpreting legal sources.

By the end of 1934 Hitler controlled the *Reichstag*, the army and the legal system. The Nazi police and security organisations had wormed their way into the fabric of society and it was now almost impossible for anyone to escape the power and grip of the Nazis.

Concentration camps

The SA and SS ran a number of new prisons called concentration camps. The first of these was opened in April 1933 in Dachau, near Munich. Others followed, including Buchenwald, Mauthausen and Sachsenhausen. Prisoners were classified into different categories, each denoted by a different coloured triangle worn by the prisoners.

Opponents of the regime were taken to concentration camps for questioning, torture and hard labour. The inmates were treated with great brutality. If someone was killed at a concentration camp, family members would receive a note saying that the inmate had died of a disease or been shot trying to escape. Few survived the experience. Moreover, the prisoners were used as slave labour, especially for extracting raw materials and manufacturing weapons.

TASKS

1. Study Source A. What does it show you about Nazi police methods?
2. Use the information in Source B and your own knowledge to explain why the Gestapo was so effective in Nazi Germany. (For guidance on how to answer this type of question, see page 141.)
3. How important were the SS and Gestapo in the Nazi police state?
4. Study Source C. What does it show you about Nazi courts?
5. Use Source D and your own knowledge to explain why the Nazis wanted to control the legal system. (For guidance on how to answer this type of question, see page 141.)
6. Describe the work of the concentration camps. (For guidance on how to answer this type of question, see page 175.)

How did the Nazis extend their control over central and local government?

With the passing of the Enabling Bill in March 1933 (see page 136), Hitler reorganised the German political system so that every part of it, at central and regional level, was under Nazi control.

The *Reichstag*

The Enabling Bill transferred the power of making laws from the *Reichstag* to the Chancellor. It was renewed every four years. Only seven more laws were passed by the *Reichstag* which rarely met and which was used as an applause machine for Nazi leaders' speeches.

The Cabinet

This was kept on by Hitler but, like the *Reichstag*, gradually lost all influence. In 1933 it met 72 times and contained several non-Nazis. By 1938 all non-Nazis had been removed and it only met once, in February of that year.

The Civil Service

Many civil servants had not been keen on democracy and the Weimar Republic. They were reasonably happy to transfer to the Third Reich. In any case, the Civil Service became more Nazi, partly because Nazis were appointed. In 1939 it was made compulsory for all civil servants to be members of the Nazi Party.

The *Führer*

In the Nazi state all power came from Hitler. He was the supreme authority in the Nazi state. As the state developed, so laws were increasingly made by the *Führer*. Hitler had the final say in all disputes and he made all the key decisions. Germany was governed by 'the will of the *Führer*'.

Reich Chancellery

This took over much of the work of the Cabinet. It was led by Hans-Heinrich Lammers, who had great influence over Hitler in the years leading up to the Second World War. He drew up many of the new laws.

State governments

On 31 March 1933 the Nazis closed down all state parliaments. They were then reorganised so that the Nazis had a majority in each state parliament. The country was divided into regions (*Gau*), each headed by a Reich Governor (*Gauleiter*). These men had the power to appoint and dismiss state officials and make state laws.

Source A Written by a leading member of the Nazi Party in 1935

The Führer is the bearer of the people's will. He is independent of all groups, associations and interests but he is bound by laws which are inherent in the nature of his people. In his will, the will of the people is realized. He shapes the collective will of the people within himself.

TASKS

1. Study Source A. What does it tell you about the role of the Führer in Nazi Germany?
2. Describe how the Nazis exercised control over central and regional government. (For guidance on how to answer this question, see page 175.)

How were propaganda and censorship used?

In March 1934 Josef Goebbels set up the Ministry for Popular Enlightenment and Propaganda to control the thoughts, beliefs and opinions of the German people. It was important for the long-term future of the Third Reich that the majority of the population believed in the ideals of the Nazi Party. All aspects of the media were censored and skilfully manipulated by Goebbels. He used a variety of methods.

Source A Goebbels explaining the use of propaganda, in a Nazi magazine

The finest kind of propaganda does not reveal itself. The best propaganda is that which works invisibly, penetrating every cell of life in such a way that the public has no idea of the aims of the propagandist.

TASK

1 What do Sources A and B suggest about the use of propaganda in Nazi Germany? (For guidance on how to answer this type of question, see page 132.)

NEWSPAPERS

Non-Nazi newspapers and magazines were closed down. Editors were told what they could print, which meant that the German people only read what the Nazis wanted them to know. Failure by the editors to comply meant arrest and concentration camp.

Source B Official orders from the Ministry of Propaganda, 1935

Photos showing members of the Reich *government at dining tables in front of rows of bottles must not be published in the future. This has given the absurd impression that members of the government are living it up.*

RADIO

All radio stations were placed under Nazi control. Cheap mass-produced radios were sold. Sets were installed in cafés and factories and loudspeakers were placed in streets. It was important that the Nazi message was heard. Hitler and Goebbels regularly made broadcasts.

Source C Workers listening to a broadcast by Hitler

CINEMA

Goebbels also realised the popularity of the cinema. More than 100 films were being made each year and audiences were topping 250 million in 1933. He was one of the first to realise its potential for propaganda. All film plots were shown to Goebbels before going into production. He realised that many Germans were bored by overtly political films. Instead, love stories and thrillers were given pro-Nazi slants. One of the best known was *Hitlerjunge Quex* (1933) which tells the story of a boy who broke away from a communist family to join the Hitler Youth, only to be murdered by communists. All film performances were accompanied by a 45-minute official newsreel which glorified Hitler and Germany and publicised Nazi achievements.

Response by candidate

Identifies and discusses evidence in support of the given interpretation.

Begins to suggest how and why these interpretations have been formed.

Identifies and discusses evidence which provides a counter interpretation.

Provides a judgement upon the given interpretation.

There is lots of evidence to support the interpretation that the Nazis were very successful in using propaganda and censorship to win the hearts and minds of the German people. Evidence One comments upon how the Nazis had made very effective use of propaganda to capture the minds of millions of Germans. By constantly using simple slogans they had brainwashed the German people into accepting Nazi beliefs. Through the use of the cinema, the radio and newspapers, they had put forward Nazi views of how Germans should live their lives. Evidence One is the view of an historian writing in a GCSE history textbook. The author would have had time to research and reflect upon what went on in Germany in the 1930s and he came to the conclusion that propaganda and censorship were powerful and effective tools. This interpretation is supported by Evidence Three which is a contemporary photograph showing a large crowd of loyal party members giving the 'Heil Hitler' salute. This image gives the impression that Germans were very supportive of the Nazi regime. However, we do not know if the photograph was staged and was deliberately produced by Goebbels's Propaganda Ministry to create the impression of mass support.

Evidence Two puts forward an alternative interpretation which disagrees with the interpretation in Evidence One. It suggests that the German people were reluctant supporters of the Nazi regime and did not really believe what was printed in the newspapers. Many Germans secretly ignored the Nazi propaganda and just gave the impression of believing it. The author says that the Nazis were never successful in turning all Germans into loyal and committed National Socialists. Evidence Two is taken from the memoirs of a Social Democrat who lived in Germany in the 1930s. The interpretation might be biased in its viewpoint as the Party had been forced out of politics. They saw the Nazis as their political opponents and it is therefore difficult to test the accuracy of their interpretation. However, having examined all three pieces of evidence I think that the interpretation put forward in Evidence One is correct as it shows that the Nazis were successful in using propaganda and censorship to brainwash the German people into becoming loyal supporters. The interpretation is backed up by Evidence Three.

Comment on candidate performance

This is a developed answer which discusses the given interpretation and identifies and uses information from Evidence One and Evidence Three as supporting sources. The content of each source is analysed and contextualised through the inclusion of own knowledge. Attention has been paid to the attributions of both sources and how this has influenced the given interpretation. A counter-interpretation has been identified in Evidence Two with the suggestion that this source may be biased in its viewpoint. Reasons for the possible biased nature of this interpretation have been suggested, and this has been linked to contextual knowledge. The answer concludes with a judgement upon the value of the given interpretation. The answer displays the characteristics of a high performing answer worthy of marks within the highest level.

15 How did Nazi racial and religious policy affect life in Germany?

Source A From a private letter by a Jewish refugee, 1933

On the blackest day of all Saturdays big trucks patrolled the Berlin streets from which Nazis shouted down through loudspeakers: 'Down with the Jews!'; 'Jews, die like beasts!' One of the most popular songs of these inhumane beasts was: 'If Jewish blood flows from the knife, things will go much better.' The words for this song were written by a Nazi poet.

This source provides evidence of the anti-Semitism which was typical of Nazi Germany. In order to win support in the years before 1932 Hitler had used the Jews as the scapegoats for many of Germany's problems, including defeat in the First World War and the Treaty of Versailles. Once in power, the Nazi propaganda machine was used to turn more and more Germans against the Jews and justify a policy of persecution. Moreover, Hitler was determined to reduce the influence of the German Catholic and Protestant Churches. Christian ideas contrasted greatly to those of the Nazi Party.

TASK

Study Source A. What does it tell you about Nazi attitudes towards Jews living in Germany?

This chapter answers the following questions:

- What was Nazi racial policy?
- Why and how did the Nazis persecute the Jews?
- How did the Nazis change relations with the Catholic and Protestant Churches?

Examination guidance

Throughout this chapter you will be given the opportunity to practise different exam-style questions and detailed guidance on how to answer question 2(a). This is a 'describe' question which requires you to display specific knowledge of an historical event. It is worth 4 marks.

What was Nazi racial policy?

Central to Nazi policy was the creation of a pure German state. This meant treating all non-German groups, especially the Jews, as second-class citizens. Hitler's theory of race was based on the idea of the 'master race' and the 'subhumans'. He tried to back up this theory by saying that the Bible showed there were only two races – the Jews and the Aryans – and that God had a special purpose for the Aryans.

Master race

The Nazis believed that the Germans were a pure race of Aryan descent – from the *Herrenvolk* or master race. They were shown in art as blond, blue-eyed, tall, lean and athletic – a people fit to master the world. However, this race had been contaminated by the 'subhumans'.

Subhumans

Jews and Slavs on the other hand were the *Untermenschen* or subhumans. Nazi propaganda portrayed Jews as evil moneylenders. Hitler regarded the Jews as an evil force and was convinced of their involvement in a world conspiracy to destroy civilisation.

Source A A poster from an exhibition, used by the Nazis to turn people against the Jews, with the caption 'The Eternal Jew'

Making the master race

Hitler believed that Germany's future was dependent on the creation of a pure Aryan racial state. This would be achieved by:

- selective breeding
- destroying the Jews.

Selective breeding meant preventing anyone who did not conform to the Aryan type from having children. The SS were part of the drive for selective breeding. They recruited men who were of Aryan blood, tall, fair-haired and blue-eyed. They were only allowed to marry women of Aryan blood.

Source B From a speech given by Hitler to Nazi supporters in 1922

There can be no compromise. There are only two possibilities. Either victory of the Aryan Master Race or the wiping out of the Aryan and the victory of the Jew.

TASKS

1. Describe Nazi racial theory. (For guidance on how to answer this type of question, see page 175.)
2. What do Sources A and B suggest about Nazi attitudes towards the Jews? (For guidance on how to answer this type of question, see page 132.)

Why and how did the Nazis persecute the Jews?

Hitler and the Nazi Party were by no means the first to think of the Jews as different and treat them with hostility as outsiders. Anti-Semitism goes back to the Middle Ages.

Source A From *Mein Kampf* written by Hitler in 1924

Was there any form of filth or crime without at least one Jew involved in it? If you cut continuously into such a sore, you find, like a maggot in a rotting body, often dazzled by the light – a Jew.

Why were the Jews persecuted? →

Jewish people have been persecuted throughout history, for example in England during the Middle Ages. This is because Jewish people stood out as different in regions across Europe. They had a different religion and different customs. Some Christians blamed the Jews for the execution of Christ and argued that Jews should be punished forever. Some Jews became moneylenders and became quite wealthy. This increased resentment and suspicion from people who owed them money or were jealous of their success. →

Hitler had spent several years in Vienna where there was a long tradition of anti-Semitism. He lived as a down-and-out and resented the wealth of many of the Viennese Jews. In the 1920s he used the Jews as scapegoats for all society's problems. He blamed them for Germany's defeat in the First World War, hyperinflation in 1923 and the Depression of 1929. →

Hitler was determined to create a pure racial state. This did not include the 100,000 Jews who were living in Germany. He wanted to eliminate the Jews from German society. He had no master-plan for achieving this, however, and until the beginning of the Second World War, a great deal of Nazi Jewish policy was unco-ordinated.

TASKS

1. Use Source A and your own knowledge to explain why Hitler saw the Jews as the enemy of Germany. (For guidance on how to answer this type of question, see page 141.)
2. Why was the cartoon (Source B) published in the early 1930s? (For guidance on how to answer this question, see page 188.)
3. Explain why the Nazis persecuted the Jews.

Source B A Nazi cartoon of the early 1930s with the title 'Jewish department store octopus'

Anti-Semitism in schools

The persecution of the Jews did not begin immediately. Hitler needed to ensure that he had the support of most of the German people for his anti-Semitic policies. This was achieved through propaganda and the use of schools. Young people especially were encouraged to hate Jews, with school lessons and textbooks putting across anti-Semitic views.

School textbooks and teaching materials were controlled by the government Ministry of Education. The government was able to put anti-Semitic material into every classroom. In addition, laws were passed to restrict the role of education for Jewish people. In October 1936 Jewish teachers were forbidden to give private tuition to German students. In November 1938 Jewish children were expelled from German schools.

Source C Jewish schoolchildren being humiliated in front of their class. The writing on the board reads 'The Jews are our greatest enemy!' and 'Beware of the Jews!'

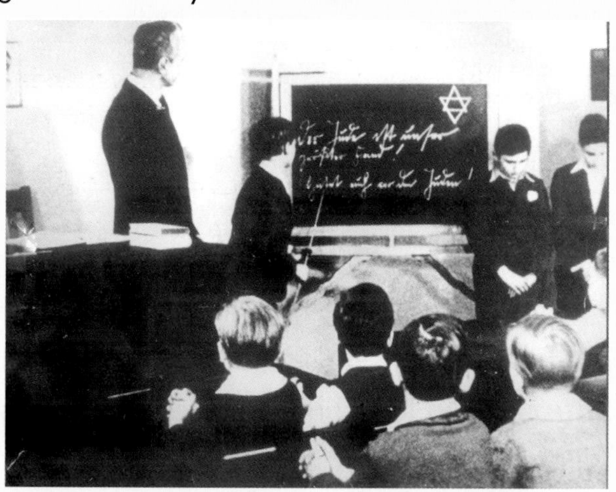

Source D From the memoirs of a German mother, written after the Second World War

One day my daughter came home humiliated. 'It was not so nice today.' 'What happened?' I asked. The teacher had sent the Aryan children to one side of the classroom, and the non-Aryans to the other. Then the teacher told the Aryans to study the appearance of the others and to point out the marks of their Jewish race. They stood separated as if by a gulf, children who had played together as friends the day before.

Source E Extract from a school textbook used in Germany in the 1930s

1. The Jewish race is much inferior to the Negro race.
2. All Jews have crooked legs, fat bellies, curly hair and look untrustworthy.
3. The Jews were responsible for the First World War.
4. They are to blame for the treaty of Versailles and hyperinflation.
5. All Jews are Communists.

TASKS

4 Study Source C. What does it show you about the treatment of Jewish school children?

5 How useful are Sources D and E to an historian studying how education was used to encourage hatred of the Jews? (For guidance on how to answer this type of question, see pages 155–56.)

6 Describe how life changed for Jewish children under the Nazis. (For guidance on how to answer this type of question, see page 175.)

Measures taken against the Jews

1933

April	The SA organised a boycott of Jewish shops and businesses. They painted 'Jude' (Jew) on windows and tried to persuade the public not to enter. Thousands of Jewish civil servants, lawyers and university teachers were sacked.
May	A new law excluded Jews from government jobs. Jewish books were burnt.
September	Jews were banned from inheriting land.

1934

Local councils banned Jews from public spaces such as parks, playing fields and swimming pools.

1935

May	Jews were no longer drafted into the army.
June	Restaurants were closed to Jews all over Germany.
September	The Nuremberg Laws were a series of measures aimed against the Jews passed on 15 September. This included the Reich Law on Citizenship, which stated that only those of German blood could be German citizens. Jews lost their citizenship, the right to vote and hold government office. The Law for the Protection of German Blood and Honour forbade marriage or sexual relations between Jews and German citizens.

1936

April	The professional activities of Jews were banned or restricted – this included vets, dentists, accountants, surveyors, teachers and nurses.
July–August	There was a deliberate lull in the anti-Jewish campaign as Germany was hosting the Olympics and wanted to give the outside world a good impression.

1937

September	For the first time in two years Hitler publicly attacked the Jews. More and more Jewish businesses were taken over.

1938

March	Jews had to register their possessions, making it easier to confiscate them.
July	Jews had to carry identity cards. Jewish doctors, dentists and lawyers were forbidden to treat Aryans.
August	Jewish men had to add the name 'Israel' to their first names, Jewish women, the name 'Sarah', to further humiliate them.
October	Jews had the red letter 'J' stamped on their passports.
November	*Kristallnacht* (see page 172). Jewish children were excluded from schools and universities.

TASKS

7 Make a copy of the table below and give examples of measures which removed Jews' political, social or economic rights. One example has been done for you.

Political	Economic	Social
	Boycott of shops	

8 Using a flow diagram, show the key changes in the lives of Jews in Germany 1933–39.

9 Describe how the position of Jews living in Germany changed during the years 1933–38. (For guidance on how to answer this type of question, see page 175.)

Kristallnacht (9 November 1938) and after

On 8 November 1938 a young Polish Jew, Herschel Grynszpan, walked into the German Embassy in Paris and shot the first official he met. He was protesting against the treatment of his parents in Germany who had been deported to Poland.

Goebbels used this as an opportunity to organise anti-Jewish demonstrations, which involved attacks on Jewish property, shops, homes and synagogues across Germany. So many windows were smashed in the campaign that the events of 9–10 November became known as *Kristallnacht*, meaning 'Crystal Night' or 'the Night of Broken Glass'. About 100 Jews were killed and 20,000 sent to concentration camps.

Many Germans were disgusted at *Kristallnacht*. Hitler and Goebbels were anxious that it should not be seen as the work of the Nazis. It was portrayed as a spontaneous act of vengeance by Germans.

Source F An account of *Kristallnacht* published in the *Daily Telegraph*, a British newspaper, on 12 November 1938

Mob law ruled in Berlin throughout the afternoon and evening as hordes of hooligans took part in an orgy of destruction. I have never seen an anti-Jewish outbreak as sickening as this. I saw fashionably dressed women clapping their hands and screaming with glee while respectable mothers held up their babies to see the 'fun'. No attempt was made by the police to stop the rioters.

Hitler officially blamed the Jews themselves for having provoked the attacks and used this as an excuse to step up the campaign against them. He decreed the following:

- The Jews to be fined 1 billion *Reichmarks* as compensation for the damage caused.
- Jews can no longer own or manage businesses or shops or employ workers.
- Jewish children can no longer attend Aryan schools.

The persecution continued in 1939.

- In January the Reich Office for Jewish Emigration was established with Reinhard Heydrich as its director. The SS now had the responsibility for eliminating Jews from Germany completely by forced emigration. They wanted other countries to take the Jews as refugees and even discussed a scheme to settle Jews in Madagascar.
- In the following months Jews were required to surrender precious metals and jewellery.
- On 30 April Jews were evicted from their homes and forced into designated Jewish accommodation or **ghettos**.
- In September Jews were forced to hand in their radio sets so they could not listen to foreign news.

Source G An account of *Kristallnacht* published in *Der Stürmer*, an anti-Semitic German newspaper, on 10 November 1938

The death of a loyal party member by the Jewish murderer has aroused spontaneous anti-Jewish demonstrations through the Reich. In many places Jewish shows have been smashed. The synagogues, from which teachings hostile to the state and people are spread, have been set on fire. Well done to those Germans who have ensured revenge for the murder of an innocent German.

TASKS

10 How useful are Sources F and G to an historian studying the events of Kristallnacht? (For guidance on how to answer this type of question, see pages 155–156.)

11 How seriously did the following measures threaten the position of Jews in Nazi Germany? Rate them 1–10, with 10 being very serious.

- Boycott of Jewish shops 1933
- Nuremberg Laws
- *Kristallnacht* 1938
- Deportation 1939

12 Was the boycott of Jewish shops the worst problem faced by Jews in Germany in the years 1933–38?

> In your answer you should discuss the seriousness of the problems faced by Jews during the years 1933–38, including the impact of the boycott of Jewish shops.

(For guidance on how to answer this type of question, see pages 195–96.)

How did the Nazis change relations with the Catholic and Protestant Churches?

Nazi ideals were opposed to the beliefs and values of the Christian Church.

Nazism	Christianity
Glorified strength and violence.	Teaches love and forgiveness.
Despised the weak.	Helps the weak.
Believed in racial superiority.	Respect for all people.
Saw Hitler as god-like figure.	Belief in God.

However, Hitler did not immediately persecute Christianity or the German Churches because Germany was essentially a Christian country. Almost two-thirds of the population was Protestant, most of whom lived in the north. Almost one-third was Catholic, most of whom lived in the south. Many saw Nazism as a protection against the atheism of communism and as an upholder of traditional family values and morals, in contrast to the immoral attitudes of the Weimar period.

Relations with the Catholic and Protestant Churches

At first Hitler co-operated with the Catholic and Protestant Churches. Eventually, however, his attempts to control them brought opposition.

The Catholic Church

In 1933 Hitler viewed the Catholic Church as a threat to his Nazi state:

- Catholics owed their first allegiance not to Hitler but to the Pope. They therefore had divided loyalties.
- There were Catholic schools and youth organisations whose message to the young was at odds with that of the Nazi Party.
- The Catholics consistently supported the Centre Party. Hitler intended to remove this party.

In 1933 Hitler decided to work with the Catholic Church and signed a concordat, or agreement, with the Pope. The Pope agreed that the Catholic Church would stay out of politics if Hitler agreed not to interfere with the Church. Within a few months Hitler had broken this agreement:

- Priests were harassed and arrested. Many criticised the Nazis and ended up in concentration camps.
- Catholic schools were interfered with and eventually abolished.
- Catholic youth movements closed down.
- Monasteries were closed.

In 1937 Pope Pius XI made his famous statement 'With Burning Anxiety' in which he attacked the Nazi system and their abuse of human rights. As a result, up to 400 Catholic priests were arrested and sent to Dachau concentration camp.

Source A From police reports in Bavaria in 1937 and 1938

The influence of the Catholic Church on the population is so strong that the Nazi spirit cannot penetrate. The local population is ever under the strong influence of the priests. These people prefer to believe what the priests say from the pulpit than the words of the best Nazi speakers.

The Protestant Church

Many Protestants opposed Nazism, which they believed conflicted greatly with their own Christian beliefs, as well as the new Reich Church. They were led by Pastor Martin Niemöller, a First World War submarine commander. In December 1933 they set up the Pastors' Emergency League for those who opposed Hitler. In the following year they set up their own Confessional Church. Niemöller was arrested in 1937 and sent to a concentration camp. The Confessional Church was banned.

Source B From a school history textbook about Nazi Germany, written in 1997

The Nazis never destroyed the established Churches in Germany. They made it difficult for Christians to worship but the churches remained open and services were held. However, Hitler succeeded in his aim of weakening the Churches as a source of resistance to his policies.

The National Reich Church

There were some Protestants who admired Hitler. They were called 'German Christians', wore Nazi uniforms and gave the German greeting '*Heil Hitler*'. Their slogan was 'The **swastika** on our chests and the Cross in our hearts'.

Source C A Protestant pastor speaking in a 'German Christian' church in 1937

We all know that if the Third Reich were to collapse today, Communism would come in its place. Therefore we must show loyalty to the Führer who has saved us from Communism and given us a better future. Support the 'German Christian' Church.

Source D Reich Bishop Müller after the consecration of the Gustav-Adolf church, Berlin, 1933

German Protestants belonged to 28 Church groups. In 1933, under Nazi pressure, they agreed to unite to form a National Reich Church. Their leader was Ludwig Müller who became the Reich Bishop, which means national leader, in September 1933. It was a deliberate attempt to Nazify the church structure. The Bible, cross and other religious objects were removed from the altar and replaced with a copy of *Mein Kampf* and a sword.

In 1935 a Ministry of Churches was set up under the leadership of Hans Kerrl. Church schools were abolished and the Nazis aimed to influence young people by promoting the Hitler Youth rather than the Church youth clubs.

TASKS

1. Eventually Hitler would have completely removed the Christian Churches and replaced them with a Nazi Church. Who or what would have taken the place of the following:
   - God
   - the Bible
   - the cross as a symbol
   - the disciples?
2. Explain why Hitler wanted to control the Church in Germany.
3. How far does Source A on page 173 support the view that the Nazis had only limited success in controlling the Church?
4. How useful are Sources B and C to an historian studying Nazi attempts to control the Church in Germany? (For guidance on how to answer this type of question, see page 155–56.)
5. Study Source D. What does it tell you about the National Reich Church?
6. Study Source D. You are an opponent of the new National Reich Church. Devise a caption for the photograph.

Examination guidance

This section provides guidance on how to answer a 'describe' question which requires you to demonstrate specific knowledge of an historical event. This is worth 4 marks.

Describe the treatment of Jews in Germany between 1933 and 1939. (4 marks)

Tips on how to answer

- Make sure you **only include information that is directly relevant**.
- It is a good idea to start your answer using the words from the question. For example: 'The treatment of Jews living in Germany … '
- Try to **include specific factual details** such as dates, events, the names of key people. The more informed your description the higher the mark you will receive.
- Aim to **cover at least two key points**.

Response by candidate

The treatment of Jews living in Germany grew increasingly harsh between 1933 and 1939. Hitler had constantly said bad things about the Jews and when he came to power in January 1933 he began to target them. In April the Nazis enforced a boycott of Jewish shops and this was followed by banning Jews from working in certain professions such as the civil service, and working as teachers, judges and doctors. In 1935 the Nuremburg Laws took away the rights of Jews to be German citizens and banned them from marrying Aryan Germans.

By the mid-1930s life for Jews was much harder and they could be arrested and held in prison or concentration camp without any trial. One of the worst actions against them took place in November 1938 and was given the name Kristallnacht. On that night SA men attacked Jewish shops and synagogues in towns across Germany, smashing the windows and setting fire to the buildings. Many Jews were killed that night. Their treatment had got much harsher by 1939.

A number of key events are dealt with in chronological order.

A good range of specific factual detail.

Covers several key points and has clear links to the question.

Section C

War and its impact on life in Germany, 1939–47

Source A From a letter written in January 1943 by Hans Scholl, the leader of the White Rose Group

The war is approaching its inevitable end. With mathematical certainty Hitler is leading the German nation to disaster. Now is the time for those Germans to act who want to avoid being lumped with the Nazi Barbarians by the outside world. Only in broadminded co-operation between the peoples of Europe can the basis be established for a new society. Freedom of speech, freedom of belief, protection of the individual citizen against criminal power – these are the foundations of a new Europe.

This section examines the effects of the war on Germany, the extent of opposition to the Nazis during the war years and the division of the defeated Germany.

The war brought great changes in Germany, particularly the effects of mass bombing on everyday life and the introduction of a policy of '**Total War**'. Moreover, the war encouraged opposition to Hitler and the Nazis from groups such as the Edelweiss Pirates and the White Rose Group and from the military, especially the July Bomb Plot. The defeat of Germany brought about the division of Germany and Berlin. Nazi leaders were arrested and put on trial at Nuremberg.

Each chapter explains a key issue and examines important lines of enquiry as outlined below:

Chapter 16: How was life affected during the war years?

- What was life like during the early years of the war, 1939–41?
- What was life like during the later war years, 1942–45?
- How were Jews treated during the war years?

Chapter 17: How much opposition was there to the Nazis in Germany during the war years?

- What opposition was there to Nazi rule within Germany from civilians?
- What opposition was there to Nazi rule within Germany from the military?

Chapter 18: What was the situation in Germany following total defeat in the war?

- How was Germany defeated?
- How was Germany punished by the Allies?
- What happened to Germany after the war?

16 How was life affected during the war years?

Source A A painting by a German artist, 1943, showing the damage caused by the Allied bombing of Germany

TASKS

Study Source A. What does it show you about the effects of the bombing on German cities by 1942?

The German people were not, at first, greatly affected by German involvement in the Second World War. However, this was to change in the years after 1942, due to the move towards a Total War economy, the effects of Allied bombing and greater and greater shortages, especially of food. Moreover, Nazi policies towards the Jews moved from persecution and forcing them out of Germany, to the introduction of the Final Solution in Nazi-occupied areas of Eastern Europe.

This chapter answers the following questions:

- What was life like during the early years of the war, 1939–41?
- What was life like during the later war years, 1942–45?
- How were Jewish people treated during the war years?

Examination guidance

Throughout this chapter you will be given the opportunity to practise different exam-style questions and detailed guidance on how to answer question 2(b). This requires you to explain the purpose behind the creation of a primary source at a particular time. It is worth 6 marks.

What was life like during the early years of the war, 1939–41?

The Second World War brought great changes to the lives of the German people.

Initial impact

At first the war had little effect on people living in Germany. ***Blitzkrieg*** brought quick victories and little suffering to civilians in German cities. There were no food shortages and each victory brought new supplies of raw materials. Lovely things such as gold, paintings and silk stockings poured into Germany. German successes in Poland and Western Europe made Hitler even more popular.

From the start, Germany followed a policy of ***autarky***, or self-sufficiency, controlling supplies of food in order to avoid shortages. Rationing was introduced as early as 1939 and one direct result was that two out of five Germans came to follow a more healthy diet than they had before the war.

All sections of the community were encouraged to take part in the war effort. Members of the **Hitler Youth** carried out a variety of tasks, including collecting metal, clothing and books as part of the recycling campaigns.

Fearing bombing, children were evacuated from Berlin in September 1940 but many soon returned. It was not until the start of large air raids by the **Allies** from 1943 onwards that mass **evacuation** took place.

Source B Heinrich Hauser recalls life in Germany in 1940 in his book *Hitler Versus Germany: A Survey of Present-Day Germany From the Inside* (1940)

Every week, groups of Hitler Youth, one week boys and the next week girls, go from house to house to collect waste from the 'Raw Materials Saving Boxes', empty food-cans, tinfoil, and old newspapers. With handbarrows they march to the outskirts of towns and villages and pick over dump heaps for old pots, kitchen ranges, rusty buckets and bed frames.

Source A Germans relax at a street café on the Unter den Linden in Berlin in 1940

Source C A Nazi district leader, writing in a newspaper in 1940

The nation is filled with a trust in the Führer such as never before existed to this extent.

Changing role of women

Although the Nazis believed that a woman's place was in the home (see page 147), they had been recruiting more and more women into industry in the years after 1937. In 1933 there were 4.2 million married women working outside the home. This number had reached 6.2 million by 1939.

Nevertheless, the Nazis were reluctant to conscript women in the early years of the war. Labour shortages led to a gradual rethink. Indeed, by the autumn of 1944 a total of 13 million men had been conscripted into the armed forces, leaving a dwindling number of workers to produce the crucial armaments needed at the war front.

As early as January 1943 women between the ages of 17 and 45 were obliged to sign up for work, although only 400,000 were finally recruited. By 1944 around 41.5 per cent of women were in the workforce.

TASKS

1. What do Sources A and C suggest about life in Nazi Germany during the early years of the war? (For guidance on how to answer this type of question, see page 132.)
2. Use Source B and your own knowledge to explain why the Nazis followed a policy of *autarky*. (For guidance on how to answer this type of question, see page 141.)
3. Why was the poster (Source D) produced in 1943? (For guidance on how to answer this type of question, see page 188.)
4. Explain why the role of women changed during the Second World War.

Source D A German poster of 1943 with the words 'One Battle, One Will, One Goal: Victory at any Price'. It features a female worker

Propaganda

Goebbels made effective use of propaganda during the Second World War in order to maintain morale at home and ensure support for the war effort. This became much more essential in the later years of the war. During the string of German victories in the first two years of the war, Nazi propaganda, especially posters, portrayed Germany as literally smashing her enemies to pieces. Goebbels claimed that between December 1941 and January 1942 Germany gave 1.5 million furs and 67 million woollen garments to help the German army (***Wehrmacht***) in Russia.

Source E A poster released in the summer of 1940. It translates as: 'Into the Dust with All Enemies of Greater Germany'

From January 1943 the nature of German propaganda changed, due to the German defeat at **Stalingrad** in the Soviet Union and the Allied bombing of Germany cities.

- German posters shouted a new message after Stalingrad – Nazi Germany was the defender of Europe's ancient civilisation against the barbarian hordes of the East. A series of posters claimed that victory for Germany was certain in the long run.
- The bombing of German cities was used to increase support for the war effort, especially the policy of 'Total War'.
- Other campaigns urged people to save fuel, work harder and even try to avoid tooth decay.

Source F A poster published in February 1943, just after the defeat at Stalingrad. It pronounces 'Victory or Bolshevik Chaos'

TASKS

5 How useful are Sources E and F to an historian studying Nazi propaganda during the Second World War? (For guidance on how to answer this type of question, see pages 155–56.)

6 Explain why propaganda was important to the Nazis during the Second World War.

What was life like during the later war years, 1942–45?

Between 1942 and 1945 German civilians were far more affected by the war.

The move to Total War was signalled by a speech at the Berlin *Sportsplatz* by Goebbels in February 1943. Goebbels called for universal labour service and the closure of all non-essential businesses.

Source A From the speech made by Goebbels at the *Sportsplatz*, February 1943

I ask you: Do you believe with the Führer and with us in the final victory of the German people? I ask you: Are you determined to follow the Führer through thick and thin in the struggle for victory and to put up even with the heaviest personal burdens? I ask you: Do you want total war?

Goebbels' move to improve production and productivity was reinforced by the appointment of Albert Speer as **Reich** Minister for Armaments and Production in September 1943. Until Speer took over, the German economy, unlike the British one, was not fully geared for war production. Consumer goods were still being produced at nearly as high a level as during peacetime. No fewer than five 'Supreme Authorities' had control over armament production. Few women were employed in the factories, which were running only one shift.

Speer overcame these problems in the following ways:

- He took over direct control of the war economy.
- Factories were given autonomy or, as Speer put it, 'self-responsibility', and each factory concentrated on a single product.
- He divided the armament field according to weapon system, with experts rather than civil servants overseeing each department.
- Over these departments was a central planning committee headed by Speer, which took increasing responsibility for war production and, as time went by, for the German economy itself.
- He closed down small firms and moved workers to bigger, more efficient factories.
- He brought in more and more foreign workers to cover labour shortages. By 1944, 29.2 per cent of all industrial workers were foreign.

Speer had the full confidence of Hitler who readily agreed to all his suggestions. Speer's work led to a great increase in productivity. One of the best examples was the use of production-line assembly in the manufacture of Panzer III tanks in 1943. This cut by 50 per cent the man hours needed in its assembly. In the manufacture of **munitions**, output per worker increased by 60 per cent between 1939 and 1944, despite the disruption caused by Allied bombing.

Source B German tank and aircraft production

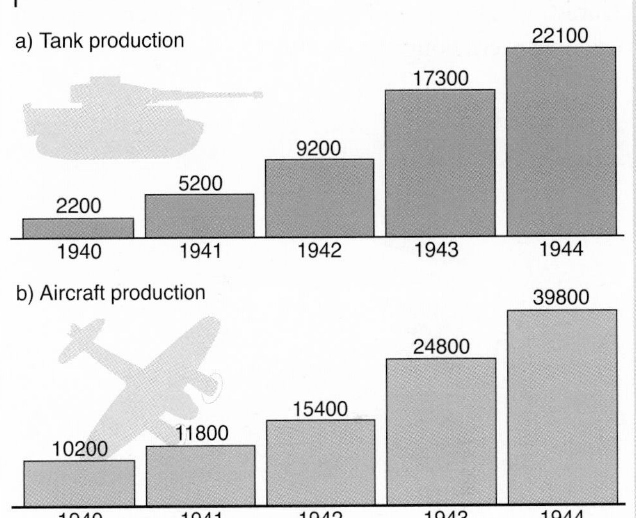

TASKS

1. Describe the policy of Total War. (For guidance on how to answer this type of question, see page 175.)
2. How successful was Albert Speer in increasing weapons production?
3. Why was Source A produced in February 1943? (For guidance on how to answer this type of question, see page 188.)
4. Study Source B. What does it tell you about Germany's war production between 1940–44?

Shortages and the black market

The Germans had to introduce food rationing at the start of the war. Nevertheless, at first the German people were allowed much more food than had been the case in the First World War.

However, as the defeats mounted, food became in even shorter supply and, in 1942, food rations were reduced. People were encouraged to use more exotic products brought in from the conquered countries, such as aubergines, fennel and Jerusalem artichokes. Ingenious recipes were devised by special groups to make use of available products. Parks and gardens in cities were dug up and used as vegetable patches.

It was not only food that was rationed. Items such as cigarettes, soap, clothing and shoes were also restricted. By 1941 women were only allowed one and a half cigarettes a day and old shoes had to be given up when new ones were bought.

Item	Ration
Bread	2.4 kg
Potatoes	3.5 kg
Meat	250 g
Cheese	60 g
Jam	175 g
Coffee	60 g
Cereal	150 g

A week's rations for one person in Germany in 1943.

Source C Some German wartime dishes

Baked udder with herbs
Stuffed calf's heart
Escalope of kohlrabi (cabbage)
Sorrel cutlets
Nettle soufflé
Daisy salad
Acorn coffee
Acorn nougat

A combination of shortages and also a sense that there was some unfairness in the distribution of commodities, with the rich and those with connections being favoured, encouraged illegal trading and the **black market**. The authorities did their best to stamp out the black market through more vigorous inspections.

TASKS

5 Describe rationing in Germany during the Second World War. (For guidance on how to answer this type of question, see page 175.)

6 Study Source C. Can you think of at least one more unusual dish appropriate for Germany during the Second World War?

Effects of Allied bombing

From 1942 the Allies – Britain and the USA – began bombing raids on German cities. These raids were designed to disrupt German war production and destroy the morale of the German civilians. They had devastating effects on Germany:

- Allied aircraft carried out a total of 1,442,280 missions over Germany. Around 2,700,000 bombs were dropped and an estimated 650,000 civilians were killed.
- A single raid on Cologne in 1942 killed 40,000 civilians.
- By the end of the war more than 3.5 million civilians had been killed.
- The centres of German cities, such as Berlin and Hamburg, became ruins.
- German civilians were also forced to work much longer hours with the introduction of a 60-hour week.
- Bombing made millions of people homeless. Many of these became refugees, leaving their towns to look for refuge elsewhere.

Source D From an eyewitness, Jacob Shultz, describing the aftermath of an air raid on Darmstadt

The hospitals were crammed. All preparations counted for nothing. You could travel without a ticket on a train. There were no windows in the trains, no schools, no doctors, no post, no telephones. You felt completely cut off from the world. To meet a friend who survived was a wonderful experience.

Source F Extracts from the diary of Goebbels

15 May 1943: Air raids are becoming more common again. But the number of planes we shoot down is huge.
29 June 1943: During the night over 800 English bombers raided Hamburg. A city of a million has been destroyed. It has given us problems that are impossible to deal with. Food must be found for the population of a million. Shelter must be found. There are 800,000 homeless people wandering up and down the streets, not knowing what to do.

Source E The centre of Dresden in 1945

TASKS

7 Study Source E. What does it tell us about the impact of the Allied air raids on Germany?

8 How useful are Sources D and F to an historian studying the effects of the Allied air raids on Germany? (For guidance on how to answer this type of question, see pages 155–56.)

People's Home Guard – the *Volkssturm*

By 1944 Germany's armed forces were heavily stretched and in September Hitler gave orders for the creation of the ***Volkssturm***. This was a type of People's Army, or Home Guard, which was intended to be used to defend Germany's cities from the Allied invasion. It was made up of men and boys who were expected to provide their own uniforms and weapons.

The *Volkssturm* lacked experience and was never a serious fighting force. Its men were poorly trained, possessed few weapons and suffered from low morale. An exception to this were some well-indoctrinated members of the Hitler Youth. They were keen to be involved and played an active role in the defence of central Berlin against the Russian assault upon the city in April 1945.

Source G Hitler's decree of 25 September 1944 setting up the *Volkssturm*

All German men aged between 16 and 60 who are capable of bearing arms are to be members. It will defend the homeland with all weapons and all means that seem appropriate.

Source H An elderly member of the *Volkssturm* recalls his involvement in the unit in the town of Fürth in northern Bavaria

I was never a soldier and so hadn't a clue about anything. After three hours of instruction from a holder of the Iron Cross, we were 'ready for action' to use a bazooka. Our platoon had twenty-three members and for these twenty-three we got given twelve weapons. I didn't get one and didn't make any effort to. I didn't understand how they worked.

Source I A German poster of 1944 advertising the role of the *Volkssturm*

TASKS

9 Why was the poster (Source I) produced in 1944? (For guidance on how to answer this type of question, see page 188.)

10 Describe the role of the People's Home Guard. (For guidance on how to answer this type of question, see page 175.)

11 Use Source H and your own knowledge to explain why the People's Home Guard were not very effective. (For guidance on how to answer this type of question, see page 141.)

How were Jewish people treated during the war years?

Shortly before the outbreak of the Second World War, the persecution of the Jews in Germany had intensified. In January 1939 the Reich Central Office for Jewish Emigration was set up, with Reinhard Heydrich as its director. The aim was forced emigration of German Jews. Madagascar, a large island off Africa, was even suggested as an area for resettlement. However, there is no evidence at this stage that the Nazis considered the mass slaughter of Jews.

The outbreak of war changed Nazi attitudes to the Jewish question in three ways:

- It allowed the more extreme treatment of the Jews without concern from world opinion.
- Early German success increased the number of Jews under Nazi control and removed the very areas they had hoped to use for forced emigration.
- It meant that the Nazis had to come up with more extreme solutions, especially because of the 3 million Jews in German-occupied west Poland.

Ghettos

This was the first solution. The Nazis gathered all the Jews into **ghettos** or 'Jewish reservations' in towns. Walls were built to keep them in. The largest ghetto was in Warsaw. Conditions in the ghettos were appalling. The Germans allowed only starvation rations and thousands died from hunger, the intense cold or the disease typhus. Around 55,000 Jews died in the Warsaw Ghetto.

Einsatzgruppen

Following the invasion of Russia in June 1941, and the German occupation of massive areas of western Russia, the Jewish problem intensified. The Nazis organised special murder squads known as the *Einsatzgruppen*. These squads moved into Russia behind the advancing German armies to round up and kill Jews. They raided towns and villages and picked out Jews, who were then marched to the outskirts of villages. Here they were forced to dig their own graves before they were shot. By 1943 it is estimated that the squads had murdered more than 2 million Russians, mainly Jews.

Source A An extract from *Notes from the Warsaw Ghetto*. This was written by a Jewish eyewitness

The most fearful sight is of freezing children. Little children with bare feet, bare knees and torn clothing stand dumbly in the streets weeping. Tonight ... I heard a tot of three or four crying. The child will probably be found frozen to death tomorrow morning, a few hours off.

Source B From the diary of Felix Landau, a member of an *Einsatzkommando*, based first in Lviv (Lwow) and then in Drohobycz

Drohobycz – 12 July 1941 ... At six in the morning I was suddenly awoken from a deep sleep. Report for an execution. Fine, so I'll just play executioner and then gravedigger, why not? ... Twenty-three had to be shot, amongst them ... two women ... We had to find a suitable spot to shoot and bury them. After a few minutes we found a place. The death candidates assembled with shovels to dig their own graves. Two of them were weeping. The others certainly have incredible courage ... Strange, I am completely unmoved. No pity, nothing. That's the way it is and then it's all over ... Valuables, watches and money are put into a pile ... The two women are lined up at one end of the grave ready to be shot first ... As the women walked to the grave they were completely composed. They turned around. Six of us had to shoot them. The job was assigned thus: three at the heart, three at the head. I took the heart.

TASKS

1. Explain why the outbreak of war led to harsher measures being taken against the Jews living under Nazi control.
2. Study Source A. What does it tell us about conditions inside the ghettos?

Source C A member of *Einsatzgruppe D* preparing to shoot a Jewish man in Vinnitsa, Ukrainian SSR, Soviet Union, in 1942. The photograph was inscribed: 'The last Jew in Vinnitsa'

The Final Solution

In the summer of 1941 a decision was taken by senior Nazi leaders to seek a permanent and final solution to the Jewish question, which was to exterminate them in death camps. Although Goering signed the order, it seems to have been mainly the idea of Himmler in order to deal with the problem of the increasing number of Jews in German-occupied areas. The decision was brought about by long-term factors, such as Hitler's hatred of the Jews and the desire to create a pure master race. More immediate factors were the massive numbers of Jews in German-occupied territories. The Nazis needed an efficient solution – extermination by gassing in death camps.

In January 1942 leading Nazis met at Wannsee in Berlin to work out the details of the 'Final Solution'. Death camps were built in Poland, far away from Germany, where Jews were to be worked to death. Work was carried out quickly on building gas chambers and crematoria at camps such as Auschwitz, Treblinka, Sobibor and Belzec. The first camp began operating on 17 March 1942 at Belzec on the eastern Polish border. By the summer of 1943 Jews from all over Europe were being transported to these camps.

The death camps

On arrival at the death camps, the Jews were divided into two groups:

- Those who were fit were put to work.
- The others were sent to the gas chambers.

The survivors were no better off than those sent to the gas chambers. They were worked to death in the labour camps. Older women, mothers with small children, pregnant women and children under ten were usually taken immediately to be executed.

Young boys would lie about their age and invent a skill or craft in order to be given work and stay alive.

TASKS

3 How useful are Sources B and C to an historian studying the activities pf the Einsatzgruppen? (For guidance on how to answer this type of question, see pages 155–56.)

Source D Errikos Sevillias, a Jew, describes his arrival at Auschwitz in 1943

*As we huddled together, the **SS** quickly separated the men from the women. They took the old and the sick and put them in a special line. They asked for twins, but no one volunteered, even though there were twins among us. The doctor who examined me held my arm down on a table and tattooed it with the number 182699. My entire body was shaved, then I was given a shower and afterwards issued with clothes which had huge red painted marks on them. This was so I could be easily spotted if I tried to escape.*

TASKS

4 How useful are Sources D and E to an historian studying the treatment of prisoners in the death camps? (For guidance on how to answer this type of question, see pages 155–56.)

5 Describe the final solution. (For guidance on how to answer this type of question, see page 175.)

Many died in the gas chambers from carbon monoxide and Zyklon B gases. The Nazi aim was to carry out the Final Solution as efficiently as possible. For example, at Treblinka, 140,000 Jews were killed each month in 1942. There was little opposition because most gas chambers were fitted out as showers so that the prisoners would not realise what was happening to them until it was too late. Bodies were burnt in ovens or left in mass pits.

Prisoners who were not gassed were given various jobs to do, with the worst being removing the dead bodies from the gas chambers. There was a strict daily routine, with roll calls for several hours per day before forced labour in mines or factories. The conditions were terrible. There was very little food, mainly bread and thin soup. Disease spread quickly. In addition, some inmates were used for medical experiments, generally without anaesthetics. Doctors were experimenting to create the perfect **Aryan** type.

By the time the camps were liberated by the Allies in 1945, up to 6 million Jews and 500,000 European gypsies, as well as countless other prisoners, had been worked to death, gassed or shot.

Source E *Roll call at Auschwitz I on a Christmas Eve*. This was painted by a camp prisoner after the war was over

Examination guidance

This section provides guidance on how to answer the question which requires you to explain the reasons for the creation of a primary source at a particular time. It is worth 6 marks.

Why was this source produced in 1943? (6 marks)

Source A A Nazi recruitment poster produced in 1943 calling on women to play a part in the war effort. The German caption reads 'Help victory by joining the air defence service'

Tips on how to answer

- Use your **knowledge of this topic area** to consider **the content of the source** and **what it shows**.
- Make use of the **information provided in the attribution** of the source – this can provide specific details such as publication date and the name of the newspaper, book or magazine in which the source first appeared. These details can help you to **identify motive** – why the source was produced at that time.
- You must support your reasoning with a reference to what was happening at the time that the source was produced. This is the **context**.
- You should spell out a **range of reasons** which address the key issue of **'why'** the source was produced at that time.

Response by candidate

Use of own knowledge to develop the content of the source and provide context.

Development of the attribution to help explain why the poster was produced in 1943.

Source A shows a Nazi recruitment poster which was produced in 1943. By 1943 the war was beginning to turn against Germany and the expansion of the Nazi empire had stopped. Germany was beginning to lose battles on several fronts, especially the Eastern Front against Russia. There was a pressing need for more Germans to become actively involved in fighting the war including women. This poster was designed to target women. It appeals to women to join the air defence service and it shows a young German woman dressed in a military uniform, giving the impression that she is doing her patriotic duty by joining up. This poster was produced after the turn of the tide in the war and it shows how the role of women in Germany was beginning to change. They were no longer expected to be just housewives and were being called upon to serve their country by helping to achieve 'victory' by joining the armed forces. They were also encouraged to take jobs in factories to release the men to fight. The poster was therefore deliberately produced to get women actively involved in fighting the war.

Comment on candidate performance

The candidate has successfully developed the content of the source and used their knowledge of this topic area to provide historical context, spelling out the importance and significance of the year 1943. Reference has been made to the turn in the tide of the war for Germany and how this triggered a change in the expectations and role of women in the war effort. A range of detailed reasons have been given to explain why the poster was produced in 1943, looking at the bigger picture of how and why women became involved in the war effort, either by joining up or entering the factories. This is a developed answer which displays the characteristics required to qualify for a mark [6] in the top level of response.

17 How much opposition was there to the Nazis in Germany during the war years?

Source A The execution of 12 Edelweiss Pirates in Cologne, November 1944

TASKS

1 Study Source A. What does it show you about opposition to Nazi rule?

2 Write a caption for the photograph as if it was published by:

a) the Propaganda Ministry of Dr Josef Goebbels

b) the Cologne branch of the Edelweiss Pirates.

The Nazi police state ensured that opposition was dangerous as it could cost you your freedom, your family or your life. Nevertheless, there were a number of groups and individuals who opposed the Nazi regime during the Second World War. These included young people such as the Edelweiss Pirates and the student group, the White Rose organisation. There was opposition from religious groups and specific individuals such as the priest Martin Niemöller and the pastor Dietrich Bonhoeffer, as well as opposition from within the German military itself. This was best demonstrated through the ill-fated Bomb Plot of July 1944.

This chapter answers the following questions:

- What opposition was there to Nazi rule within Germany from civilians?
- What opposition was there to Nazi rule within Germany from the military?

Examination guidance

Throughout this chapter you will be given the opportunity to practise different exam-style questions and detailed guidance on how to answer question 3. This is an essay question which requires you to evaluate two sides of an argument. It is worth 12 marks, with an additional 3 marks for SPaG.

What opposition was there to Nazi rule within Germany from civilians?

The Nazis faced opposition during the war from several youth groups as well as from religious leaders.

Young people

Not all young people accepted attempts to convert them to Nazi ideas through education and youth movements. By the end of the 1930s a number of gangs emerged that opposed Nazi attempts to control all aspects of their life. As the war developed, however, these gangs began to organise opposition to the war itself.

The Edelweiss Pirates

Many of the gangs eventually became part of a national resistance group known as the Edelweiss Pirates, named after the distinctive edelweiss flower they used as an emblem. Pirates wore check shirts and dark trousers. At weekends they would go on hikes, meet other groups and hope to beat up Hitler Youth patrols. The local groups gave themselves very distinctive names, such as the Roving Dudes, Kittelbach Pirates and the Navajos.

During the Second World War they collected propaganda leaflets dropped by Allied bombers and pushed them through people's doors. They also provided shelter to deserters from the armed forces. In November 1944 Barthel Schink, the 16-year-old leader of the Cologne Pirates, was one of 12 members of this group publically hanged by the **Gestapo**. They were denied a trial and were collectively charged with killing five people and planning an attack on the Gestapo headquarters in Cologne.

Source B A song from the Edelweiss Pirates

Hark the hearty fellows sing
Strum that banjo, pluck the string!
And the lassies all join in.
We're getting rid of Hitler,
And he can't do a thing.

We march by banks of Ruhr and Rhine
And smash the Hitler Youth in twain.
Our song is freedom, love and life,
We're pirates of the Edelweiss.

Source A The Edelweiss Pirates. This photograph appeared in a Nazi training manual for the Gestapo. The caption described them as 'A wild group from Cologne'

Swing groups

These were groups of mainly upper-middle-class youths that developed in large cities such as Hamburg, Berlin, Frankfurt and Dresden during the late 1930s. They rejected the ideals of the Hitler Youth and developed a rival culture. The groups met in bars, nightclubs and houses and played American black and Jewish music as well as swing. The Nazis felt threatened by their activities and closed the bars and made some arrests.

Source C From a report by the Reich youth leadership in 1942

The formation of groups of young people outside the Hitler Youth was on the increase a few years before the war. This has particularly increased during the war, to such a degree that a serious risk of the political, moral and criminal breakdown of youth must be said to exist.

The White Rose Group

The White Rose Group was set up by Hans and Sophie Scholl and Professor Kurt Huber at Munich University in 1941. Hans Scholl was a medical student who had served as a medical orderly on the Russian Front and had seen, first hand, the atrocities that were carried out against Jews and Poles and other non-Aryans. They believed that if they publicised these atrocities, then many Germans would support them in opposing the Nazis. The White Rose was a symbol of their belief in justice. They issued six different pamphlets trying to make people aware of the Nazi atrocities.

Source D Three of the leaders of the White Rose Group. On the left, Hans Scholl, in the centre Sophie Scholl and, on the right, Christoph Probst

Source E Extract from a White Rose pamphlet, 1943

Everyone has the right to an honest and workable government which guarantees the freedom of the individual and ensures the property of all ... Our present 'state' is a dictatorship of evil ... Why do you not rise up ... ? Sabotage armaments and war industry plants; sabotage meetings, festivals, organisations, anything which National Socialism has created. Hinder the smooth operation of the war machine.

These leaflets had to be issued anonymously, and were left in public places, on doorsteps or in mailboxes. They painted anti-Nazi messages on building walls during the night. However, on 18 February 1943 they were seen giving out leaflets by a janitor at Munich University, who was a Nazi Party member. The janitor informed the Gestapo and they were arrested, tortured and hanged. Sophie Scholl had her leg broken during Gestapo interrogation and had to limp to the scaffold on crutches.

TASKS

1. Describe the activities of the Edelweiss Pirates and the White Rose Group.
   (For guidance on how to answer this type of question, see page 175.)
2. What do Sources A and B suggest about the activities of the Edelweiss Pirates?
   (For guidance on how to answer this type of question, see page 132.)
3. How useful are Sources C and E to an historian studying opposition to Nazi rule during the war years? (For guidance on how to answer this question, see pages 155–56.)
4. Working in pairs, design a poster advertising the aims/activities of either the Edelweiss Pirates or the White Rose Group. The aim of the poster is to recruit new members.

Religious groups

Once the true nature of Hitler's regime was recognised, the Nazis also faced opposition from religious groups and individuals within Germany itself.

Martin Niemöller

Niemöller was a U-boat commander during the First World War but became a pastor in the German Protestant Church. In 1933 he welcomed Nazism, believing that Hitler would restore the greatness of Germany and reverse the Treaty of Versailles. However, his views changed when the Nazis set up the Reich Church, which Niemöller believed was much more about Nazism than Christianity. In 1934 he established the rival German Confessional Church, which made clear differences between the two. Over the next three years, Niemöller frequently spoke out in public against the Nazi regime. He was arrested and eventually imprisoned in Sachsenhausen concentration camp as a 'personal prisoner of the *Führer*'. Niemöller survived the next seven years and was alive when the concentration camp was liberated by the Allies in 1945. He died in 1984.

Source F A poem thought to be written by Niemöller in the early 1940s describing the Nazi persecution of specific groups

First they came for the ***communists****, and I did not speak out – because I was not a communist;*
Then they came for the trade unionists, and I did not speak out – because I was not a trade unionist;
Then they came for the Jews, and I did not speak out – because I was not a Jew;
Then they came for me – and there was no one left to speak out for me.

Dietrich Bonhoeffer

Bonhoeffer was a Church leader who, in 1934, helped Niemöller found the Confessional Church. He believed that Christianity could not accept Nazi racist views and that churchmen had to be free to preach against the Nazis. He openly spoke out against the Nazis, especially the Nuremberg Laws of 1935. In 1937 the Gestapo banned him from preaching. In 1939 Bonhoeffer joined the Abwehr, the German counter-intelligence service, within which a secret group was working to overthrow Hitler. He helped set up 'Operation 7', which assisted a small number of Jews to escape to Switzerland. In October 1942 Bonhoeffer was arrested by the Gestapo for plotting against Hitler. He was eventually transferred to Flossenburg concentration camp where, in April 1945, not long before the camp was liberated, he was executed by the SS.

Von Galen

Bishop Clemens von Galen was a Catholic bishop of Munster. At first he welcomed Hitler's rise to power and, although he criticised Hitler's racial policies, he believed that the Nazis would help save the Church from the atheism of **communism**. However, from 1934 onwards, having experienced Hitler's consolidation of power, he began to preach sermons attacking Nazi policies. In 1941 von Galen gave a string of sermons protesting against Nazi policies on euthanasia, Gestapo terror, forced sterilisations and concentration camps. About euthanasia he wrote: 'These are people, our brothers and sisters; maybe their life is unproductive, but productivity is not a justification for killing.'

He became known as the 'Lion of Munster', too popular to be punished. However, he was arrested after the July 1944 Bomb Plot, but released in 1945. He died in 1946.

TASKS

5 Use Source F and your own knowledge to explain why Niemöller opposed the Nazis. (For guidance on how to answer this type of question, see page 141.)

6 Explain why Bishop von Galen was arrested by the Gestapo.

7 Working in pairs, make a list to show the similarities and differences between the three religious leaders. Refer to their background, views and deaths.

What opposition was there to Nazi rule within Germany from the military?

The most serious opposition to Hitler came from within the army.

Growing discontent within the military

The main conservative opposition group during the war was the Kreisau Circle. This was a mixed group including aristocrats, **socialists**, clergymen and foreign office officials. It was named after the Silesian estate of Count Helmuth von Moltke where meetings of the circle took place from 1940. The aim of the group was to draw up plans for the period after Hitler's downfall. They produced a programme called *Principles for the New Order of Germany* but they had no plans to assassinate Hitler. Von Moltke was arrested in January 1944 for speaking out against the Third Reich. After his arrest, some members of the circle continued his work and developed links with Colonel von Stauffenberg.

The army leaders had reluctantly supported Hitler during the early years of the war when German armies had, for the most part, been successful. However, defeats, especially on the Eastern Front, brought opposition from within the army, led by General Ludwig Beck. He had resigned his post in the army in 1938 because he disagreed with Hitler's plans to challenge the Treaty of Versailles.

Together with Karl Goerdeler, a Nazi official, he had helped to organise two assassination attempts upon Hitler's life in March and November 1943, both of which failed. In July 1944 these men gave their full backing to plans by Colonel Claus von Stauffenberg to kill Hitler using a bomb.

Von Stauffenberg and the Bomb Plot

Claus von Stauffenberg was born into an aristocratic family in 1907. He had distinguished himself in the early years of the Second World War. However, he also witnessed the defeats on the Russian front where, in 1942, he had been badly wounded, losing his left eye, right arm and two fingers of his left hand. He was appalled by the brutality of the SS, especially the mass murder of Jews, and became convinced that it was the duty of the army commanders to remove Hitler.

Source A Stauffenberg in a letter, just before the July Plot

I know that he who will act will go down in history as a traitor but he who can and does not, will be a traitor to his conscience. If I did not act to stop this senseless killing, I should never be able to face the widows and orphans of the war.

He devised 'Operation Valkyrie', which involved using a bomb in a briefcase to kill Hitler. In May 1944 Stauffenberg was appointed as Chief-of-Staff to the Home Army Commander. This position enabled him to make preparations to lead the Home Army in support of the plot, once Hitler was dead. In addition, it gave him access to Hitler himself. After the assassination, the plotters intended to declare martial law, set up a temporary government and negotiate peace with the Allies.

Source B A script of a radio broadcast the plotters intended to make after Hitler's death

Hitler had only contempt for truth and right. In place of truth he put propaganda; in place of right he put violence. Propaganda and the Gestapo were his means of staying in power. In place of this the new Reich *Government will establish a state in accordance with the Christian traditions of the Western World. Based on the principles of civic duty, loyalty, service, and achievement for the common good, as well as respect for the individual and the natural rights of a human being.*

The events

On 20 July 1944 Stauffenberg took a briefcase containing two kilos of plastic explosive to a military conference at Obersalzberg in East Prussia. He was disturbed whilst setting the detonator and was only able to take one kilo into the room. He placed it under a large oak table, two metres away from Hitler. Someone else at the meeting moved the briefcase just behind one of the legs of the table. Stauffenberg then made the excuse of a pretend phone call, left the room and headed for an airstrip, where a plane was waiting to take him to Berlin.

Hitler was leaning across the table, studying a map, when the bomb exploded. One person died immediately and a further three died later. Hitler, however, shielded by the solid oak table leg, was still very much alive. He suffered only bruises and a perforated eardrum.

Source C Goering visits the room where the bomb blast took place

Although the assassination attempt had failed, the plot might still have succeeded if the leaders had acted quickly and decisively. However, the time taken by Stauffenberg to return to Berlin caused a fatal delay. It gave time for news of Hitler's survival to reach the other conspirators. Furthermore, the conspirators failed to cut all communications from Obersalzberg.

The effects of the plot

- Stauffenberg was arrested when he reached Berlin and shot.
- Beck committed suicide.
- Hitler took savage revenge on all those involved in the 'July' plot. In total, 5746 people were executed, including Stauffenberg and Beck. The dead included 19 generals and 27 colonels.
- The failure of the plot brought the German army under the tight control of the SS.
- Every member of the German army was required to reswear his loyalty oath, by name, to Hitler on 24 July 1944.
- The military salute was replaced throughout the armed forces with the German greeting in which the arm was outstretched and the salutation '***Heil Hitler***' was given.
- There was no early end to the war, which dragged on until May 1945.

TASKS

1. Use Source A and your own knowledge to explain why Stauffenberg plotted against Hitler. (For guidance on how to answer this type of question, see page 141.)
2. Study Source C. What does it show you about the July Bomb plot?
3. Describe the events of the July Bomb plot. (For guidance on how to answer this type of question, see page 175.)
4. Explain why the July Plot failed.
5. Devise either a newspaper headline or radio broadcast to be put out by the Nazis immediately after the failed assassination attempt.

Examination guidance

This section provides guidance on how to answer an essay question. The question carries 12 marks and up to an additional 3 marks will be awarded for spelling, punctuation and grammar (SPaG).

To what extent did the most serious opposition to the Nazis in Germany during the war years come from the German military? (12 marks)

> In your answer you should discuss the seriousness of the opposition from a variety of groups, including the German military.

See page 196 for more guidance on how to structure your essay to the question above.

Tips on how to answer

- You need to **develop a two-sided answer** which has balance and good support.
- You should **start by discussing the factor mentioned in the question**, using your factual knowledge to explain why this factor is important.
- You then need to **consider the counter-argument** by using your knowledge to examine other relevant factors.
- These points need to be discussed in some detail, starting a new paragraph for each point.
- Aim to link the paragraphs by using words such as 'other factors include', 'also important', 'in addition to', 'however'.
- **Avoid generalised comments** – the more specific your observations the higher mark you will get, providing the factual information is relevant to the question.
- **Conclude your answer with a link back to the question, making a judgement** about the importance of the factor listed in the question when ranked against the other factors you have discussed.
- You should aim to write between one and two sides of a page.

Now you have a go

To what extent did opposition from religious groups within Germany present the most serious challenge to Nazi rule during the war years? (12 marks)

> In your answer you should discuss the seriousness of the opposition from a variety of groups, including religious groups.

Introduction which links to the question.

Deals with the key factor mentioned in the question.

Provides precise details to support the argument.

Begins the counter-argument. Using the term 'however' makes it clear you are now looking at other factors.

Other factors are discussed such as youth groups, university students, the Church.

A new paragraph is started for each new factor.

A good reasoned conclusion which provides a clear judgement linked back to the question.

Response by candidate

During the war years opposition to Nazi rule within Germany became more open and more widespread. Opposition emerged from several sections of society but it varied in its strength and its effectiveness.

Amongst the most serious of all opposition was that from a section of the German military. In July 1944 a group of top generals who had regular meetings with Hitler used their position to try to assassinate him by blowing him up. They placed a bomb in ...

While this attempt came close to killing Hitler it ultimately failed. <u>However</u>, there were other opposition groups that emerged across Germany in protest at Nazi rule. Some young people such as the Swing Kids rebelled by listening to jazz music and ...

Likewise, students in Munich University who belonged to the White Rose group also displayed open opposition by ...

Religious groups also became more open in their criticism of Nazi policies during the war years. The Catholic Archbishop of Munster, von Galen, criticised the euthanasia policy and Protestant priests were equally critical of Nazi actions ...

The war was a heavy drain on Nazi resources and this made it easier for ordinary people to risk types of opposition. Some listened to BBC broadcasts on their radio sets to find out what was really happening in the war, others ...

Resistance and opposition to Nazi rule became more common and more open during the war years. This opposition came from many sections of society, from the German youth groups, from university students, from church leaders and from ordinary individuals. However, the greatest threat came from the military, from a group of top generals who came closest to killing Hitler in July 1944. This showed that many Germans were unhappy with Nazi rule and were prepared to oppose it.

18 What was the situation in Germany following total defeat in the war?

Source A Map of Europe, 1943, showing the German and Italian occupation of Europe

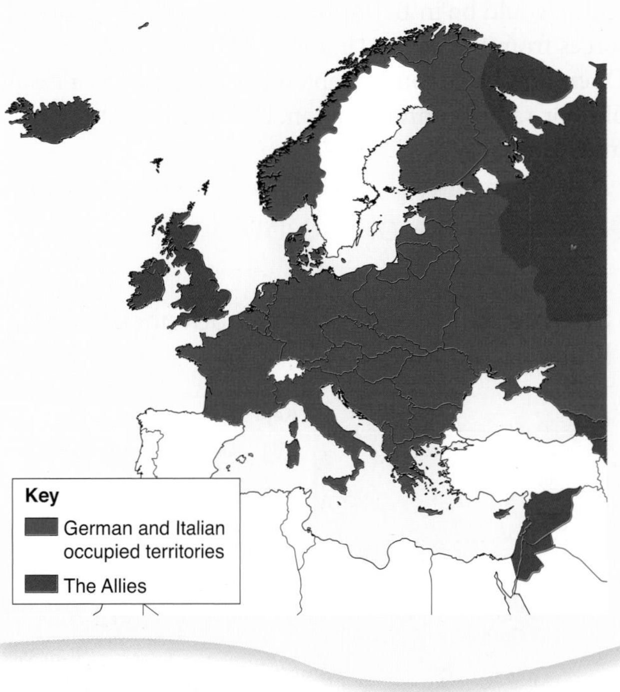

TASK

Study Source A. What does it show you about German occupation of Europe?

By the end of 1942, the Allies felt that the tide was turning in their favour. In North Africa, following the Battle of El Alamein (October–November 1942), German forces were forced to retreat. They then faced the Allied landings in Morocco and Algeria and were eventually pushed out of North Africa. The remaining German troops there surrendered in May 1943. These Allied victories were followed by the invasion of Sicily in July and the Italian mainland in September. Italy surrendered that month.

1943 was also a turning point for the Soviet Union when the siege of Stalingrad was lifted. In July 1943 the Germans were defeated at the Battle of Kursk, where they lost 2000 tanks, and the Soviet Union then began to advance westwards at a rapid rate.

German attempts to starve Britain into submission in the Battle of the Atlantic had failed by 1943 and its U-boats were no longer a major threat. A second front was established in June 1944, when the Normandy landings took place. Paris was liberated in August but Allied progress was slow. However, Hitler's last gamble at the Battle of the Bulge failed and Germany was then occupied by the Allies and divided into four military zones. The captured Nazi leaders were put on trial at Nuremberg.

This chapter answers the following questions:

- How was Germany defeated?
- How was Germany punished by the Allies?
- What happened to Germany after the war?

Examination guidance

In this chapter you will be given the opportunity to practise different exam-style questions.

How was Germany defeated?

Allied advances in the West, 1944–45

Source A One of the Normandy invasion beaches, on D-Day, 6 June 1944

TASK

1 Study Source A. What does it show you about the Allied landings in Normandy on 6 June 1944?

On 6 June 1944 the Allies secured a second front (the other being the Eastern Front) by staging landings of troops from England in Normandy. These were known as the **D-Day Landings**. After the successful establishment of secure areas, the Allies found it difficult to break out into Normandy but eventually did so and, on 25 August, Paris was liberated.

After this, the Allies moved towards Belgium and Luxembourg, but as the autumn approached, the advances towards Germany slowed down. In his desire to hasten the end of the war in the West, General Montgomery suggested an airborne attack behind the German lines. This was codenamed Operation Market Garden. Montgomery's plan was to secure key Rhine bridges so that the Allied forces could advance rapidly northwards and wheel into the lowlands of Germany, thereby skirting around the German defences. It was estimated that success would mean that the Western Allies would be in Berlin by Christmas 1944, before forces from the Soviet Union would arrive. The Operation began on 17 September but failed as a result of poor radio communication, bad weather and poor intelligence.

The Battle of the Bulge

Source B Map of German advances at the Battle of the Bulge

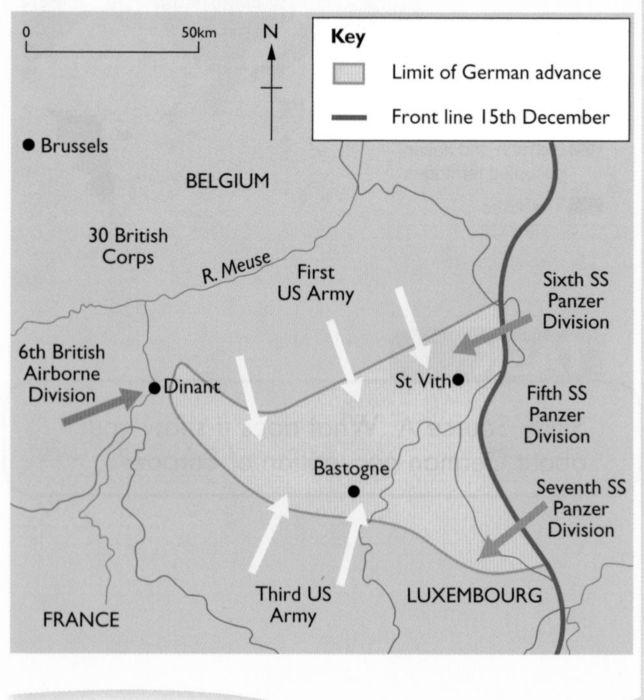

In December 1944 Hitler made his last attempt to defeat the Allies in the West. He wanted to split the Allied forces and prevent them using the port of Antwerp in Holland.

The offensive was made through the Ardennes and achieved total surprise. The attack was launched on 16 December and the Germans made rapid advances into Belgium and Luxembourg, creating a 'bulge' in the American lines (see Source B). There was savage fighting. The US suffered about 80,000 casualties and the Germans about 100,000.

However, the results of the Battle of the Bulge were devastating for the Germans. Their final reserves had been used and German forces were pushed back in the West and the East – they could no longer hold back the Allies' juggernaut. On 9 March 1945 the Allies at last pushed across the River Rhine at Remagen and, in late April, Soviet forces attacked Berlin.

Hitler refused to contemplate ending the war. Moreover, the German people were terrified of the Russians and fought desperately to keep them at bay.

TASKS

2 Explain why Operation Market Garden was launched.

3 Study Source B. What does it show you about the Battle of the Bulge?

4 Explain why the Battle of the Bulge was a failure for Germany.

5 Describe the war on the Eastern Front between 1943–45. (For guidance on how to answer this type of question, see page 175.)

Developments on the Eastern Front, 1943–45

By the summer of 1943 the Germans were outnumbered three to one in terms of tanks, and the Soviet Union was manufacturing them at an astonishing rate. The Germans were faced by an enemy that seemed to have limitless numbers of soldiers and vast amounts of war material and it could not hold back the Soviet forces. What marked out the war in the East was the intensity, savagery and scale. Not only were millions of soldiers killed but also millions of civilians. No one knows the exact number of dead Soviet civilians, but the figure is between 7 and 20 million. The Germans considered the Soviet civilians as subhumans (*Untermenschen*) and hence they were not accorded normal human treatment.

Source C Map showing the key events on the Eastern Front, 1941–45

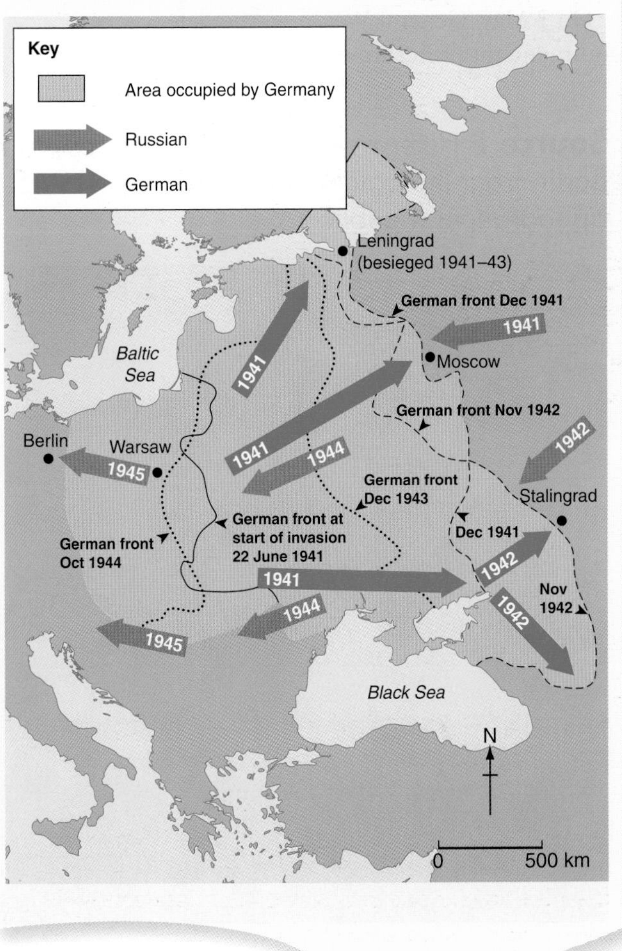

The fall of Berlin

There were no German troops occupying the Soviet Union by the end of 1944. Soviet forces liberated Warsaw in Poland on 17 January, Budapest in Hungary on 11 February and Vienna in Austria on 13 April.

The final Soviet attack on Berlin began on 16 April with an assault by around 1.5 million soldiers, 6300 tanks and 8500 aircraft. Millions of shells were fired into Berlin – a city that had already experienced two years of relentless bombing raids by the British and Americans. Berlin was surrounded by 24 April and combat deteriorated into house-to-house fighting. Having been surrounded, there were about 100,000 German soldiers (who were by now mainly old men – members of the *Volkssturm* – or members of the Hitler Youth) and they stood little chance against the highly trained Soviet forces.

As Soviet forces moved into Berlin, they became difficult to control and discipline broke down, especially when stocks of alcohol were found. There was rape, looting and violence on a huge scale.

On 2 May, General Weidling, the defence commandant of Berlin, ordered the surrender of German defending forces to the Red Army. However, it was not until 8 May that the last German troops surrendered, as a result of Germany's official surrender. About 300,000 Soviet troops had been killed or wounded in the battle for the city.

Source D From *Laughter Wasn't Rationed* by Dorothea von Schwanenfluegel, a German who was living in Berlin in 1945. She was writing in 1999

We noticed a sad looking young boy across the street standing behind some bushes in a self-dug shallow trench. I went over to him and found a mere child in a uniform many sizes too large for him, with an anti-tank grenade lying beside him. Tears were running down his face, and he was obviously very frightened of everyone. I very softly asked him what he was doing there. He told me that he had been ordered to lie in wait here, and when a Soviet tank approached he was to run under it and explode the grenade. I asked how that would work, but he didn't know.

Source E Hitler awarding the Iron Cross to members of the Hitler Youth who were defending Berlin from the Soviet attack, 20 April 1945. This was Hitler's 56th birthday and his last appearance in public

Source F A Berlin housewife writing in April 1945

The radio announced that Hitler had come out of his safe bombproof bunker to talk with the fourteen- to sixteen-year-old boys who had 'volunteered' for the 'honour' to be accepted into the SS and to die for their Führer in the defence of Berlin. What a cruel lie! These boys did not volunteer, but had no choice, because boys who were found hiding were hanged as traitors by the SS as a warning that, 'he who was not brave enough to fight had to die'. When trees were not available, people were strung up on lamp posts. They were hanging everywhere, military and civilian, men and women, ordinary citizens who had been executed by a small group of fanatics.

Source G A Soviet soldier placing the Soviet flag on the *Reichstag* building in Berlin, 2 May 1945

TASKS

6 How useful are Sources E and F to an historian studying the end of the Nazi regime in 1945? (For guidance on how to answer this type of question, see pages 155–56.)

7 What do Sources D and G suggest about the fall of Berlin? (For guidance on how to answer this type of question, see page 132.)

8 Study Source G. Why do you think it was important for the Soviet Union to fly its flag over Berlin in May 1945?

9 Re-read pages 198–201. Construct a timeline from 6 June 1944 to 8 May 1945 showing the key events. Place British/US events on one side of the line, and Soviet Union events on the other.

10 Describe the Soviet attack on Berlin. (For advice on how to answer this type of question, see page 175.)

The death of Hitler

During the Soviet attack on Berlin, Hitler was in his underground bunker in the Reich Chancellery, cut off from the reality of the world outside. At last accepting that the war could not be won, and that there was no escape, he made his final plans. Around midnight on 28 April, Hitler married Eva Braun. Interestingly, in keeping with Nazi requirements, the official had to ask both Hitler and Eva Braun whether they were of pure Aryan blood and whether they were free from hereditary illnesses.

After the wedding, Hitler then wrote his political testament in which he claimed that the war and Germany's misfortunes had been caused by international Jewry. He also expelled Himmler and Goering from the Nazi Party on grounds of betrayal. He then divided his own posts between Admiral Dönitz and Goebbels. Dönitz was to succeed him as Head of State and Supreme Commander of the Armed Forces and Goebbels was to be Head of Government and also Chancellor.

On 30 April, Hitler committed suicide – together with Eva. He intended using cyanide capsules and had them tested on his dog Blondi. The dog was taken to the Reich Chancellery garden and killed along with her puppies.

Hitler had made it clear that both his and his wife's body should be burned. He had heard what had happened to Mussolini's corpse, which had gone on public display in Milan, and did not want his body to be viewed in a similar way. At 3.30p.m., the bodies of Hitler and his wife were found in their private quarters by Martin Bormann and Josef Goebbels. There was a bullet hole in Hitler's right temple and Eva had died from swallowing poison. The bodies were then wrapped in blankets and taken to the entrance of the Chancellery, where they were soaked in petrol and set alight.

Chancellery guards later indicated that the two bodies were thoroughly burnt and unrecognisable. What remained of the bodies was found by Soviet troops on 4 May and taken away for examination. The Soviet authorities had Fritz Echtmann, a dental technician who had worked for Hitler's dentist, examine a jaw bone and two bridges from the remains. Echtmann used existing records and was able to identify both Hitler and his wife.

On 1 May, Goebbels committed suicide with his wife in the Chancellery (having administered poison to their six children). The other top Nazi in the Chancellery, Martin Bormann, is thought to have fled on 2 May. Grand Admiral Dönitz then appointed Schwerin von Krosigk as Chancellor and they attempted to form a government. Himmler and Goering were excluded. Dönitz retained Keitel and Jodl as *Wehrmacht* leaders.

TASKS

11 Describe Hitler's final days in the bunker. (For guidance on how to answer this type of question, see page 175.)

12 Explain why Hitler committed suicide in April 1945.

Other factors why Germany was defeated

- The **RAF** and **USAAF** destroyed industrial complexes, roads, bridges, railway yards and munitions factories. However, the output of German industry did not decline until early 1945 and it is difficult to measure the impact of the bombing campaign on civilians. It has been estimated that about 600,000 German civilians were killed as a result of Allied bombing.
- The Allies had access to tremendous industrial resources against which Germany and its allies found it impossible to compete.
- The invasion of the Soviet Union meant that Hitler had to fight a war on two fronts and, in addition, he had to send several divisions to assist Italy in North Africa and then in Italy itself.
- The war at sea was a failure for Germany. The U-boat threat was a major problem in 1942 when almost 1200 Allied ships were sunk. But technical developments – sonar, depth charges and centimetric radar – helped the Allies to combat the U-boats. The Allies were able to replace destroyed ships and, in 1944, only 117 Allied ships were sunk by U-boats.

Source H A Soviet cartoon from 1942 showing Hitler being strangled by the Allied powers

Source I Map of German areas bombed by the Allies in the Second World War

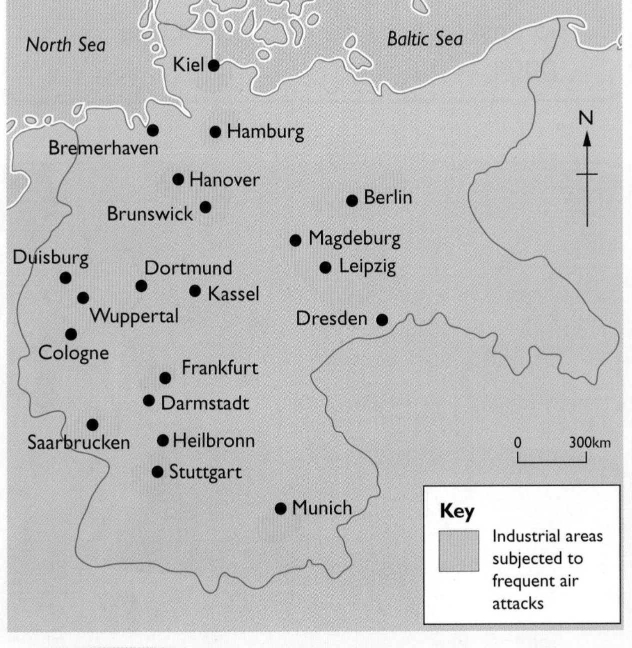

- German treatment of the civilians in the countries that they occupied led to the growth of resistance or partisan groups. These groups, especially in France, were given Allied assistance and meant that Germany had to keep many soldiers based in areas away from the actual fighting.
- Historians often cite the errors caused by Hitler meddling in military affairs, for example, the halting of German tanks outside Dunkirk, the refusal to allow his troops to retreat from Stalingrad and the belief that the Normandy invasion was a feint. In addition, Hitler was faced with three powerful leaders, Churchill, Roosevelt and Stalin, who inspired their peoples throughout the war years.
- Ordinary people in Britain and the USA were united in the belief that they were fighting to rid Europe of tyranny. In addition, they felt that their sacrifices were worth enduring in order to forge a better future for the world.

TASKS

13 Devise a caption for Source H.

14 Why was the cartoon (Source H) produced in 1942? (For guidance on how to answer this type of question, see page 188.)

15 Study Source I. What does it show you about the Allied bombing of Germany?

16 Was the impact of Allied bombing the most important reason for the defeat of Germany in 1945?

> In your answer you should discuss the impact of the various factors which caused the defeat of Germany, including the effects of the Allied bombing.

(For guidance on how to answer this type of question, see pages 195–96.)

The surrender of Germany

Following the events in the Chancellery (see page 202) Admiral Dönitz began negotiations with US General Eisenhower at Rheims in France, hoping to gain better terms than with the Soviet Union. He wanted to ensure that as many German troops as possible did not have to surrender to the Soviet Union. Eisenhower, however, insisted that Germany make a complete and unconditional surrender on all fronts. If there was no surrender then Eisenhower threatened to resume air raids. Dönitz then accepted that he had no option but to surrender and his representative, Chief of the Operations Staff of the Armed Forces High Command, Alfred Jodl, signed the surrender documents.

The first Instrument of Surrender, the official document indicating the end of fighting, was signed at Rheims, France at 2.41a.m. on 7 May 1945. The German High Command issued orders to all forces under its command to cease active operations at exactly 11.01p.m. on 8 May. A second Act of Military Surrender was signed on 8 May because Stalin felt that the Soviet representative of the previous day had not been senior enough.

Germany at the end of the war

Inside Germany, the devastation caused by the war was extensive. Around 3.25 million soldiers and 3.6 million civilians had been killed and the country was swarming with refugees. Millions fled the advancing Soviet forces and after the surrender millions of Germans were expelled from Poland, Hungary and Czechoslovakia. More than 25 per cent of all homes had been destroyed and only about 45 per cent of schools remained intact. Almost all major towns and cities lay in rubble.

The economy was in ruins and the transport system was non-existent. Money had become worthless and bartering became the means of exchange.

TASKS

17 Suggest reasons why Eisenhower refused to make separate terms with the Germans.

18 Why were German people frightened of the Soviet forces?

19 Describe the condition of Germany in May 1945. (For guidance on how to answer this type of question, see page 175.)

An aerial photo showing the damage to Anhalter station near the Potsdamer Platz in Berlin, taken in 1945. It was one of the city's largest stations and was badly damaged by Allied bombs.

How was Germany punished by the Allies?

The Allies agreed that Germany should never again have the opportunity to destroy European peace as it had in the two world wars. A key aim of the Allies was to prevent the resurgence of a powerful and aggressive Germany. Accordingly, decisions were made at the Yalta and Potsdam Conferences and it was accepted that Germany would have to be **demilitarised**, denazified, and democratised.

The Yalta Conference, February 1945

By early 1945 Germany was near to defeat, with Allied armies closing in on Berlin. The three Allied leaders were the Soviet leader Stalin, US President Roosevelt, and British Prime Minister Churchill (their nickname was the 'Big Three'). They met at Yalta in February 1945 to consider what to do with Germany and Europe once victory was achieved. They were still fearful of Hitler and were able mainly to agree on key issues. However, Stalin wanted the Germans to pay huge **reparations** but Roosevelt and Churchill agreed that it was not sensible to punish Germany too harshly. The Big Three could not agree on what to do with Poland. Final decisions were made at Potsdam, in July and August that year.

With regard to Germany, they agreed the following:

- The Soviet Union would enter the war against Japan once Germany had surrendered.
- To divide Germany into four zones: US, British, French and Soviet (see map, page 206).
- To divide Berlin into four zones in the same way (see map, page 206).
- To hunt down and try Nazi war criminals in an international court of justice.
- To allow countries that had been liberated from occupation by the German army to have free elections to choose the government they wanted.

The Potsdam Conference, July 1945

In the five months between the conferences, a number of changes took place that greatly affected relations and the outcome of the conference at Potsdam. Soviet troops liberated countries in Eastern Europe but did not remove their military presence. By July they occupied Latvia, Lithuania, Estonia, Finland, Czechoslovakia, Hungary, Bulgaria and Romania.

At Potsdam, the Allies agreed the following:

- To divide Germany and Berlin as per the Yalta agreement. Each of the four zones of Germany and four sectors of Berlin was occupied and administered by one of the Allies (see map on page 206).
- To demilitarise Germany.
- To re-establish democracy in Germany, including free elections, a free press and freedom of speech.
- That Germany had to pay reparations to the Allies in equipment and materials. Most of this would go to the Soviet Union, which had suffered most. The Soviet Union would be given a quarter of the industrial goods made in the western zones in return for food and coal from the Soviet zone.
- To ban the Nazi Party. Nazis were removed from important positions and leading Nazis were put on trial for war crimes at Nuremberg in 1946.
- That Poland's frontier was to be moved westwards to the rivers Oder and Neisse, acquiring German territory.

TASKS

1. Explain why the Yalta Conference took place.
2. Describe the decisions made about Germany at the Potsdam Conference. (For guidance on how to answer this type of question, see page 175.)
3. Study Source A on page 206. Suggest reasons why the division of Berlin was a problem for the Allies and Germany.

Source A Map showing the division of Germany and Berlin in 1948

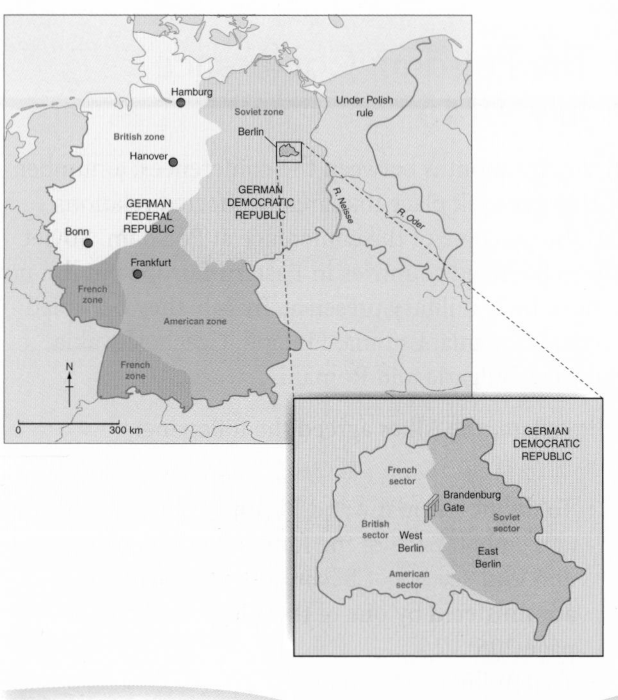

Source B A cartoon published in the *St Louis Post-Despatch* in 1945. The caption read 'Witness for the prosecution'

© *St Louis Post-Despatch*, used with permission, State Historical Society of Missouri, Columbia

The Nuremberg Trials

The Allies agreed to put on trial leading members of Nazi Germany as war criminals. Twenty two senior ranking Nazis were tried at Nuremberg, a place chosen because of its association with the development of the Nazi Party. The defendants were accused of conspiring to:

- wage war
- commit crimes against peace
- commit crimes against humanity (including the newly defined crime of genocide)
- commit war crimes such as abuse and murder of prisoners.

The trials began on 21 November 1945 and ended on 1 October 1946.

Almost 200 other Nazis were tried at Nuremberg, of whom 142 were found guilty of at least one of the charges. Twenty-four defendants received death sentences, of which 11 were subsequently amended to lifetime imprisonments, another 20 were sentenced to lifetime imprisonment, 98 were given prison sentences and 35 were acquitted. Four defendants had to be removed from trials due to illness, and four more committed suicide during the trials.

The defendants at Nuremberg. Front row, from left to right: Hermann Goering, Rudolf Hess, Joachim von Ribbentrop, Wilhelm Keitel, Ernst Kaltenbrunner, Alfred Rosenberg, Hans Frank, Wilhelm Frick, Julius Streicher, Walther Funk, Hjalmar Schacht. Back row from left to right: Karl Dönitz, Erich Raeder, Baldur von Schirach, Fritz Sauckel, Alfred Jodl, Franz von Papen, Arthur Seyss-Inquart, Albert Speer, Konstantin van Neurath, Hans Fritzsche.

Source C Table showing the fate of senior Nazis

Josef Goebbels	Suicide in the *Reich* Chancellery	1 May 1945
Heinrich Himmler	Suicide after capture	23 May 1945
Hermann Goering	Suicide after trial and before execution	15 October 1946
Robert Ley	Suicide while awaiting trial	25 October 1945
Joachim von Ribbentrop	Tried and hanged	16 October 1946
Field Marshal Wilhelm Keitel	Tried and hanged	16 October 1946
Alfred Jodl	Tried and hanged	16 October 1946
Wilhelm Frick	Tried and hanged	16 October 1946
Arthur Seyss-Inquart	Tried and hanged	16 October 1946
Fritz Sauckel	Tried and hanged	16 October 1946
Hans Frank	Tried and hanged	16 October 1946
Ernst Kaltenbrunner	Tried and hanged	16 October 1946
Julius Streicher	Tried and hanged	16 October 1946
Albert Speer	20 years in prison	
Rudolf Hess	Life imprisonment	Committed suicide in jail, 1987
Admiral Dönitz	10 years in prison	
Admiral Erich Raeder	Life imprisonment	
Baldur von Schirach	20 years in prison	

Source D Cartoon by David Low commenting on the end of the Nuremberg Trials. It was published in the *Evening Standard* newspaper, 4 October 1946

THE READERS: "WELL, THAT'S THE END OF THE NAZIS"

TASKS

4 Study Source B. What does it show you about the Nuremberg Trials?

5 Describe the events of the Nuremberg Trials. (For guidance on how to answer this type of question, see page 175.)

6 Research: study Source C and find out what position each person held in the Nazi Party.

7 Why was the cartoon (Source D) published in 1946? (For guidance on how to answer this type of question, see page 188.)

8 In groups of three or four, discuss whether you think the punishments given out at Nuremberg were fair or not.

What happened to Germany after the war?

Denazification

Denazification was the Allies' policy of removing traces of the Nazi regime from German society, culture, press, economy, judiciary and politics. The Allies not only had to punish and remove the senior members of the Nazi Party, they wanted to ensure that Nazism was removed from everyday life. By early 1947 the Allies held 90,000 Nazis in detention and almost 2 million were forbidden to work as anything but manual labourers.

Denazification in Germany was accomplished through a series of directives issued by the Allied Control Council, which oversaw the running of Germany in the aftermath of the war. Some of its key decisions about denazification were:

- 30 August 1945: the wearing of the uniform of the German army was prohibited.
- 10 October 1945: the National Socialist Party was dissolved and its revival was totally prohibited.
- 1 December 1945: all German military units dissolved.
- 12 January 1946: a set of comprehensive criteria for the removal from public office of those who had been more than nominal participants in the Nazi Party's activities. The category of persons to which the directive applied were those who had held significant positions in the Nazi Party or those who had joined prior to 1937, the time when membership became compulsory for German citizens.
- 13 May 1946: the publication and dissemination of Nazi or militarist literature was banned.

Special courts were set up to examine the extent of involvement of party members in the Nazi regime and to determine if they were suitable to play a part in the reconstruction of post-war Germany. The Allies relied on statements from other people regarding the accused's involvement in National Socialism. These statements earned the nickname of *Persilscheine*, (Persil certificate, after the soap powder).

Source A Part of the denazification process – the renaming of a German street in 1946

The process of denazification differed in each zone of occupation but it became very difficult, almost impossible, to examine all party members thoroughly. Many former Nazi Party members were able to escape justice, much to the regret of many Germans. Some even became members of the new governments of the two Germanys in the 1950s. The work of the investigators was far from straightforward because it was not easy to distinguish those who were responsible for Nazi activities from those who were simply followers.

On 13 May 1946, the Allied Control Council issued a directive for the confiscation of all media that could contribute to Nazism or militarism. As a consequence, a list was drawn up of more than 30,000 book titles, ranging from school textbooks to poetry, which were banned. All copies of books on the list were confiscated and destroyed; possession of a book on the list was made a punishable offence.

In the US zone, there were attempts to denazify by controlling the media. By July 1946 the Allies had taken control of 37 German newspapers, 6 radio stations, 314 theatres, 642 cinemas, 101 magazines, 237 book publishers and 7384 book dealers and printers.

In the Soviet zone, a number of special camps were set up where alleged Nazis were interned. However, people were sometimes arrested without cause and did not receive a fair trial – some were not even tried at all. It is thought that more than 40,000 died in the camps.

Germany in 1947

By 1947 great steps had been taken to put Germany on the road to some semblance of recovery. However, the zones of occupation began to reflect the ideologies of the Allies. In the three Western zones (American, British and French) **capitalism** and democracy were being introduced. In the Soviet zone, communism was introduced and though there were several political parties, democracy was a sham. Moreover, Germany became part of what became known as the Cold War – the growing hostility between the USA and the Soviet Union and their allies. Winston Churchill used the phrase 'Iron Curtain' to describe the division in Europe between the West (US and its Allies) and the East (Soviet Union and its Allies). He said that the division ran along the borders of the German occupation zones.

In 1947, Britain and the USA merged their zones and further decisions that year indicated that the likelihood of reuniting Germany was disappearing. The USA issued the Truman Doctrine, stating that it would halt the spread of communism. This was followed with the Marshall Plan which aimed to revive Europe's economies. The Soviet Union had already set up COMINFORM to develop communist economic and social systems in the countries and areas it controlled, including its German zone. In 1949, two separate countries were created from the occupation zones. The Federal Republic of Germany emerged from the three Western zones and the German Democratic Republic from the Soviet zone. Two Germanys, East and West, continued to exist until reunification in 1990.

TASKS

1. Study Source A. What does it show you about the process of denazification?
2. Suggest reasons why 'almost 2 million Nazis were forbidden to work as anything but manual labourers'.
3. Describe the work of the Allied Control Council. (For guidance on how to answer this type of question, see page 175.)
4. What was meant by the term *Persilscheine*?
5. Explain why it was important for the Allies to control the media in post-war Germany.
6. How far would you agree with the statement that 'between 1919 and 1947 Germany was a country in transition'?

Examination guidance

Here is an opportunity for you to practise some of the questions that have appeared in previous chapters. The questions cover all the questions that appear on the Unit One examination paper and are worth 53 marks in total. The first question is on page 118, the second two are here.

Question 2

This question is about the impact made by the Nazis on the lives of many German people.

(a) Describe the main changes made by the Nazis to the lives of women in Germany. (4 marks)

- For guidance, see page 175.

Source F An image showing a Jew and German girl, printed in a Nazi school textbook (1937)

(b) Why was Source F produced in the late 1930s? (6 marks)

- For guidance, see page 188.

Historians have made different interpretations about Nazi employment policy. These three pieces of evidence can be used to interpret Nazi employment policy. Study these and answer the question that follows.

Evidence one An interpretation about Nazi employment policy written by an historian in the 1950s. He argues that the Nazis didn't create many jobs

Under the Nazis there was much 'invisible' unemployment. The number of unemployed Jews was great but they were not counted as being unemployed. Another source of 'invisible' unemployment was the sacking of women from their jobs. None of these people were included among the unemployed in the official statistics. Part-time workers were counted as fully employed.

Evidence two An interpretation by a German woman reflecting on her experiences in Nazi Germany for a BBC television programme in 1979. She argues that the Nazis provided many jobs

My mother and father went to hear Adolf Hitler give a speech at a rally in town. The next morning they told us children how he wanted to be on the side of the unemployed. My mother wept for joy as we would no longer be poor because Hitler knew how to get jobs for us.

Evidence three This evidence is from Nazi Government official statistics showing the numbers recorded as unemployed in Germany between 1933 and 1939

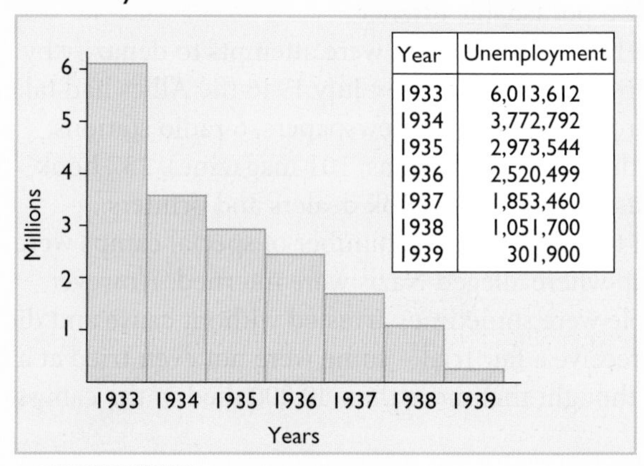

Year	Unemployment
1933	6,013,612
1934	3,772,792
1935	2,973,544
1936	2,520,499
1937	1,853,460
1938	1,051,700
1939	301,900

(c) One interpretation is that the Nazis had solved the problem of unemployment in Germany by 1939. How far do you agree with this interpretation? (10 marks)

- For guidance, see pages 165–66.

Question 3

This question is about opposition to the Nazis within Germany during the war years 1939–45.

(a) To what extent did the most serious opposition to the Nazis in Germany during the war years come from youth groups? (12 marks & 3 marks for SPaG)

- For guidance, see pages 195–96.

GLOSSARY

Allies Supporting countries
Anarchism Belief in removing all forms of government
Anti-Saloon League An organisation founded in 1895 which campaigned for Prohibition
Anti-Semitism Hatred and persecution of the Jews
Armistice The ending of hostilities in a war
Aryan Nazi term for a non-Jewish German, someone of supposedly 'pure' German stock
Autarky Self-sufficiency

'Back to Normalcy' Warren Harding's slogan promising a return to the more carefree days of 1917 – before the USA entered the First World War
Bible Belt Area of southern USA where Christian belief is strong
Black market Illegal trade in goods which are in short supply
Black Power Movement Movement in support of improved rights for black Americans, which was prepared to use more violent methods
Blitzkrieg Lightning war. The new method used by the German armed forces in 1939
Bolshevik Revolution Communist takeover in Russia in October 1917
Bolsheviks Members of the Russian Social Democrat party, who followed Lenin and carried out a communist revolution in Russia in 1917
Boom Period of economic prosperity
Bootlegger Illegal maker and distributor of alcohol
Bull market A time when share prices are rising
'Buying on the margin' Borrowing money to buy shares on the stock market

Capitalism A system under which businesses are owned privately and people are able to make a profit
Coalition government A government of two or more political parties
Colony A group of settlers in a new country controlled by a mother country
Commercial aviation Airlines used for business and to make a profit
Communism A theory that society should be classless, private property abolished, and land and business owned collectively
Communists Followers of the ideas of Karl Marx, who believe in the theory of communism
Congress The US equivalent of parliament. Congress is split into two parts, the Senate and the House of Representatives
Conscription Compulsory military service for a certain period of time
Constituent Assembly A group of representatives elected to set up a new constitution
Consumer goods Manufactured goods that satisfy personal needs – vacuum cleaners, for example
Consumerism An increase in the production of consumer goods on the grounds that high spending is the basis of a sound economy

Credit Money available for borrowing

Dawes Plan Introduced in 1924 to reduce Germany's annual reparation payments
D-Day Landings Name given to Allied landings in Normandy in June 1944.
Deficit spending Spending by governments financed by borrowing
Depression A period of extended and severe decline in a nation's economy, marked by low production and high unemployment
Demilitarised Removal of all armed forces
DNVP *Deutsche National Volks Partei*, the German National People's Party

Evacuation Removing women and children from a place of danger to safety

Federal government The central government of the USA, based in Washington DC
Federal Reserve Board Organisation which controls the Federal Reserve – a national system of reserve cash available to banks
Federal structure System in which power is divided between a central government (*Reichstag*) and regional governments (*Länder*)
Flapper A young woman who flouted the norms of dress and behaviour in the 1920s
Free City Not under the control of any country
Führerprinzip The leadership principle; the idea that the Nazi Party and Germany should have one leader obeyed by all
Fundamentalists Religious group who went to church regularly and believed in the Bible

General strike A strike of workers in most, if not all, trades
Gestapo *Geheime Staats Polizei,* Secret State Police
Ghetto A city neighbourhood inhabited by a minority who live there because of social and economic pressure
Gleichschaltung Bringing people into the identical way of thinking and behaving. Usually translated as co-ordination
Governor The elected head of a state within the USA
Gramophone A record player

Heil Hitler Form of salute to Hitler
Hire purchase A system of credit whereby a person may purchase an item by making regular payments whilst having the use of it
Hitler Youth Organisation set up for the young in Germany to convert them to Nazi ideas
Hobo An unemployed wanderer seeking a job
Hyperinflation Extremely high inflation, where the value of money becomes almost worthless

Import duties Taxes placed on goods brought from foreign countries
Income tax Payment from wages/salaries to the government treasury
Industrialists Someone who owns and/or runs an industry or factory

Inflation A general increase in prices and a fall in the purchasing power of money
Isolationism A policy of deliberately staying out of world affairs. The USA was isolationist between the two world wars

Jim Crow Laws A series of laws which brought about segregation and discrimination against black Americans in the southern states of the USA

Kaiser The German Emperor
KPD The German Communist Party
Kristallnacht 'Night of the Broken Glass', when the windows of Jewish premises were smashed

Laissez-faire A policy of no direct government interference in the economy
Länder Regional states of Germany
League of Nations The international body established after the First World War in order to maintain peace
Lynching Put a person to death by hanging without a legal trial

Mass production Manufacture of goods on a large scale
Mechanisation The use of machines
Minimum wage The lowest wage per hour that someone can be paid
Munitions Ammunition/weapons produced for the armed forces

National Association for the Advancement of Coloured People (NAACP) Set up in 1909 to achieve better conditions for black Americans
Nationalise To change from private ownership to state ownership
Nationalist Party Shortened form of the German National People's Party (DNVP)
Nazi-Nationalist government Coalition of NSDAP and DNVP after January 1933
NSDAP Nazi Party

'Open Door' policy Free admission of immigrants

Plebiscite Direct vote of the electorate on an important public issue
Pogroms An organised massacre of Jews
Prohibition Banning of sale and consumption of alcohol
Proportional Representation The number of votes won in an election determined the number of seats in the *Reichstag*

Rackets Schemes for obtaining money by illegal methods
RAD The Labour Front
Radicalism A belief in more extreme change
RAF Royal Air Force
Red Scare Term used in the USA after the communist revolution in Russia in 1917. It was the fear that immigrants from Eastern Europe would bring ideas about a communist revolution to the USA
Reich In German, this has many meanings – state, kingdom, empire. When used by the Nazis it tended to mean empire or Germany
Reparations War damages to be paid by Germany
Republic A state in which the government is carried out by the people or their elected representatives
Republican Supporter of the Republican Party. Its main ideas were to keep taxes low, limit the powers of the federal government, follow policies which favoured business and encourage people to be self-sufficient
'Rugged individualism' The American ideal that individuals are responsible for their own lives without help from anyone else; they stand or fall by their own efforts

SD *Sicherheitsdienst* – Security Service
Sharecropper Farm workers who did not own their land; they were given a share of the crops instead of a wage
Socialist Those who believe in state ownership
Speakeasy An illegal drinking shop
SS *Schutzstaffel* – originally, Hitler's private bodyguard; but eventually grew to have very wide ranging powers
Stalingrad City of Tsaritsyn was renamed Stalingrad in 1925
Stock market The place where stocks and shares were bought and sold on a daily basis
Stocks and shares Certificates of ownership in a company
Supreme Court The highest federal court in the USA. It consists of nine judges, chosen by the president, who make sure that the president and Congress obey the rules of the Constitution
Swastika Emblem of the Nazi Party

Tariff An import duty; a tax on foreign goods coming into a country
Temperance Movement An organisation which sought to outlaw the sale of alcoholic beverages
The 'Great Migration' Movement of farm workers in the USA in the 1930s
The Great Depression Slump in the economy in the 1930s which led to high unemployment
Total War A war in which all available weapons and resources are used
Trade union Organisations set up to protect and improve the rights of workers

Universal Negro Improvement Association (UNIA) A self-help organisation for black Americans set up in 1914 by Marcus Garvey
USAAF The United States Airforce

Volkssturm A German militia set up by Hitler in 1944 to recruit younger and older German males

Wall Street Crash 29 October 1929, when more than 16 million shares were traded in panic selling, triggering further sales and leading to world economic crisis
Wall Street Stock Exchange Base of New York's stock market
WASP White Anglo-Saxon Protestant
Wehrmacht German army
White supremacy The theory that white people are naturally superior to people of other races
Women's movement A united effort to improve the social, economic and political position of women

Xenophobia An irrational fear or hatred of foreigners

Young Plan Plan to reduce Germany's reparations payments, introduced in 1929

INDEX